MYTHS & LEGENDS

of the
Second World War

MYTHS & LEGENDS
of the
Second World War

JAMES HAYWARD

SUTTON PUBLISHING

First published in 2003 by
Sutton Publishing Limited · Phoenix Mill
Thrupp · Stroud · Gloucestershire · GL5 2BU

British Library Cataloguing in Publication Data
A catalogue record for this book is available from the British Library.

ISBN 0 7509 3047 0

Typeset in 10/12pt Photina.
Typesetting and origination by
Sutton Publishing Limited.
Printed and bound in England by
J.H. Haynes & Co. Ltd, Sparkford.

Contents

Acknowledgements

The author owes a particular debt of gratitude to Nigel Bewley, Terence Burchell, Nicholas and Dawn Champion, Terry Charman, David Collyer, Peter Dachert, Clive Dunn, Lowell Dyson, Ian English, Julian Foynes, James Herbert, Robert Jackson, Richard Knight, Chris Lewis, Bob Moore, Roger Morgan, Ian Munroe, Mick Muttitt, Roy Nesbit, Robin Prior, Winston Ramsey, Neil Storey, Richard Townsley, T.H. Waterhouse and Nigel West. Many more people have assisted in the research and preparation of this book, although any errors in the text are mine and not theirs.

I also extend my sincere thanks to the following libraries and institutions: The Imperial War Museum, Cambridge University Library, The British (Newspaper) Library, PA News Library, Norfolk County Libraries. And to all at Sutton Publishing, in particular Jonathan Falconer, Elizabeth Stone and Nick Reynolds.

Although every effort has been made to contact copyright holders, this has not been possible in every case. If I have omitted to give due credit to any individual or organisation I offer my sincere apologies.

Introduction: True Lies

When I began researching this book, which is a sequel of sorts to my earlier study *Myths & Legends of the First World War*, I naively assumed that there would be less raw material to analyse. After all, by 1939 the world had moved on twenty years, the populace were wiser, and had the benefit both of bitter experience and the wireless. This is true to a point, for in these pages the connoisseur will find few tales quite as tall as those of the Angel of Mons, or the Kaiser's corpse factory, or fiendish Hun plots to undermine the moral stamina of British troops through the use of homosexual agents.

And yet, as we see in Chapter One, a whole raft of First World War rumours were resurrected during the first eighteen months of the war. Myths fade like flowers, only to bloom elsewhere as soon as the climate and season are suitable. The same fictive poisoned sweets passed out by German soldiers in Belgium in 1914 were dropped by the *Luftwaffe* over Poland in 1939, and by the USAAF on Germany in 1944. Most of these resurrection myths were by-products of the spy mania common to both conflicts, with the 'Alien Peril' and 'Hidden Hand' now replaced by the equally chimerical fifth column. In Britain in both conflicts these panics were specifically engineered to keep the population on its toes, and to justify widespread internment, and differed only by degree. Whereas in 1914 dachshund dogs had been kicked and stoned on the streets, in 1939 they were merely denigrated in cartoons and portrayed with swastikas drawn on their backs. Although xenophobia was still widespread, the hatred was leavened by humour, in which Adolf Hitler was found wanting a testicle, and German parachutists were inclined to descend from the skies dressed as pantomime priests and nuns.

As with my earlier book, I was surprised to find that no previous writer had compiled a truly comprehensive study. Of course, there are several well-known books which deal with particular areas, such as *The Myth of the Blitz* by Angus Calder (1991), *Unreliable Witness* (1986) and *Counterfeit Spies* (1998) by Nigel West, and *Double Standards* (2001), which covers most aspects of the Rudolf Hess affair. There is also an abundance of large format books dealing with sundry 'secrets' and 'mysteries' on a superficial level, while John Keegan's scholarly dissection of *The Battle for History* (1995) is concerned more with controversy than with myth. One reason, perhaps, for this absence is that the substance of many myths and legends is fundamentally banal, and provides no firm foundation on which to build any wide-ranging academic thesis. Another is that some areas will never be considered legitimate topics of research for the military historian, in particular the occult, and the fantastical reports of extraterrestrial Foo Fighters from 1944 to 1945. But a myth is a myth, a legend a legend, and all justify exploration between the covers of this book.

Although most of the fictions explored in the following chapters share little in common, and cannot easily be arranged to form a seamless narrative thread, they do raise an obvious question: how are myths and legends created? The detailed answer differs from case to case, as Lord Arthur Ponsonby discovered when compiling his landmark compendium *Falsehood in Wartime*, first published in 1928, and revived in 1940. That said, several general patterns may be discerned. One certain cause is the lack of available hard facts in wartime, often due to poor communications from the Front, or deliberate censorship. What Mass Observation founder Tom Harrisson termed 'home made news' is then manufactured to fill the vacuum, as were the fictions christened 'outside information' by diarist Naomi Royde Smith, often by people only too keen to appear in the know to their immediate social circle. In this way we can isolate a basic desire for certainty, where in fact none exists, and simple one-upmanship.

Another cause is the insatiable appetite of the man in the street, and in the front line, for lurid tales based on death, destruction and epic misfortune visited upon others, whether friend or foe. On the Allied side at least, the term '*Schadenfreude*' would have been condemned as unpatriotic. The syndrome is explored in some depth in the US Army lecture on The Rumor Racket reproduced as Appendix Two, and in the following passage by Tom Driberg from his collection *Colonnade*, concerning the aftermath of a raid on London in October 1940:

> I looked at the ruin of a house in which, I knew, one man had been killed. A bystander said to me, 'They say there's dozens buried down there still. They ought to call for volunteers from the street. Why don't they call for volunteers?'
>
> 'Who says there's dozens buried down there still?' I interrupted sharply.
>
> He gave me a dirty look, mumbled 'Chap who was here just now said so,' edged away; a moment later I heard him say to a woman, 'They say there's dozens buried down there still. They ought to call for volunteers . . .'

Other myths arise by virtue of dishonest invention by unscrupulous writers, either through financial necessity or greed. Another stimulus is the need for secrecy, in particular the silence surrounding Enigma and Ultra, which persisted until 1974 and gave rise to persistent myths, including that of the deliberate sacrifice of Coventry. To the causal list we may also add deliberate deception operations and outright propaganda, such as the doomed Polish lancers of 1939, the flaming English Channel of 1940, the rouged German airmen of 1941, and the carrot-gobbling night fighter pilots of the RAF.

The question of whether there truly existed in Britain an indomitable 'Dunkirk spirit' or 'Myth of the Blitz' has been argued by several capable historians in recent years, including Angus Calder and Clive Ponting. Indeed Tom Harrisson himself lambasted many Home Front myths about national unity and heroism, homing in on the snobbish nature of the establishment, the inadequacy of provision made for air raids, and the dismay and even derision aroused among those who suffered the brunt of the bombing. However, this study makes no pretence of being a social history, and is instead nothing more ambitious than an objective record of myth, legend, falsehood and controversy. Indeed it must stand as one of the few non-fiction books which makes a virtue of the fact that nothing in it is true.

The opening months of any war are invariably the most fertile for myth, and so it is that Chapters One, Two, Three, Five and Six of this book form a cohesive whole, since they deal in turn with spy mania, followed by Dunkirk, the invasion scare and the Blitz. Much of this period is viewed from a British standpoint, but by no means all of it. Stand-alone chapters on supposed war crimes by British troops at Arras in May 1940 (Chapter Four), and the tangled history of The Man Who Never Was (Chapter Nine), involve greater detail, and reveal in turn how flawed research and unflinching self-interest respectively can contribute to myth. Given that Adolf Hitler would probably top most polls of evildoers in the twentieth century, it is scarcely surprising that Führer myths deserve a chapter of their own, although it is interesting to note that his closest rival, Stalin, remains essentially myth free, at least in the West. Chapters Eleven and Twelve are essentially a miscellany of legends based on land and air operations, from which two salient points emerge. Whenever a major military operation goes disastrously wrong, a myth inevitably rises in its wake. And whenever a major figure or celebrity is killed – be they Glenn Miller, Gunter Prien or Adolf Hitler – stories inevitably circulate that they are not dead at all. Then again, fifty years later the same is true of Elvis Presley.

Although I cannot pretend this book will alter anyone's perception of the Second World War, a few facts emerge which have too often been ignored. The widespread killing of suspected fifth columnists in France, Belgium and Holland, invariably on the basis of little or no evidence, reflects credit on no one, including the British Expeditionary Force. That fact that the total number of killings and summary executions probably ran into the low thousands during a campaign which lasted little more than a month is particularly disturbing. Most war histories have failed to recognise the fact that the burning sea myth of 1940 was the first significant British propaganda victory of the Second World War, and did much to convince Americans that Britain was not yet beaten. There is strong evidence that British military intelligence has often practised deceptions with the aid of corpses, and enjoyed closer links with its *Abwehr* counterparts than previously thought. And although often derided as little more than a joke, mistakenly pitting cavalry against tanks in the misguided belief that German armour was constructed from wood and canvas, in the light of the information contained in Chapter Three it is hard to escape the conclusion that the Polish army was the only force which put up serious or determined opposition to the *Wehrmacht* before 1941.

This study is also defined by those areas I have chosen to omit. For reasons of space and cohesion I have been obliged to leave certain areas unexamined. Although this book contains chapters devoted to land and air myths, the detailed examination of the *Royal Oak* disaster in Chapter Two left little further naval material. The fiction of secret U-boat bases on the Donegal coast remains just that, and was laid bare by Nigel West in his book *Counterfeit Spies*, while the wartime tale that German submarines put to sea with a grisly stock of cold-stored severed limbs to simulate their own sinking is an obvious product of propaganda. Many myths continue to attach to the resistance movement in Europe, and almost certainly deserve a book of their own, while the subject of Holocaust denial remains both delicate and litigious. The main reason I chose not to explore the latter subject is that specious claims that the Holocaust never occurred, or took place on a far smaller scale than is generally accepted, are a postwar creation, whereas I have tried to focus only on myths and legends which first arose between 1939 and 1945. For the same reason I have side-stepped several subjects which might more properly be labelled conspiracy theories, such as the charge that Roosevelt, forewarned by Churchill of the attack on Pearl Harbor, allowed it to proceed in order to bring the United States into the European war.

It is clear that the overripe 'corpse factory' fiction of 1917 had a detrimental effect on the way in which the Ministry of Information steered British reporting of Nazi atrocities against the Jews. But that is not a myth, and probably had no practical effect. The misconception that the incalculable human suffering inflicted at Auschwitz could have been alleviated by Allied bombing is convincingly exploded by William Rubinstein in his book *The Myth of Rescue* (1997). The subject of area bombing over Germany is another controversy which falls outside the scope of this book, and readers are instead directed towards *The Bomber War* (2001) by Robin Neillands, whose earlier study of British generalship on the Western Front between 1914 and 1918 did so much to explode those hoary old myths about donkeys and lions. Yet another body of research which deserves to be read more widely, yet does not fall within the remit of this book, can be found in *Other Casualties*, written by James Bacque in 1989. This detailed investigation into the mass deaths of German prisoners of war after April 1945 reveals a truly numbing statistic, albeit one which has been challenged, that no fewer than 750,000 died of malnutrition and disease while held in deliberately inadequate French and American camps. That the Allies had right on their side during the Second World War is one of the few absolutes of the conflict. However, the mass killing of unarmed enemy prisoners between April 1945 and 1948 is an unwelcome lesson which still remains to be learned by many, let alone forgotten.

But that is neither myth nor legend. For the fictions, read on.

James Hayward
February 2003

CHAPTER ONE

Dressed as Nuns

In the opening chapter of my book *Myths & Legends of the First World War*, I described how Britain was gripped by a feverish spy mania during the first few months of the conflict, in which anyone – or anything – German or faintly alien was viewed with hostility and scorn. Dachshunds were stoned in the streets, delicatessens and pork butchers attacked and looted, and enamelled advertising signs examined for coded instructions to spies. Tennis courts were identified as gun platforms, and matches struck in London streets reported as signals to German U-boats and Gothas. Spies and saboteurs were identified on every street corner, usually masquerading as waiters and barbers, with others in service as maids or governesses, their steamer trunks packed full of bombs. Some enemy agents, it was said, had been arrested in female attire, or dressed as nurses. Everywhere, it seemed, there was signalling to airships, some of them invisible, to which the latter replied by dropping poisoned sweets over cities to kill children. No rumour was too ridiculous, no exaggeration too great.

Little of this alarmism had any foundation in fact, and following the Armistice a marked degree of disenchantment flowed from the exposed falsehoods of the Crucified Canadian, the corpse rendering factory, and the often pornographic stories of bestial outrage committed by the Kaiser's army on its march through Belgium in 1914. It is all the more fascinating, therefore, that so many of these First World War myths and legends were dusted off, re-labelled, and sold as new in 1939 and 1940, as Poland, Denmark, Norway, Holland, Belgium and finally France were overrun. Poisoned sweets, murderous spies, treacherous maidservants, secret signals, even the enamel sign story – all, like Lazarus, rose up from the dead as soon as hostilities commenced. Just as the Kaiser was said to have been insane, so too was Adolf Hitler. One rumour current in Britain during the first few days of the war was that which held that the Führer had 'gone off with a gun and shot himself'. A lie, it is said, never lives to be old, and so it was that this particular falsehood soon perished, to be replaced with a more pleasing (and less easily disproved) legend that the German leader was equipped with a solitary testicle. This subject is discussed at length in Chapter Seven.

Although 1939 and 1940 spy mania never escalated into the panic of 1914, the First World War rumour of the familiar figure or 'friendly enemy' was revised and updated. The original version involved a young woman suddenly and unexpectedly confronted in Piccadilly by her fiancé, an officer in the Prussian Guards, who cut her dead before making his escape by means of a passing omnibus or taxi. In the updated version, in one town or another (Dover and Crewe were among the locations cited) a tradesman was said to have called at a newly let house to solicit orders. When the door was opened, the horrified vendor found himself facing the same brutal Prussian who had commanded the prisoner-of-war camp in which he had rotted two decades earlier. In his memoir *Friend or Foe*, self-styled 'spycatcher' Oreste Pinto records a supposed chance meeting with a senior Dutch Nazi on a London street, although Pinto is a highly unreliable witness and the incident probably an invention.

Another feature common to the first few days of both conflicts were the widespread and almost gleeful rumours of mass destruction. Just as the British Expeditionary Force of 1914 was said to have suffered extinction-level casualties immediately upon arriving in France, and the British fleet mauled in the North Sea, early in September 1939 word spread of various towns being heavily bombarded from sea and air. At the same time, each air raid warning was followed by wild speculation as to the awful fate which had befallen some faraway part of the country. While it is doubtful that anyone actually wished to see the devastation of Hartlepool, Scarborough and Lowestoft repeated, the morbid appetite of some seems to have extended far beyond weary resignation.

From early September 1939 onwards false spy reports were returned from the fighting in Poland, many of them sponsored by official sources. German paratroops were reported fighting in Polish uniforms, assisted by ethnic *Volksdeutsche* dressed in distinctive or eccentric clothing, while the general brutality of German troops was said to include the use of civilians as human shields, and a reluctance to take prisoners. It was claimed German aircraft had dropped poisoned chocolates and cigarettes, while other reports told of tobacco leaves strewn across meadows so that cattle, alarmed by the odour of nicotine, would starve. When the *Luftwaffe* ran short of bombs, chunks of rail and other scrap metal were thrown from aircraft. Although there was no repeat of the sustained atrocity propaganda manufactured by the Allies in 1914–15, it is clear that the Polish authorities took a conscious decision to manufacture certain fictions, the most flagrant of which involved the use of poison gas. At a press call in London on 3 September, the Polish Ambassador announced that the German air force had begun dropping gas bombs, while on the 5th it was reported from Warsaw that

German bombers have dropped asphyxiating bombs, and many people have been injured and burned. There were particularly many casualties among children. . . Enemy warplanes dropped little balloons filled with poison gas, which were collected by children in the streets. Analysis established they were filled with Yperite gas.

On the basis of this report, questions were raised in the Commons. On the ground German agents and saboteurs were said to have poisoned water supplies with mustard gas, while a rumour spread in Germany that Britain was supplying gas shells to the Poles. With all sides keen to prevent the outbreak of chemical warfare, these charges were rapidly quashed, Lord Halifax reminding the House of Lords on 14 September that Germany had ratified the Geneva Protocol which proscribed gas as a weapon of war. A German counter-claim that Polish 'poison gas mines' had caused casualties near Jaslo made little headway, and despite claims of atrocities on both sides it is clear that in Britain at least a general mood of scepticism prevailed. A prescient letter published in several papers on 9 September, above the pseudonym Everyman, deplored some of the wilder reports printed during the first week of the war:

Already the truth appears to be the first casualty in some papers. The first news of the war in Poland suggesting that women and children were especially aimed at . . . One paper carried a story of poisoned chocolates dropped on Polish towns, and children dying as a result. . . Can we not determine to fight this war without lies of the corpse factory description? A just cause should be fought on truth, and truth alone.

However, the voice of reason (or disenchantment) was little heard. Just as tales of poisoned chocolates and sweets were hoary relics of the First World War, so too were widespread rumours of signalling to enemy aircraft. This paranoia was no doubt fuelled by the bombing of civilians during the Spanish Civil War, which had also produced a new name for the alien and spy peril: the fifth column. The phrase is attributed to General Emilio Mola, who in October 1936 claimed to have four columns of troops waiting to march on Madrid, and a fifth inside ready to rise and fight for Franco. In fact there was no Nationalist organisation in the city, and no solid proof that the general himself phrased the threat in these terms. Nevertheless the phrase was taken up by British newspapers, and borrowed by Ernest Hemingway as the title of his 1939 play about life and love in besieged Madrid.

As in the First World War, phantom signalling by fifth columnists in Poland took a number of forms. Miniature wireless transmitters were hidden in tombs, chimneys and trees, while others daubed markers on roofs, or painted chimneys white, or heaped straw from hayricks in suspicious patterns. Crops and pasture were said to have been planted or cut according to pre-arranged plans, while at night signals were flashed by means of lamps, fires and matches. One spy was even identified 'by his German shoes'. If these activities were largely illusory, the result was all too real. In Poland untold numbers of suspects were arrested or killed on the basis of little or no evidence. In the town of Thorn alone, 34 were shot for signalling with mirrors and flags, while supposed sniping in Bydgoszcz on 3 September led to a reprisal dubbed Bloody Sunday. Hans Roos, in his *History of Modern Poland*, observes that some 7,000 German and ethnic German civilians were deported, murdered or simply shot out of hand in the wave of national hatred which swept the country, this despite the fact that a considerable number of ethnic Germans were fighting in the Polish army. The same fictions, and the same summary justice, would be repeated across Holland, Belgium and France eight months later.

In reality, the assistance offered by German *Volksdeutsche* in Poland seems to have been largely uncoordinated. Many helped clear roads, repaired vehicles, fed troops and acted as guides, but this falls some way short of the mythic bands of killers and saboteurs. *Abwehr* units (including Brandenburg troops) did operate in civilian clothes to secure key objectives at the outset of the campaign, but not in the garb of priests or monks, or any of the more outlandish disguises commonly ascribed to the Polish fifth column. Since no airborne troops were deployed in Poland, none fought in Polish uniforms, as early reports suggested.

After six months of Bore or Phoney War, on 9 April 1940 German forces invaded Denmark. The country was taken wholly by surprise and overrun in a single day. Against this background, it is easy to understand why rumours quickly spread that German troops had hidden in the holds of ships which docked in Copenhagen some days before, and in freight cars on the Warnemunde–Gjedser ferry, to issue forth 'like the Greeks out of the Trojan horse' at the critical moment. In Northern Schleswig rumours of underhand tactics also extended to poisoned water supplies, although the foreign press were less interested in this particular story than in the nefarious activities of the dread fifth column. According to *The Times*:

> Members of the large German colony undoubtedly played pre-arranged roles, as did a number of German reserve officers in civilian clothes who had obtained Danish visas in the guise of commercial travellers.

On the same day Norway too was attacked. Here it was also rumoured that German forces were smuggled into target ports by ship, while an armed fifth column already in place in Oslo passed on false orders, cut telephone wires, and sabotaged a mine barrage. Many, it was said, had entered the country in the guise of salesmen, tourists and even foster-children. These reports reached the British government on the same day and were accepted as factual. A widely syndicated report by Leland Stowe, of the *Chicago Daily News*, left a sinister and lasting impression:

> Norway's capital and great seaports were not captured by armed force. They were seized with unparalleled speed by means of a gigantic conspiracy which must undoubtedly rank among the most audacious and most perfectly oiled political plots of the past century. By bribery and

extraordinary infiltration on the part of Nazi agents, and by treason on
the part of a few highly placed Norwegian civilians and defence officials,
the German dictatorship built its original Trojan Horse inside Norway.

Everywhere the portrait painted was of powerless Allies fighting an invisible
enemy capable of diabolical cunning. One British sapper, evacuated after the
abortive attack on Trondheim in May, lamented: 'The place was full of spies.
Every move we made was known to the Germans almost as soon as we
made it.' The truth is that the hastily assembled expeditionary force sent to
Norway largely comprised ill-equipped Territorials, and failed to mount an
effective counter-attack despite outnumbering the German defenders at
Trondheim by six to one. On land the Norwegian campaign was an
ignominious shambles, although the Royal Navy did manage to inflict
decisive damage on its German counterpart.

Again, the reality of the supposed 'Trojan Horse' was very different. In
Denmark, *Volksdeutsche* did little beyond offering the invading force an
enthusiastic welcome, while covert actions along the frontier were
undertaken by *Abwehr* operatives, rather than a Danish fifth column. No
German troops hid in ships; instead they simply crossed the Baltic on board
ferries and naval vessels on the day and took the Danes by surprise. As early
as 6 May the Norwegian foreign minister announced publicly that he had
still to discover a single authenticated case of treachery, but this statement
was little reported. Although in Norway the name of the former foreign
minister, Vidkun Quisling, would become synonymous with treachery, he
was not taken seriously by Germany and his Nasjonal Samling followers took
no real part in the battle. Although Quisling did succeed in seizing a radio
station in order to proclaim himself Prime Minister, it was not until 1942
that his German masters permitted him to use this title. In his definitive
1953 study, *The German Fifth Column in the Second World War*, Dutch
historian Louis de Jong concluded that in both Denmark and Norway no
special forces were deployed other than regular airborne troops. An official
Norwegian enquiry into whether any prominent member of the Nasjonal
Samling played an active part in the German invasion reached a similarly
negative conclusion. Hitler and his generals wished to keep their plans
completely secret, and instead German planners relied principally on tourist
guides such as Baedeker.

Although most core fifth column myths were already in place by May
1940, it was the invasion of Holland on 10 May which saw the greatest
flowering of falsehoods. German paratroops now came to replace the dreaded
Uhlans of 1914 in the iconography of myth, due in part to the sheer number
deployed against Holland: some 4,500 paratroopers and a fleet of 430
transport aircraft. However the heightened Dutch hysteria probably owes
something to the fact that Holland had remained neutral during the First
World War, and thus had had no recent reminder that in war truth is always
the first casualty.

The facts run as follows. In Holland the German airborne arm undertook three main operations. Paratroops of the 7th Flieger Division captured three key bridges over the River Maas, while at Rotterdam a dozen seaplanes landed 120 men, who then seized several key bridges. Less successfully, a force landed from transport planes at The Hague was almost destroyed, and failed in its object of capturing Queen Wilhelmina and her government. Allied to the spectacular conquest of the Belgian fortress at Eban Emael by just 55 combat engineers landed by glider, the overall achievement of German airborne forces in the Low Countries was considerable. However, their victory came at a high cost, with 3,900 of almost 11,000 men killed, wounded and captured, 220 Ju 52 transports destroyed, and almost every parachute lost.

From the outset fantastical reports emerged in Holland, and quickly fed back to Britain. On the night of 10 May the Home Office issued a statement warning of enemy paratroops 'wearing uniforms calculated to deceive observers', who should immediately report suspicious jumpers to the nearest police station. On the same day an Air Ministry circular warned that German paratroopers might descend with their arms raised above their heads, as if to surrender, but in fact holding primed grenades. The following day it was reported that 200 parachutists dressed in British uniforms had landed in The Hague. On 13 May the *Daily Express* ran the following, almost comically alarmist report:

> On the first day of the invasion parachutists dropped out of the sky like a vast flock of vultures. Most of them were disguised in Allied or Dutch uniforms, others came down in the uniform of Dutch policemen and began to direct the population in the streets and mislead the army. One 'policeman' told a group of isolated Dutch troops that their friends were round the corner. When the Dutch troops turned the corner, German troops, barricaded across the road, slaughtered them . . .
>
> But, most fantastic of all, the steward of an English ship said that he and the crew had watched parachutists descend in women's clothing. They wore blouses and skirts and each carried a sub-machine-gun. The steward could not tell if they were women or men disguised as women. Several eye-witnesses in the boat confirmed it, and said that others had come down disguised as priests, peasants and civilians . . .
>
> As machine-guns came out of the sky like unnatural lighting peppering the streets below, the Fifth Column crept out of their homes in German uniforms, heavily armed. Holland had combed out the Fifth Column for weeks before, but as the doors opened at 3 am the men who had been proclaimed anti-Nazis and refugees from Germany, held rifles.

In a similar vein, the *Daily Telegraph* told of lethal delivery boys with hand grenades in their baskets, in league with female spies who signalled their allegiance by clapping at their windows. In a litany of 'every kind of trick to sap confidence and cause confusion', the *Daily Express* listed 'poisoned chocolates and wine' as well as 'spies disguised as priests and postmen and housemaids'. Another typical report appeared in the *Eastern Daily Press* on the same date:

> Holland's internal defence organisation is matching in alertness the valour of her fighting troops at the front as parachute invaders and the Fifth Column enemy strike at the heart of the country. German parachutists disguised as clergymen and peasants, as well as others in the uniforms of the Dutch forces, have been rounded up in several towns, while hundreds of Fifth Column suspects have been arrested. . . The Press Association correspondent saw one large building surrounded by police with fixed bayonets, while others climbed onto the roof and finally chased and shot a man who had been giving signals to enemy aircraft.
>
> A detachment of Dutch soldiers was attacked yesterday near the Hague by a group of 'Dutchmen' who proved to be German soldiers. It is recalled that as long ago as last August a store of about 2000 uniforms of Dutch postmen, railway officials, gendarmes and soldiers had been seen by a resident stacked up in the local offices of a small German village in Westphalia. The reasons for these collections is now revealed.

The sheer volume and similarity of these reports suggests they were the deliberate creation of official propagandists, possibly from Department EH, a small subsection of MI6 charged with the creation of propaganda. The charge of underhand tactics, and disregard for the laws and usages of war, largely replaced the overt atrocity propaganda of 1914–18, with books such as *The Rape of the Netherlands* (1940) and *Belgium in Bondage* (1943) offering far less than their lurid titles promised. However, the alleged use of human shields was revived, as is clear from *The War* cover reproduced in the plate section, and an official Dutch communiqué circulated by British United Press:

> Some of the parachutists had forced motor coach drivers at pistol point to take them to certain places, shielded by Dutch civilians, but they were afterwards annihilated by our tanks. It seems that German soldiers are not able to fight without using civilians as shields.

From Brussels it was reported that German parachutists jumped equipped with dummies, used to simulate death on landing, allowing the parachutist to make good his escape. At Ostend they were said to have dropped in sky-blue uniforms beneath transparent canopies, so as to remain semi-invisible during their descent. In fact no German paratroops were dropped anywhere in Belgium, although another fiction was born when the Air Ministry announced on 14 May that German paratroops were released like bombs through a hole in the floor of their transports – 'the pilot pulls a lever and out they go'.

Outlandish as these fictions seem now, in May 1940 many of them were taken seriously by the Joint Intelligence Committee, and perhaps by Churchill, who wrote to Roosevelt on the 18th warning that Britain 'must expect to be attacked on the Dutch model before very long'. Many senior officers fell prey to the scare, including Admiral Sir Bertram Ramsay, the naval commander at Dover, who reported:

> Indications of numerous acts of sabotage and Fifth Column activity in Dover, eg communications leakages, fixed defences sabotaged, second-hand cars purchased at fantastic prices and left at various parking places.

On 31 May General Ironside, then Commander-in-Chief Home Forces, recorded in his diary that:

> Fifth Column reports coming in from everywhere. A man with an arm-band and a swastika pulled up near an important aerodrome in the Southern Command. Important telegraph poles marked, suspicious men moving at night all over the country . . .

Indeed on 2 July Ironside recorded confidently that 'there is signalling going on all over the place' and 'people quite definitely preparing aerodromes' while at the same time (and apparently without irony) noting with regret that no one seemed able to obtain any evidence.

Even as late as September 1940, Home Guard units in London were formally instructed to watch for signalling to aircraft. In 1941 the Ministry of Information resorted to faking refugee memoirs, for example *The Diary of a Dutch Boy Refugee* by the wholly fictive Dirk van der Heide, while in 1942 films such as *The Foreman Went to France* and *Went The Day Well?* continued to peddle well-worn fifth column stereotypes. Returning to 1940, MI5 actually dispatched officers to examine telegraph poles across the southern counties, while the RAF flew patrols to check the countryside for suspicious markings in fields. A revealing first-hand account of the abortive investigation of a scoutmaster thought to be involved in jamming a Chain Home radar station at West Beckham in Norfolk is given by R.V. Jones in his book *Most Secret War*.

Nor were the Dutch military immune. In his account *The Ordeal of the Frontier Battalion*, published in 1945, E.P. Weber recalled:

> One cannot name a single commander in the Dutch army who, according to rumour, has not been killed at least once. Over the roads along which our troops are to march poison gas has been observed. Whenever chocolates are found they should be destroyed, because they are sure to be poisoned. In our grenades there was supposed to be sand instead of gunpowder, and the rumour went that casemates had crumbled at the first shot because the concrete was no good.

Paratroops and parachute saboteurs were frequently run together to form a single menace from the air, as in the following report from 14 May. On this

date a large British contingent from Holland returned by sea, including sundry
consular officials, newsmen and the entire Sadlers Wells Ballet Company.

All the passengers had a great deal to say concerning Germany's Fifth
Column in Holland. Many Nazi supporters, even domestic servants, went to
the aid of the parachutists who appeared in all manner of disguises as
dustmen, clergymen, policemen and postmen. They frequently knocked at a
private house and at the point of their revolver demanded civilian clothing.
Many paratroops who had been taken prisoner were boys of 16 and 17.
They did not know what fighting meant and they told a Dutch officer that
they had been pushed out of the plane when over their objective. One carried
with him his last letter from his mother and her picture. He said he had
made up his mind when he set out that he would never live to see her again.

Little if any of this was true, and as we shall see in Chapter Six, the
technique of spreading useful disinformation via travellers and passengers
would be repeated later in 1940 when the myth of a failed German invasion
attempt was actively promoted in America. Among the evacuees returning
from Holland was Sir Neville Bland, the British Minister to the Dutch
government in The Hague, who quickly prepared a report on the 'Fifth
Column Menace'. This thousand-word fantasy included the following
disinformation:

All boys of 16 to 18, completely sodden with Hitler's ideas, and with nothing
else in their minds but to cause as much death and destruction as they could
before being killed themselves. They dropped on the roofs of houses, in open
spaces – even in private gardens . . .

Bland also told how a detachment of German troops were led to a vital bridge
by a German maidservant, and warned that when the moment came, the fifth
column in Britain would

At once embark on widespread sabotage and attacks on civilians and
military indiscriminately. The paltriest kitchen maid not only can be, but
generally is, a menace to the safety of the country . . . and we cannot
conclude from the experiences of the last war that 'the enemy in our
midst' is no less dangerous than it was then. I have not the least doubt
that, when the signal is given, as it will scarcely fail to be when Hitler so
decides, there will be satellites of the monster all over the country who
will at once embark on widespread sabotage and attacks on civilians and
the military indiscriminately. We cannot afford to take this risk. ALL
Germans and Austrians, at least, ought to be interned at once.

Some credit Bland with importing the worst of the paratroop and fifth column
myths into Britain, yet most had already appeared in the press. At the same

time Department EH prepared a report titled 'Operations in Holland', containing the now-familiar litany of bizarre disguises, poisoned cigarettes, and peasant girls armed with machine-guns. In truth the main purpose of the Bland report was to help justify the mass internment of male aliens, which the Home Secretary had ordered on 13 May.

Myth and reality were blurred further still on 16 May when the Dutch foreign minister, E.N. van Kleffens, stated for the first time that enemy parachutists had landed dressed as nuns. This picturesque image would in time become an integral thread in the mythology of the fifth column. Van Kleffens fed the falsehood first to the French press, which meant that it did not immediately catch fire in Britain. By the end of May paratroop myths had expanded beyond sky-blue uniforms, dummies and female attire to include Hunnish brutality. It was said that some dead jumpers found in Holland 'had obviously been shot in the back – presumably by their officers in the plane when they displayed an undue reluctance to take the drop into space'. A late report at the end of May from Norway held that some Germans were being kicked out of their transports without parachutes: 'These soldiers are ordered or thrown out of low-flying aeroplanes onto patches of snow on the hill slopes, in the hope that some of them will escape without broken limbs.' This absurd tale was perhaps inspired by the fact that a significant number of German paratroops were killed by canopies which failed to open.

While conceding that some of these 'well-armed desperadoes' had landed 'dressed as women and girls', *The War Illustrated* was prepared to accord the *Fallschirmjäger* a measure of respect:

> The parachute soldier is a formidable invader. He may bring with him a collapsible bicycle and may even carry a portable tent; with his iron rations he can keep going until he obtains food from the country; should he be able to make contact with a Fifth Columnist he is sure to help.

As in Poland and Scandinavia, fifth column activity in Holland was negligible. Stories of poisoned meat, water and cigarettes were unfounded, as were signalling scares involving lights and 'large swastikas' burnt in fields, and the fiction that an armed band tried to storm the central police station in The Hague. Instead German Brandenburg units dressed in makeshift Dutch uniforms did attempt to capture several key border crossings, but succeeded only at Gennep, where such a unit held the bridge until relieved by an armoured train. As elsewhere, the Dutch 'Trojan Horse' myth gained currency from a natural reluctance to attribute failure to the poor performance of their own troops in open combat, or face up to the fact that two days before the invasion, the German military attaché in The Hague had inspected Holland's defences by the simple expedient of conducting a tour of local tulip fields.

The same phantom menace ran riot through Belgium and France. In Belgium the security service, which should have known better, warned that

German parachutists had landed in several parts of the country, dressed as civilians and equipped with miniature wireless transmitters. In fact no parachute troops were dropped anywhere in Belgium or France. Nevertheless on the 14 May it was officially announced that enemy agents 'dressed in light brown uniforms with buttons stamped with the swastika' had repeatedly attacked the police. Another story ran that among Dutch refugees were SS men in ringletted wigs and false beards, posing as orthodox Jews from Amsterdam. An official order was even issued that all advertising for Pacha chicory was to be removed:

Complicity on someone's part had permitted the Germans to put on the back of them indications useful to parachutists landing in the locality. . . He needed only to find the nearest Pacha chicory sign, which might be in a grocery shop or along a public highway, and on its back he would find cryptic indications giving him the location of the nearest German agent and how to find him . . . This was later confirmed by repeated radio warnings.

The story was no less false than in 1914, when precisely the same myth had attached to advertising for selected brands of food, usually Maggi soup. Indeed the humble chicory root was held in great odium in Belgium in May 1940. While the rapid fall of the fortress at Eban Emael was attributed to death rays and poison gas, the following year an American magazine claimed the fort had been blown up by German saboteurs, who in peacetime had grown chicory in nearby caves, and surreptitiously packed the caverns with explosives.

Several books published in 1940 and 1941 faithfully promulgated any number of tall stories, the most popular being *Through the Dark Night* by the prolific James Lansdale Hodson, who had been in Belgium and France as a war correspondent for the *Sketch*. Viewed with the benefit of hindsight, it is clear that Hodson (and others) considered the spread of true lies as a legitimate activity in wartime, and some of his copy was undoubtedly provided by the War Office and the Ministry of Information. On 13 May he recorded

A Belgian lady of title I met today in Brussels told me, 'The Germans have been dropping booby traps shaped as watches and writing-pencils and trinkets. When picked up they have exploded; and the Maire has now issued a warning proclamation' . . . Near Brussels six Germans were captured dressed as nuns – a familiar story, but in this case well-authenticated.

As well as dropping men dressed as women, and adolescents with automatic pistols, it appeared that the shiftless *Luftwaffe* was not beneath employing women as aircrew:

I heard of a machine brought down in Flanders which had three girls in it as pilot, navigator and gunner, with a male sergeant. But my officer informant had the story second hand only, though he said the man who told him was reliable and saw them.

In Louvain, so Hodson learned

One man much suspected burnt the Belgian flag in the market place with loud protestations that he couldn't have it falling into German hands. Was the smoke a signal? Nobody knew.

From the Royal Ulster Rifles, near the town of Bossuyt, he heard

Hereabouts news and rumours of Fifth Columnists at work were plentiful, including spies dressed as British officers visiting headquarters – tales mostly unverified. But at all events an arrow of the type used by the enemy to locate HQ was found in a ploughed field – a large arrow fashioned in the soil, with three gramophone records at the tail.

The First World War myth of sinister officer spies, resurrected in the popular film *The Foreman Went to France*, was also repeated by Hodson in relation to the withdrawal from the Dyle by the Duke of Wellington's Regiment:

Men in British uniform acted suspiciously and may well have been spies. First a Guards colonel who asked them to break orders and take up a new position, second a brigade major who said the road was impassable when it was not, and third a brigadier who ordered a bridge in Tournai to be blown despite protests that it was still much needed.

And from the Black Watch:

A regiment the Black Watch relieved told them that a hundred Germans had crossed the bridge in threes, dressed in battle-dress, and singing 'Tipperary' . . . Some of the Germans killed were wearing clothes of khaki material – possibly parachutists.

And from the Royal Scots:

A Scots soldier told how they captured some parachutists dressed as Belgians, but lost a comrade doing it – 'for,' he said, 'the Germans held up their hands, but one raised in surrender held a grenade which, as we got near, he threw.'

Similarly propagandist accounts by Douglas Williams (*The New Contemptibles*, 1940) and Bernard Gray (*War Reporter*, 1941) also peddled stock myths of signals, snipers, sleepers and crop signs. However, few were truly contemporary and fail to stand up as reliable historical sources.

The canard that enemy personnel were abroad dressed as nuns is one of the most enduring and colourful legends of the Second World War, but was almost certainly a deliberate fiction. The story was perhaps intended to portray the enemy as both godless and perverse, without resorting to the crucifixion stories circulated during the First World War. The myth was born in Paris on 16 May, when the Dutch foreign minister, van Kleffens, staged a distraught press call at which he claimed that German parachutists had descended on Holland 'by the thousand' dressed 'in the cassocks of priests and in the garb of nuns or nurses'. Later in 1940 his book *The Rape of the Netherlands* would slavishly repeat each and every fifth column myth ad nauseam.

The nun story took time to catch on, and appears in very few contemporary diaries, although an RAMC captain, J.H. Patterson, describes an amusing incident near Tournai on 19 May. After ordering his CSM to inspect a suspicious column of nuns, Patterson noted that particular attention was paid to hands, feet and chins, resulting in a verdict that the sisters were definitely female. The accounts later given by several BEF veterans of encounters with hairy-handed nuns in hobnailed boots are no less dubious than supposed first-hand sightings of the Angel of Mons, reported in 1915 several months after the fact. For instance, this story offered by Williams in *The New Contemptibles*:

At one place, a British officer stumbled upon several Germans undressing in a wood and putting on nuns' clothing. A horse cart awaited them nearby in which, no doubt, they intended to penetrate the British lines. Needless to say, they did not continue their journey.

Even as late as 1961, historian Richard Collier was prepared to accept an almost identical report at face value:

Gunner William Brewer and four mates, retreating to Dunkirk, were drinking tea near a farmhouse when Bombardier 'Geordie' Allen came doubling white-faced. 'Did you ever see a bloody nun shaving?' Stealing across the pasture, all five men saw what they'd always taken to be the tallest of tales: two German paratroopers, white coifs discarded, crucifixes dangling, shaving behind a haystack. Seconds later, the 'nuns' fell dying, riddled with .303 fire, the blood a dark spreading stain on the black habits.

The nun myth was particularly popular in France, including the tale of a nun unmasked as a Nazi thug and killed on the spot by an angry mob. Indeed the poet Jean Cocteau is said to have observed that 'along all the roads in France, only nuns fastening their puttees were to be seen'.

In Britain the nun myth seems not to have caught on until the end of May. On the 24th a Ministry of Information Home Intelligence summary noted 'the usual crop of rumours about "hairy-handed nuns" and parachutists', together with 'a house full of blind refugees which were alleged to be in possession of machine-guns'. On the same date, beneath the headline 'Sister of Mercy Caught Shaving', the *Eastern Daily Press* reported:

Miss Elsie Seddon, one of six Salvation Army social workers who reached England yesterday . . . told how on one of the many occasions she had to leave her car for shelter in roadside woods from enemy bombers French soldiers pounced upon her. They apparently believed that she was either a parachutist or a spy. When she proved her identity they apologised and explained that only a day or so ago they had found a 'sister of mercy' hastily shaving in the same woods. 'She' was a German parachutist.

Suspicious nuns quickly became a popular talking point, a fact reflected in Mass Observation reporting. A diary entry on 30 May by Naomi Mitchison illustrates the point:

We discussed German agents in disguise. Archie said he had often noticed what big feet nuns had, and probably the half of them were men. The conversation, as Scottish Presbyterian conversations do, then became extremely ribald.

That in Britain the story was never more than a joke is clear from John Lehmann's biography of Leonard and Virginia Woolf:

A rather absurd spy mania broke out, and a few days after the fall of Paris, Leonard, his poise recovered, produced a wonderful story of how, on a train journey to London, Virginia had insisted in a stage whisper that a perfectly innocent nun who got into their carriage was a Nazi paratrooper in disguise.

An odd variation on the masculine nun theme was noted by diarist Margery Allingham in *The Oaken Heart*:

The weekly comic papers had nothing on the new Jerry in the matter of invention. Startled soldiers told you extraordinary tales of trickery, among them stories of fierce long-haired women in Belgian farms who turned out to be stalwart Nazis carrying disguise to the point of farce.

The tale of the bogus nun captured the popular imagination like no other, and was singled out for special attention in a broadcast by Harold Nicolson, then Parliamentary Secretary to the Ministry of Information. On the subject of the chatterbug, he warned:

He will say that his brother in law – chatterbugs always have innumerable brothers in law – was in the train from Derby when a nun entered and started to read a religious book. The book dropped from her lap, and as she stooped to retrieve it she disclosed a manly wrist complete with a tattooed inset of Adolf Hitler.

Despite the fact that De Jong's carefully researched account of the fifth column myth appeared in translation as early as 1956, the picturesque falsehood of nuns in hobnailed boots remained alive and well for decades to come, one American history offering as late as 1976:

In Heugot's, a bistro just behind the Place du Palais Bourbon, a startling transformation took place when a nun who for months had made regular collections among the political clients patronising the bistro appeared as a man – and a German. As Cocteau pointed out, there were 'nuns' everywhere, since penetrating the disguise was a delicate matter.

Nuns aside, perhaps the most ridiculous fifth column rumour of all was exported from Luxembourg, which told of a false travelling circus which crossed the border from Germany, whose personnel comprised entirely military men. Across France various station masters were said to have been unmasked as spies, along with the usual stock reports of airborne saboteurs, suspicious lights, false orders, poisoned sweets and human shields. Arras was said to have been captured by parachutists, who jumped at night carrying flaming torches, while in Paris there were daily reports of paratroops descending on public parks. The idea that fifth columnists contrived to scare refugees onto the roads, and direct them so as to hamper troop movements, would also seem to be French in origin. Another French myth credited German motorised units with the fantastical ability to fuel their vehicles with water, to which a small but evidently miraculous pellet was added.

The fifth column myth in France was boosted on 21 May when the Prime Minister, Paul Reynaud, declared that the bridges over the Meuse had been betrayed, when in fact their loss was due to military incompetence. Suspected fifth column agents were treated in the same brutal way as in Poland, with French units ordered to shoot all strangers unable to account for their presence in any given district. In a single incident at Abbeville no fewer than 22 were shot out of hand, while probably thousands more were killed in woodlands or on roadsides. The summary execution of downed aircrew was also commonplace. The published diary of a French horse transport captain, Daniel Barlone, reveals something of the credulity which underpinned this orgy of violence in France:

The Fifth Column really does exist; every night blue, green and red lights appear everywhere. A regiment cannot remain two hours in a tiny spot without being invariably bombed with enormous bombs . . . Dispenser Charbonnier, at our hospital, had five persons shot, one a beautiful young girl; by showing lights and curtains of different colours, they had guided

German aircraft, signalling to them and thereby causing fires in the neighbouring chemical factory.

Six months after France had fallen, André Morize, who worked at the Ministry of Information before fleeing the country, did much to spread the fifth column myth abroad in America. In a much remarked article published in the *Sunday Star*, Morize described 'entire regiments' of German sleepers in Holland, and reported that spies had bribed French communists to sabotage war production. Some in the US military establishment took these claims seriously, with Major-General Robert Richardson warning the War Department that he had it 'on good authority' that 'the typewriter industry is riddled with Fifth Columnists'. Indeed in February 1942 no fewer than 30 citizens of Japanese extraction were arrested for signalling during the celebrated phantom air raid on Los Angeles, examined in Chapter 12.

What motive underpinned these outlandish falsehoods? Clearly, many on the Allied side had a vested interest in ascribing the German victories to an underhand secret weapon, rather than poor leadership and military incompetence. Yet as we have seen, many in the British military and political establishment, including Churchill, Ramsay and Ironside, gave these myths full credit, Churchill even offering that there were 20,000 organised Nazis in Britain. Indeed the sinking of the *Royal Oak* in Scapa Flow in October 1939, and a series of mysterious explosions at the gunpowder factory at Waltham Abbey two months later, convinced many of the reality of a dangerous fifth column in Britain. According to R.V. Jones, both MI5 and the RAF continued to chase shadows long into the Battle of Britain:

> Great zeal was expended by security officers in chasing reports of fireworks being let off while German aircraft were overhead. Our countryside was scanned by aircraft of the RAF looking for suspicious patterns laid out on the ground which might serve as landmarks to aid the navigation of German bombers. More than one farmer was surprised by a call from security officers to explain why he had mown his hay in such a manner as to leave a striking pattern which could be see from the air. One chapel, whose gardener had unconsciously laid out paths in the pattern of an enormous arrow as seen from the air, and which did indeed point roughly in the direction of an ammunition dump ten miles away, was raided as a suspected Fifth Column Headquarters.

A similar account was given by a 21 Squadron officer stationed at RAF Watton in Norfolk, Wing Commander P. Meston:

> My best friend, Flight Lieutenant David Watson, one day asked me if I had noticed anything unusual about the countryside. I authorised a flight and we took off to investigate. After about 20 minutes David asked if I could see anything abnormal. I replied that I couldn't. I still remember his reply 'Look

at the bloody lime heaps' and then it came into focus. The heaps were in straight lines across the country, complete with arrows. We followed the lines but couldn't make sense of them. We reported this to our squadron CO and eventually it reached the station commander, Group Captain Vincent, who chided the CO for listening to two young pilots who had let their imagination run riot. Nevertheless he took a look himself and informed higher authority. Next day the place was swarming with MI5 and we were told to shut up and not mention this to anyone. About a year later we learned, quite by accident, that the lime heaps were markers for the German airborne invasion of the UK, and that in addition there were prepared airfields with filled-in ditches and fold-down hedges.

As might be expected, actual prosecutions for fifth column activity were few and far between. A former Mosleyite named Saxon-Steer received seven years for pasting up a flyer for the New British Broadcasting Service in a telephone kiosk, while in December 1940 a landlady named Dorothy O'Grady was sentenced to death for cutting telephone wires on the Isle of Wight, although later it emerged that her confession was false. The only remotely serious case was that of Marie Ingram, a German-born woman married to an RAF sergeant, who conspired with a number of former BUF members in the Southsea area to wheedle military information from serving soldiers, and infiltrate the local Home Guard to obtain arms and ammunition. On her conviction in July 1940 Ingram was jailed for ten years, and an accomplice named Swift for fourteen.

Even if the Ingram case convinced some of the reality of the fifth column threat, belief in the myth went deeper still. Some historians have concluded that the fifth column menace was deliberately fabricated to support mass internment in Britain, and in this there is a great deal of truth. Between January and April 1940 several British papers, including the *Sunday Dispatch* and the *Daily Mail*, attempted to whip up a storm about the 'enemy alien menace', which comprised 'fascists, communists, peace fanatics and alien refugees in league with Berlin and Moscow', as well as the IRA. In February, the *Evening Standard* even claimed that the Gestapo was busy 'employing Jews to spy in England'. However, such reports made little headway, and other papers were more cautious. *The Times* warned against the 'hysterics' of the last war, pointing out that most aliens had come to Britain as bona fide refugees from Nazi persecution, and had already passed through several vetting procedures. The *Daily Express* took a similar view, concluding that 'all liberal-minded persons, all who value freedom and liberty in life, should stand against every recrudescence of the witch-hunt, no matter what form it should take'.

Even after the invasion of Norway and Denmark, it seems that the majority of the British public refused to take the fifth column seriously. Naomi Royde-Smith, whose book *Outside Information* (1941) takes the form of 'a diary of rumours' heard around Winchester, recorded the following:

After the withdrawal from Norway, Quisling rumours ran like wildfire. My early tea was brought up one Sunday morning with the announcement that the Town Clerk had been arrested as a spy. Sleepy though I was I refused to believe this news. It was entirely untrue. There is, however, a circumstantial tale of a local clergyman's daughter who was able to denounce as a spy a British officer quartered on the vicarage. She heard him going late at night to the lavatory – but he never pulled the plug! This un-English behaviour excited her suspicion, she reported it, and her guest was discovered to be signalling with a flashlight from the window of the retreat.

During the last week in April, Mass Observation conducted an extensive enquiry into attitudes towards the fifth column. The result was revealing:

We found that the majority of people hardly realised what the phrase meant. We also found that the level of ordinary people's feelings was much less intense than that expressed in some papers. Detailed interviewing in several areas in London and Western Scotland produced less than one person in a hundred who spontaneously suggested that the refugees ought to be interned en masse.

There can be little doubt that the fantastical reports concocted by Bland and Department EH were prepared with this end in mind, and passed on to the Ministry of Information as the basis for articles offered to British newspapers. The same disinformation was also circulated in America, notably in a series of four articles written by Colonel William Donovan published by the *New York Times* in August, clearly based on information supplied during his celebrated intelligence mission to Britain between 14 July and 4 August. By December 1941, and the attack by Japan on Pearl Harbor, these same stock signalling and alien myths were being reported in America as fact, as we shall see in Chapter Twelve. Whether this concerted campaign to convince the British public of the reality of the fifth column menace bore fruit is doubtful, for in July a Gallup Poll revealed that a mere 43 per cent of the general public wanted all aliens interned. And on at least one occasion, magistrates dismissed a case against a German-born woman who was prosecuted for allegedly flashing signals to enemy aircraft with a torch.

There was however another pressing reason to keep the population alarmed by fifth column fantasy. On 10 May, the day that Holland, Belgium and France were attacked, Churchill replaced Chamberlain as Prime Minister, and the great invasion scare began in earnest. The diary of his private secretary, John Colville, records a revealing conversation with Churchill at Chequers on 12 July:

He emphasised that the great invasion scare (which we only ceased to deride six weeks ago) *is serving a most useful purpose: it is well on the way to providing us with the finest offensive army we have ever possessed, and it is keeping every man and woman tuned to a high pitch of readiness. He does not wish the scare to abate therefore,* and although personally he doubts whether invasion is a serious menace he intends to give that impression, and to talk about long and dangerous vigils, etc, when he broadcasts on Sunday.

The italics are mine, and serve to emphasise a tried and trusted method which was employed time and again during the Second World War. In May 1941, when German airborne troops captured the island of Crete, word was spread that parachutists had descended disguised as Greeks and New Zealanders. And on 2 March 1942, in announcing that Japanese troops were attacking Java, the BBC reported that the enemy had approached an Allied post disguised as British soldiers. In reality, race alone would have sufficed to betray such a ruse. But the reality seldom extinguishes myth.

CHAPTER TWO

The Royal Oak

During the first few months of the war, two disastrous events did much to convince some in Britain that the fifth column posed a clear and present danger. One was a series of devastating explosions at the Royal Gunpowder factory at Waltham Abbey on 18 January 1940, the cause of which was never determined with certainty, and the other the sinking of the battleship *Royal Oak* while lying at anchor in Scapa Flow on 14 October 1939. The events of Black Saturday at Scapa, in which 833 officers and men lost their lives, have given rise to a whole raft of myths and legends, including sabotage, watchmaking spies and mutinous submarine crews. The loss of the *Royal Oak* makes for an interesting case study, not least because it demonstrates just how readily disaster is mythologised.

The facts of Black Saturday can be covered briefly. At midnight on a clear moonless night Lieutenant Gunther Prien navigated his submarine U47 through Kirk Sound, the northernmost of the eastern entrances to the naval anchorage at Scapa Flow. Moving on the surface, the submarine slipped between blockships, taking advantage of slack, poorly maintained defences. Inside the Flow, Prien spotted a battleship, which he mistakenly identified as *Repulse*, and fired off a salvo of three torpedoes. Only one of these hit, striking right forward of the *Royal Oak* and inflicting little damage on the massive ship. Indeed officers who went to investigate the explosion concluded it had originated inside the ship, and raised no general alarm. Prien was therefore able to reload his tubes and loose off a second salvo, two of which hit home. Within thirteen minutes *Royal Oak* capsized with massive loss of life, since a power failure meant that no order was given to abandon ship. Prien withdrew, and returned safely to Germany, where he was decorated with the Iron Cross for his outstanding seamanship and courage. The attack was by any measure an admirable feat of arms, and an unmitigated disaster for the Royal Navy.

Because the anchorage at Scapa Flow had long been considered impregnable, investigators initially guessed that the first explosion had been internal, and in turn ignited the ship's Inflammable Store. Other possibilities tabled included mines dropped by aircraft, and sabotage – a belief which remained particularly strong among surviving members of the crew. In the days which followed rumours reached fever pitch, so much so that a possible author of the crime was identified in the form of the 'Saboteur of Lyness', a naval base on the island of Hoy. It was not until some time later that the BBC intercepted a German news item in which it was claimed that a lone German U-boat had been responsible for the sinking. Finally, on 18 October, Prien was introduced to a gathering of press correspondents in Berlin, as CBS newsman William Shirer recorded in his *Berlin Diary*:

> Prien is thirty, clean-cut, cocky, a fanatical Nazi, and obviously capable . . . He told us little of how he did it. He said he had no trouble getting past the boom protecting the bay. I got the impression, though he said nothing to justify it, that he must have followed a British craft, perhaps a minesweeper, into the base. British negligence must have been something terrific.

It had indeed. The Admiralty Board of Inquiry established that at the material time there had been at least eleven significant flaws in the Flow's defences, including gaps in the booms and inadequate lookouts and patrols. Whether or not the various investigators from MI5 and the Naval Intelligence Division were aware of these lapses at the time, it was noted that there had been no recent German aerial reconnaissance before U47 slipped in, and so it was widely believed that Prien must have been helped by a spy. Certainly it was a fair assumption that Prien had the benefit of inside information. For surely he would not have risked penetrating the Grand Fleet anchorage without being certain of finding a worthwhile target, and the operation required a detailed knowledge of the channels, block ships and defences. Indeed Scapa Flow frequently harboured no capital ships at all, and the *Royal Oak* had returned only two days previously.

MI5, NID and Special Branch personnel descended on Orkney en masse in an attempt to trace the agent who had made Prien's exploit possible. They failed, and instead managed only to turn up a suspicious Italian photographer who ran a camera shop in Inverness, and was promptly interned. This marked a serious defeat for British intelligence, and in particular for Major-General Sir Vernon Kell, the head of MI5, whose confidence that all German agents in Britain had been rounded up at the outbreak of war was critically undermined. Kell seems to have been held responsible for this apparent lapse in security, and following the explosions at Waltham Abbey two months later was removed from his post.

Remarkably, two years later an American journalist succeeded where the combined might of various British intelligence agencies had failed. On 16 May 1942 the *Saturday Evening Post* carried an article on 'U-Boat Espionage' written by Curt Reiss, himself a political exile from Austria. According to Reiss, the submarine which sank *Royal Oak* had been guided through the anchorage by a

German spy who, prior to the outbreak of war, had posed as a Swiss watchmaker in Kirkwall, the nearest town to Scapa Flow. Reiss claimed the spy had established on 11 October that two entrances to the Flow were not closed by anti-submarine nets, and after sending back a coded message rendezvoused with a German submarine on the 13th:

> The man, whose last name begins with a W, was neither a Swiss or a watchmaker, but a German lieutenant commander working for the German U-boat Espionage . . . The naval inquiry board in London had little difficulty in finding out that watchmaker W had disappeared. His deserted car was found in the morning after the sinking in the vicinity of Scapa Flow.

In fact no such information had been uncovered by the Admiralty Board of Inquiry, and the story written by Reiss was a fabrication. According to a later investigation by the author Ladislas Ferago, Reiss had been duped by an unnamed, impoverished fellow journalist:

> The spy was dreamed up and the entire story of his exploit fabricated by a Central European newspaperman living as a refugee in New York. He had been prominent in his profession in Europe, but had fallen on hard times in the United States . . . He was respected and trusted as a reputable journalist on the strength of his past record. He found it relatively easy, therefore, to merchandise his sensationalistic confections to American news associations, magazines, and fellow writers, including Reiss, who were looking for dramatic material about the European scene for articles which were then in great demand in the literary market . . . And it was on this grapevine that the British authorities picked it up. They checked it out by the simple process of an MI5 agent in New York interviewing the inventor, and accepting his veracity at face value.

It is unclear whether or not some in the British intelligence community accepted the spy story as true, although no doubt the NID would have been happy to do so. Three years later, the fictive tale of the Swiss watchmaker was revived and expanded by another journalist in the United States, this time Kurt Singer. Like Reiss, Singer had been born in Austria, and had published well-received biographies of Hermann Göring and Pastor Niemoller. In 1945 he published a lesser work titled *Spies and Traitors in World War II*, which included a chapter on 'The Man Who Really Sank the Royal Oak'. By this account, the spy was a German named Alfred Wehring, who arrived in Kirkwall in 1927 having assumed the identity of Albert Oertel, a Swiss watchmaker. Singer was a prolific author of books on crime, espionage, movies and the occult, and also produced a large quantity of pulp cowboy fiction. Between 1945 and 1959 he reworked his account of the phantom of Scapa Flow several times, including chapters in *More Spy Stories* (1955) and *Spy Omnibus* (1959). Bearing in mind that British intelligence had drawn nothing but blanks when chasing the phantom spy in 1939, the level of detail provided by Singer in 1959 clearly betrays its basis as fiction:

In 1927, twelve years before Hitler launched his attempt at world domination, there came to Britain from Switzerland a somewhat retiring and bespectacled little man answering to the name of Albert Oertel. He told the immigration authorities that he was a watchmaker and would very much like to carry on his trade in the United Kingdom . . . In truth Switzerland was not his native land. Nor was his real name Albert Oertel, though that was certainly the name on his passport. The watchmaker from Switzerland was in reality Alfred Wehring, an ex-German naval officer who had served the Kaiser with distinction in World War 1. After the 1918 surrender, Germany had little to offer its former officers. Wehring spent the next four years in restless idleness. Then, in 1923, Admiral Canaris, then quietly reconstructing Germany's spy system and who held a high opinion of the young naval officer, offered him a post in the organisation. It was a new line of work for Wehring, but he was thankful to become active again.

In reality, Wilhelm Canaris did not become head of the *Abwehr* until January 1935. Singer goes on to record that Wehring/Oertel served a lengthy apprenticeship in the watch trade, and in time became a proficient craftsman in readiness for an important secret mission:

Equipped with a passport provided by Admiral Canaris in the name of Albert Oertel, nationality Swiss, Wehring came to Britain and in due course settled down in the pleasant, old-world town of Kirkwall in the Orkneys, not far from Scapa Flow. At first he worked for a local jeweller whom he persuaded to take in watch and clock repairs instead of sending them to Leith . . . His work was excellent, and he soon earned quite a reputation. It was not long before he opened a shop of his own in one of Kirkwall's quaint, narrow streets. It was a small place, rather like that in Dickens's Old Curiosity Shop, where Wehring, alias Oertel, sold fancy goods and souvenirs and, of course, carried on with repairing clocks and watches. The people among whom he now lived liked Oertel. He was pleasant, courteous, apparently honest, and his business enjoyed considerable patronage. Several of his customers invited him into their homes. He made many friends. Life in the coastal town was indeed enjoyable, so much so that in 1932 Oertel completed the process of assimilation by becoming a naturalized British subject.

Singer also wrote that Wehring was in wireless communication with his *Abwehr* masters in Holland, regularly scoured the countryside armed with maps and binoculars, and that he travelled to Rotterdam in September 1939 for a secret briefing about the long-planned submarine attack on Scapa Flow. All of which was demonstrably false. Several investigators, including Nigel West, Wolfgang Frank, Alexander McKee and Gerald Snyder, have all conducted extensive enquiries in the Orkneys, and found no trace of anyone remotely resembling Wehring/Oertel. Home Office records reveal that no one named Wehring, Oertel or any other name attached to the phantom spy applied to become a naturalised British subject, and in 1959 the leading watchmaker and jeweller on Orkney, a Mr Hourston, confirmed to McKee that Oertel had never been in business, or existed. In 1976 all fifteen living survivors of U47's original crew of 44 confirmed that no spy had played any part in the mission. Prien's commander, Admiral Karl Dönitz, published his memoirs in 1958, and he too denied any knowledge of Wehring. In 1983 Orkney's chief librarian confirmed in a letter to Nigel West that

> No watchmaker, Swiss or otherwise, worked in Orkney at that time, either on his own or in the employment of any of the local watchmakers. The name Albert Oertel is pure invention, probably derived from the name of the Albert Hotel in Kirkwall.

In fact Singer seems to have become lost in his own web of intrigue, for he gives two conflicting versions of Wehring's eventual fate. In his original account, published in 1945, the author offers that Prien and 'submarine B-06' kept a pre-arranged rendezvous with Wehring 'close to the easternmost tip of Pomona Island' and picked him up in a rubber dinghy. Wehring then handed over his plans and assisted Prien in penetrating Scapa Flow. Their mission completed, the spy returned to Kiel with the jubilant crew:

> In the midst of the celebration, one man not in uniform slipped away from the dock to which submarine B-06 was moored. Though the newspapers gave citations to everyone of the crew by name, not a word was said about this civilian. The man had not been invited to the banquet.

By 1959 the plot had changed, for Singer now placed Wehring on dry land on the night of the attack:

> The subsequent history of the man who posed as Albert Oertel is shrouded in mystery. It is known that he left Kirkwall shortly after the disaster, suddenly and without explanation. He was serving in his shop one day. The next day he was gone. Some say that he was picked up under cover of darkness by a German submarine and taken back to Kiel. No record of this was found in the official papers captured by the Allies, nor was there any indication that he was given further assignments elsewhere.

In the decade after the war's end, several other accounts published in Europe and America promulgated the myth of the phantom spy. In Britain a former Czech resistance fighter named Edward Spiro wrote a series of less than reliable books on intelligence matters under the pseudonym E.H. Cookridge. The first of these, *Secrets of the British Secret Service*, published in 1947, contained an essentially identical account of the sinking of *Royal Oak*, albeit with names and nationalities altered:

> In 1927 . . . a Dutch citizen, Mijnheer Joachim Van Schullerman, arrived in England, as the representative of a Swiss firm of watchmakers and jewellers . . . By 1932, as he had been a resident for five years in Britain, Schullerman applied to the Scottish Office for naturalization. Everyone in Kirkwall knew him well, and it was not difficult to find a few leading citizens to vouch for him. The papers went through without a hitch.

According to Cookridge, Van Schullerman was in fact a German naval captain named Kurt von Müller:

> Knight of the Iron Cross, Knight of the Military Merit Order personally awarded by the Kaiser for gallantry at the Battles of Jutland and the Kattegat, he had endured the shame of watching the defeated German navy sail into surrender at Scapa Flow in 1918.

Like Singer, Cookridge invented a wealth of personal detail, including a trip to Rotterdam in September 1939, on the pretext of visiting his terminally ill mother:

> A few days after his visit to Rotterdam Schullerman returned to Scotland, clad in deep mourning. He received plenty of sympathy as he told how he had arrived a few hours too late to comfort his mother. People noted how terribly cut up the little man was during the following fortnight. He seemed to have no zest for life, and often did not trouble to take the shutters down from his tiny shop, doubtless spending his time in meditation and prayer in the back room.

Cookridge also duplicated Singer's original ending, while adding a twist of his own:

> In Kiel a great celebration was held as the submarine entered the dock. Admiral Dönitz was there to congratulate the captain and crew. Few people bothered about the short, stoutish man in civilian clothes who unobtrusively emerged from the conning tower and was hurried to a waiting aeroplane which took off for Berlin . . .
> The omission of Müller from the long list of awards seems to indicate that Canaris had a plan to use his henchman's abilities in some other direction later, but it is certain he never played an active part in espionage in the British sphere. His name appears for a time as an official in charge of departments of the *Nachrichtendienst* in Holland and France, and then disappears into oblivion. So far he has escaped the Allied dragnet, and unfortunately it must be admitted that a man who could play the part of a

watchmaker unfalteringly for twelve years would have little difficulty in posing as an anti-Nazi or Displaced Person in some quiet corner of the occupied Reich.

In truth, it was displaced persons such as Singer, Spiro and the anonymous 'central European' discussed by Farago who lie at the heart of the fiction, no doubt finding themselves short of funds in a strange land, and unable to resist falsifying history in exchange for a feature fee or modest advance from a publisher. That is almost certainly the root of the tale of Wehring/Oertel/von Müller, although perhaps the strangest twist came in 1956 with the publication of *The Schellenberg Memoirs*. Since early 1940 Walter Schellenberg had been head of the *Sicherheitsdienst*, the SS intelligence service, and died in Italy in 1952 after serving three years in prison for war crimes. His purported autobiography, although assembled from questionable sources, was authenticated by the distinguished academic and historian Alan Bullock. Despite these credentials, however, Schellenberg's account of the phantom of Scapa Flow was almost identical to that given by Reiss and Singer more than a decade earlier, and does much to support the view that *The Schellenberg Memoirs* are bogus.

How important intelligently planned long-range preparatory work can be – and how rewarding in the end – is shown by the successful operation of the German U-boat Commander, Captain Prien, against the British naval base at Scapa Flow in October 1940 [*sic*]. The success of this operation was made possible by careful preparatory work over a period of fifteen years. Alfred Wehring had been a Captain in the German Imperial Navy and later joined the military sector of the Secret Service. After the First World War he became a traveller for a German watch factory. Working all the time under orders from the Secret Service, he learned the watchmaker's trade thoroughly in Switzerland. In 1927, under the name of Albert Oertel and with a Swiss passport, he settled in England. In 1932 he became a naturalized British subject, and soon afterwards opened a small jewellery shop at Kirkwall in the Orkneys, near Scapa Flow, whence from time to time he sent us reports on the movements of the British Home Fleet.

It was in the beginning of October 1939, that he sent us the important information that the eastern approach to Scapa Flow through the Kierkesund was not closed off by anti-submarine nets but only by hulks lying relatively far apart. On receipt of this information Admiral Dönitz ordered Captain Prien to attack any British warships in Scapa Flow . . . The sinking of this battleship took less than fifteen minutes – but fifteen years of patient and arduous work by Alfred Wehring had been the necessary foundation for this supremely successful mission.

Since no spy existed, Schellenberg either lied, or else had little to do with writing or editing his own book. Yet another American account, penned by a former intelligence officer named Christopher Felix in 1963, managed to confuse both Wehring's occupation and the vessel sunk by U47:

A notable example of the 'sleeper' agent was the innkeeper whom the Germans introduced into the British naval base of Scapa Flow not long after the First World War. He didn't stir during all the years until the outbreak of the Second World War; he was then able to provide the information which permitted a Nazi submarine to sneak into Scapa Flow early in the war, torpedo HMS *Ark Royal* [sic], and escape untouched.

Despite the wealth of evidence that Wehring never existed, the phantom of Scapa Flow continues to haunt the pages of supposedly serious histories. As recently as 1984 a study of the *Abwehr* by Lauren Paine rehearsed the same hoary tale of the Swiss watchmaker in Kirkwall, who had observed the *Royal Oak* 'enter the protected roadstead without having to wait until the submarine nets were lowered, which meant that the ship was vulnerable from the east'.

At least one account identifies the spy not as Wehring, but as Gunter Prien himself. According to Geoffrey Cousins, who published *The Story of Scapa Flow* in 1965, Prien undertook a solo spy mission to Orkney while a member of the Hitler Youth. No source for this information is given by Cousins, and no year. Nonetheless, by this version:

It was in pursuit of his dreams and ambitions that he spent a holiday on Orkney, apparently just a young German tourist but, in reality, a spy. On his walks to inspect ancient monuments, to watch the seabirds and study the flora of the islands, he observed and recorded in his mind many facts about Scapa Flow and the islands enclosing it, facts which had no antiquarian, ornithological or botanical significance but which were to help him when the time came to plan his great enterprise . . .
    Time after time, his wanderings took him down the road from Kirkwall, past Scapa Pier, to where he could watch the swirling current as the tide ebbed and flowed between the rocks. He studied this channel in all kinds of weather and at all heights of tide, and from his observations deduced that there was a way into Scapa Flow through Holm Sound. A way which would require skill, courage and luck, but still a way . . . Prien stored all the information he had gained and returned to Germany, where, in due course, he joined the submarine service.

Prien is generally assumed to have been killed in March 1941, when U47 was sunk by the destroyer HMS *Wolverine*, and so was unable to confirm the truth (or otherwise) of this new slant on the story. However his own short biography, published in Germany in 1940 as *My Way Towards Scapa Flow*, and in translation as *I Sank the Royal Oak* in 1954, makes no mention of any such holiday or exploit. Indeed Prien gave no indication that he had ever set foot on British soil.

Yet another spy variant was conjured by Richard Deacon, the pseudonym used by journalist Donald McCormick. In *The Silent War*, his book on naval intelligence first published in 1978, Deacon dismissed the possibility that Alfred Wehring existed outside the imagination of Reiss and Singer, but then proceeded to construct an equally elaborate fantasy based on the supposed existence of another German agent on Orkney. An entry in U47's log timed at 01.20 hours on 14 October records that the headlights of a car travelling along the coast road between St Mary and Kirkwall briefly settled on the submarine, before the vehicle sped off in the direction of Scapa Flow. Prien feared his boat had been spotted, but no alarm was raised, and U47 continued on its way unmolested.

Despite the best efforts of the Admiralty Board of Enquiry, the driver of the car was never identified. Against this background, Deacon wondered:

What is interesting is that the mysterious car driver proved as elusive as Oertel: he was never located. Is one possible explanation that the car driver was one of Canaris' undercover agents whose job it was to frustrate Prien's mission? Bizarre as such a theory may seem, it is not improbable . . . Canaris would go along with Dönitz to a certain extent, but from what we know about him it is more than likely that he would not wish to see the Royal Navy suffer too heavy a blow. One ship lost, perhaps, but more than that would be unthinkable. Did he send an agent in a car to flash his headlights and then drive off with the aim of frightening Prien into believing that he had been discovered, thus making him stop at one act of sabotage, instead of sinking other capital ships?

Even if Canaris harboured Allied sympathies at this early stage in the war, Deacon's theory is scarcely credible, not least because such a plan would have left far too much to chance. In any event, in 1980 the likely driver of the car was revealed to be a garage proprietor and taxi driver, one Robbie Tulloch, who had been busy running fares to a dance in St Mary's.

An altogether different theory was advanced by Alexander McKee in 1959, who in *Black Saturday* claimed not only that Wehring was a fiction, but that Prien and U47 never penetrated Scapa Flow. McKee based his startling conclusion on several factors, including a supposed lack of torpedo fragments, or any spent torpedoes fired by Prien which failed to find a target. In addition, McKee cited depth and tide data, and supposed discrepancies in the account of the action written up in U47's log. In fact parts from two other German Siemens torpedoes were located by scuba divers in 1973. Whatever view is taken of McKee's conclusions, however, it remains the case that many *Royal Oak* survivors refused to believe their ship was hit by torpedoes, or that Prien entered the Flow at all. Most pointed to the fact that stores stencilled with the name *Royal Oak* had been left on the dockside for some time, although how many hundreds of kilograms of explosive could have been smuggled on board is quite another matter. Besides which, *Royal Oak's* main magazines did not explode.

After diving and salvage operations began, a raft of other more ghoulish rumours began to circulate, as McKee records:

On Sunday, the 15th, diving operations began. What the divers found there echoes still. There were bodies leaning out of the wreck, half in and half out of the portholes; there were corpses in the full, jammed by falling gear; and on the seabed, the bloated corpses of drowned swimmers floated more or less upright, executing in the tides a macabre underwater dance . . . One of the divers, a Portsmouth man, had had a son on the *Royal Oak*; he was still in the hull . . . The scenes found below were still being passed on among the Orkney Defence Force years afterwards; it was said that divers had come up, crazed with horror . . . Stories were going round among survivors that certain named divers had told them either that the explosions were definitely internal, or that the hull had been blown outwards.

As H.J. Weaver observed in 1980, the loss of the *Royal Oak* is not a matter of dusty history in Kirkwall. Shops keep a stock of books on the disaster, summer visitors hire boats to make pilgrimages to the site of the wreck, and 'if you come across a group of men engaged in deep discussion it is an even chance that they are arguing about whether or not Lieutenant Prien ever saw the inside of Scapa Flow'. Profitability prolongs any myth.

In addition to the tale that Prien had carried out his own solo reconnaissance of Scapa Flow years earlier, it was falsely claimed that he was responsible for sinking the *Arandora Star* in July 1940, on which some 600 German, Austrian and Italian internees perished while en route to Canada. After 1941 it was widely rumoured in Germany that the celebrated U-boat ace had not died in action at all, but in a bathing accident, or else in a concentration camp following a court-martial for mutiny. Other variants insisted that he had been executed by firing squad, and that his crew were sent as punishment to a labour corps on the Russian Front. Wolfgang Frank, author of a booklet published in 1949 titled *What Really Happened to Prien?*, recorded his own experience of these rumours at the end of the war:

When the German armed forces surrendered I was out on patrol with another U-boat as war correspondent; we put into a Norwegian fjord and were taken prisoner, and I did not return from captivity to Germany till the autumn of 1945. I was amazed at the rumours, all of the same nature, current not only about Prien, but also about other U-boat commanders and *Luftwaffe* aces. The various versions I heard agreed up to a point: Prien had, so the story ran, refused to put to sea in an unseaworthy boat. Dönitz had had him court-martialled for mutiny, he had been found guilty and sent to the military penal institute at Torgau, from where he had later been transferred to the concentration camp at Esterwegen. There, I was told, he died; according to one version of starvation; according to another stood up against a wall and shot before the arrival of the Allied troops.

As late as 1949 these rumours were still in circulation. On 3 March of that year the *Braunschweiger Zeitung* published the following letter, written by one Hellmut Kuckat of Isenbuttel:

> Prien was neither drowned while bathing nor did he fail to return from an operational patrol. He died on the Wolchow in the ranks of a punishment battalion. A naval lieutenant who was a friend of Prien showed me a snapshot of his grave surmounted by a wooden cross on which his name and rank were painted. Prien and his whole crew were sent to a punishment battalion on the Russian front for making false tonnage claims of sinkings and exaggerating tonnage.

When questioned further by Frank, Kuckat elaborated thus:

> I base my statements on talks with a former naval lieutenant who was in my regiment in the Russian front in the autumn of 1944, having been degraded and transferred to our unit from the said punishment battalion. Unfortunately we were separated in the subsequent retreat. I have only recently returned home from Siberia and regret that after all that has happened to me in the meantime I cannot remember his name. I am aware that my story may appear incredible, but I can only pledge my word that I have no other motive than to throw some light on these mysterious happenings in the war.

Although others claimed to have recognised or encountered Prien in various camps, this particular story is just another in the long line of 'false death' myths common to both world wars. During the First World War, countless dignitaries and establishment figures were rumoured to have been exposed as spies and shot at dawn, including the chief of the scouting movement, Robert Baden-Powell, pioneer aviator Claude Graham-White and Admiral Sir John Jellicoe. Conversely, a legend arose that Lord Kitchener had not perished when HMS *Hampshire* was mined off Orkney in June 1916, and was instead alive in a frozen case awaiting his country's next call. The cult of the undead celebrity grew stronger after the Second World War, and extended to include Adolf Hitler, Wilhelm Canaris, Martin Bormann, Glenn Miller and Joseph Kennedy, as we shall later see.

CHAPTER THREE

The Miracle of Dunkirk

During the course of nine days between 26 May and 3 June 1940, almost 338,000 Allied troops were evacuated by sea from the port of Dunkirk and the surrounding beaches. Myth and legend shroud what was described then – as now – as a miracle, with tales of troops drilling in threes on the Mole, marking time in the surf, and demanding regulation haircuts before departing French soil. To this litany may be added countless motorcycle stunts, innumerable games of cricket on the dunes, and entire divisions lifted by the fabled armada of Little Ships.

In truth, Operation Dynamo was the final page in a chapter of disaster. Yet at the time propagandists wrote up the evacuation as 'one of the most wonderful episodes in our history', in which the British Expeditionary Force had 'marched to Dunkirk to glory's tune'. No phrase seemed too ambitious: while the BBC declared that the BEF had 'come back in glory', the *Daily Telegraph* hailed 'DEFEAT TURNED TO VICTORY', a reversal of fortune which the *Daily Mirror* in turn praised as 'BLOODY MARVELLOUS'. The *Sunday Dispatch* even managed to elevate the deliverance of the BEF into a supernatural odyssey, worthy of the legend of the Angel of Mons:

> The English Channel, that notoriously rough stretch of water which has brought distress to so many holiday-makers in happier times, became as calm and as smooth as a pond . . . and while the smooth sea was aiding our ships, a fog was shielding our troops from devastating attack by the enemy's air strength.

It has long been accepted that the campaign fought by the Allies in Flanders and France was a débâcle, involving gross errors of strategy and tactics, as well as widespread panic, desertion and summary executions. For the French, moreover, the cherished mythology of Dunkirk was inverted to become one of abandonment and betrayal by her British ally. Within the confines of a single chapter it is impossible to fully explore the various myths and legends surrounding Operation Dynamo, and the entirety of the British campaign in May and June of 1940. Nevertheless, the following is an overview of the falsehoods and misconceptions commonly encountered.

One persistent myth is that the ill-fated BEF was a plucky little army defeated by sheer weight of numbers alone. In May 1940 the *Wehrmacht* was numerically inferior to the Allies, with 135 divisions and 2.7 million men deployed against an Allied – that is, French, Belgian, Dutch and British – force of 130 divisions and 3.7 million men. The French army alone was able, at least on paper, to field more tanks and front line aircraft than its German opponents. Indeed only 5 per cent of the German strength comprised armoured Panzer divisions, in which fully 90 per cent of the tanks were obsolete training models or Czech vehicles. For the BEF, however, the situation was far worse. It had no proper armoured component until 21 May, with only 24 of the tanks in theatre armed with anything heavier than a machine-gun. Anti-tank guns were in such short supply that further guns had to be purchased from the French in great haste.

Although the BEF was entirely motorised, much of its transport was made up of unreliable vehicles requisitioned from civilian firms in Britain. Most of the Territorial divisions which arrived between January and April 1940 were hastily improvised, short of regular officers, and of varying quality. Training was scant and unimaginative, leadership often mediocre, and for communications most infantry units in France depended on the seldom reliable public telephone system. Many officers were never even issued with revolvers, and the only ammunition available for many 3-inch mortars was smoke. The sub-machine-gun, first developed by Germany in 1918, was still spurned as a Chicago-style gangster weapon, fit for use only by cowards and automatons. According to the correspondent James Hodson:

> The general view is that much of the German infantry is poor and will not face bayonets, but that his storm troops often wear armour from throat to waist, and, thus protected, stand upright, armed with 'Tommy guns' and turn these to and fro at pretty short range like a hose.

Although little remembered today, gas panics were commonplace among inexperienced troops. On 17 September 1939, exactly two weeks after the outbreak of war, the British Mission at Vauban Madelon cabled the War Office with the alarming news that 'Germans using gas Western Front today'. The erroneous report was probably French in origin, and was not passed on to the Cabinet, despite prearranged War Office procedure. Following the German attack in May gas panics became an almost daily occurrence. A vivid description of a gas alert on a front of several miles is given by Bernard Gray in his book *War Reporter*. For one group of Hampshires at Bachy, the odour from an upset bottle of nail varnish fuelled suspicions that fifth columnists were spraying the area with phosgene gas. For the Coldstream Guards, on 14 May, the trigger was the sight of several lorryloads of Belgian troops driving past at 'a panic-stricken speed' wearing respirators; for another unit it was the 'obscene' appearance of an oxygen cylinder dropped from an aircraft. Tracer bullets, coal gas and 'an enormous yellow billowy cloud' of smoke from a burning fuel dump also caused alarms elsewhere.

Other falsehoods which gained currency on the Western Front in April and May 1940 included the canard that the German Siegfried Line had been constructed in haste from inferior concrete, and would crumble as soon as the first shell hit home. It was also said that a large proportion of German tanks were dummies constructed from wood and canvas, a legend which had first made the rounds early in 1939, after an English motorist supposedly collided with one while touring Bavaria. After the German attack on 10 May it was said that German officers had to prod their reluctant troops forward at gunpoint, and that *Luftwaffe* aircraft were crewed by women. Rumours also flew that other nations had declared war on Germany, including Russia, America, Italy and Finland: all, to a point, echo the celebrated legend of 'Russians in England' in August and September of 1914.

So far as the British public was aware, the BEF was superbly trained, and lavishly equipped with modern weapons. But as we have seen, the truth was very different. Indeed the most damning indictment of the preparedness of the British army came from Major-General Bernard Montgomery, who in 1940 commanded 3 Division, reckoned by some to be the best formation in the entire BEF:

In September 1939 the British Army was totally unfit to fight a first-class war on the continent of Europe. It had for long been considered that in the event of another war with Germany the British contribution to the defence of the West should consist mainly of the naval and air forces . . . In the years preceding the outbreak of war no large-scale exercises with troops had been held in England for some time. Indeed the regular army was unfit to take part in a realistic exercise . . . There was somewhere in France one Army tank brigade. For myself, I never saw any of its tanks during the winter or during the active operations in May. And we were the nation which had invented the tank and were the first to use it in battle, in 1916. It must be said to our shame that we sent our army into that most modern war with weapons and equipment that were quite inadequate, and we had only ourselves to blame for the disasters which early overtook us in the field when fighting began in 1940.

The situation improved little between September 1939 and May 1940. Like Montgomery, few British troops saw a single British tank in France, this despite the fact that the War Office adhered to the outmoded view that the tank was primarily an infantry support weapon, rather than a mobile spearhead. By May 1940 Britain had only 24 tanks in France armed with two-pounder (37 mm) guns, the remaining 76 'infantry' tanks carrying a single machine-gun. None had proper wireless equipment, and most were destroyed during the so-called 'counter attack' south of Arras on 21 May. That same day the 1st Armoured Division was landed at Cherbourg, but itself lost 65 tanks on 27 May while supporting a French attack towards Abbeville.

That the Battle of France was lost in just six weeks was due largely to poor strategy and inertia on the part of the French themselves. Nevertheless, command decisions within the BEF were also flawed. On 10 May Gort's army abandoned the fixed defences on which it had toiled for months, and rushed to advance 75 miles east into Belgium, to the line of the River Dyle. The German breakthrough at Sedan on 14 May left the BEF's right flank fatally exposed. Gort and his staff had expected a static and slow-moving campaign, with the result that communications quickly collapsed under this unforeseen strain. Although there had been sufficient motor transport for the planned advance, this proved inadequate for an improvised retreat on roads choked with refugees. These problems were exacerbated by an acute shortage of fuel. In all respects the decision to advance into Belgium was a supremely poor one, and contributed much to the overall disaster that befell the BEF. So too did Gort's decision to split his headquarters and intelligence staffs between Lille and Arras. Despite the fact that there were countless engagements in which British troops displayed gallantry and *élan*, the simple fact is that as a whole, and at all times, the BEF failed to function effectively as an army.

Accounts of how discipline cracked in some British units during May are legion, yet it would seem there were significant problems throughout the phoney war period. As soon as the BEF landed in France in September 1939, professional criminals within the ranks established contact with French receivers, and began to plunder the British supply lines to feed the French black market. Vehicles arriving from Britain were stripped of spares, tools and accessories, while cigarettes, clothing, cutlery and razor blades were 'scrounged' and pilfered by the lorryload. Following an alarming report prepared by a senior Scotland Yard Detective, George Hatherill, the War Office had no option but to hastily assemble a body of 500 men with police experience for immediate dispatch to France. For as Hatherill had discovered:

At almost every port, railway siding and depot I visited it was the same story. Vast quantities of all kinds of disposable commodities were disappearing, often within hours of being landed. Helped by the blackout, by inadequate precautions in buildings and compounds, and the fact that all units of the Provost-Marshal's office and the Corps of Military Police were overworked and understaffed, thieves and black-marketeers were reaping a tremendous harvest.

With 'nothing to see but sugar beet and rain', drunkenness and violence earned British units a poor reputation in many billeting areas. Major D.F. Callander of the 1st Cameronians described his men as 'very rugged indeed', with a high incidence of venereal disease and difficult to handle when drunk. In the region of six had to be staked out each night, suspended above the ground, by way of punishment, even in extreme cold. Yet mere drinking and whoring palls beside an unpleasant fact revealed by Tom Willy, a Royal Artillery gunner:

Twice the 30th Field Regiment I was with held identification parades after girls had been raped. The girls picked out the guilty people but their pals gave them alibis and they got away with it.

An infantry officer, Lieutenant Peter Hadley, published a frank account of the retreat to Dunkirk in 1944:

The BEF of 1940 started the Flanders campaign full of a self-confidence due principally to newspaper and other propaganda emphasising the strength and preparedness of the Allied armies. But with the rapid German advance it became gradually and increasingly clear that the Allies were in fact inferior, and that self-confidence had been born of delusion. Blasted from this stronghold, morale fell back to the alternative position where it became dependent on discipline alone.

Even in 1944, this admission was strong meat, and four years earlier would certainly have been censored. Instead, in 1940, and in defeat, the BEF was eulogised as a glorious, defiant force. Witness this testimonial from *The New Contemptibles*, written by *Daily Express* war correspondent Douglas Williams:

Not one man failed in his task. Whether he was regular, militiaman or territorial, whether attached to a crack unit with a past history of battle trophies, or to a newly-formed labour unit recruited since the war, one and all fought with the magnificent gallantry that has always made the British soldier, when caught in a trap, the most dangerous of all . . . The disaster was, to a large extent, redeemed and dignified by innumerable individual acts of heroism and courage.

But this is mere propaganda. It has already been noted that many of the Territorial divisions lacked adequate training and equipment, and careful study reveals that no second line brigade survived its first serious contact with the enemy, or significantly delayed the German advance. Indeed during the first eleven days of the campaign the BEF sustained just 500 casualties. As early as 21 May, in the Belgian town of Wortegem, Peter Hadley described a 'disorderly mob' of British soldiers routed by a false report of approaching German armour:

Down the street towards us was straggling a disorderly mob of soldiers, grimy, bloodstained, and obviously badly scared, who pointed wildly up to the church behind them. 'The Boches are up there!' they shouted . . . And they hurried on, looking (if the truth be told) very much like the popular

British conception of the Italian army . . . Then came a more remarkable sight. [We] lit upon a grey-haired captain who was participating in the inglorious cortège.

The description of a friendly-fire incident on a canal bridge near Brussels, given by Alf Hewitt of the South Lancashires, speaks volumes as to the fragile relationship between allies at the sharp end. After a passing body of Belgian troops mistook Hewitt's section for Germans, and opened fire:

There was nothing we could do but retaliate. We weren't a rabble like they were, we were well-trained infantry. We had two Bren guns. The action went on for about a minute and then somebody among them blew a whistle and they stopped firing and we sorted ourselves out . . . When we had a count-up this Belgian officer was crying like a baby . . . We killed 17 of them and wounded many more. It showed we were a bit more efficient than they were. It was regrettable but we were rather pleased. That was our first action at close quarters, and we had come out of it well.

One of the most disquieting aspects of the retreat to Dunkirk was the large number of executions without trial. The enthusiasm of the French authorities for summary justice has already been discussed in Chapter One, yet British units also took part – if not with the same degree of alacrity, then without marked reluctance. At Helchin the Grenadier Guards – described as 'automatons' by one reporter in the field – executed at least seventeen suspected fifth columnists, while the official history of the Coldstream records, in the vicinity of Coyghem:

May 22nd was likewise quiet, the only excitement being provided by Fifth Columnists among the local inhabitants, a number of whom had to be arrested and shot.

It was the Grenadiers, too, who were later obliged to shoot a number of panic-stricken servicemen at Furnes in order to stabilise the Dunkirk perimeter. This robust approach was not restricted to the Guards. An RASC driver named Cole claimed to have taken part in a firing squad at Tournai, at which eight supposed spies were executed. Driver Cole boasted of prising forth eight bullets from the corpses with his jack-knife, 'a private memento that war was hell'. Elsewhere Major John Matthew, also of the RASC, records a distasteful scene enacted at his divisional headquarters:

At the entrance were a very tall, heavily built priest and a little elderly peasant, each of them with two soldiers with rifles cocked and fixed bayonets . . . They were suspected spies awaiting interrogation. Later on, as I came out of the HQ buildings in bright moonlight, the smaller one was being questioned by a French liaison officer, with a revolver pressed into his tummy, and as I passed the little man just collapsed in a heap under the strain. Shortly afterwards they were marched off under escort, whether for further interrogation or for shooting I don't know. Probably the latter, as in a very short time the escort came back without them, one of them wearing the priest's hat.

Behaviour of this kind is more redolent of German *Einsatzgruppen* than British line infantry, and might rightly be described as an atrocity. Yet it was not unusual. Signaller S.L. Rhodda, who never saw a single German, records an incident as his column passed a straggle of refugees. After a pigeon fluttered suspiciously from a male civilian, he was set upon by other refugees, after which:

A couple of Redcaps drove up and whisked him off. About five minutes later, as we moved off, we heard a small burst of rifle fire. An officer of the Redcaps then came along the column warning us to watch out for spies releasing pigeons carrying information to the Germans.

The experience of Anthony Rhodes, a lieutenant with the Royal Horse Artillery, included the shooting of a 'bogus doctor', supposedly dropped by parachute and 'carrying a small leather case which was really a sub-machine-gun'. The interrogation of no fewer than 100 suspected spies by a lone Field Security Police officer in a single day is graphically described in his account *Sword of Bone*, reproduced in full as Appendix One. Here it must suffice to record a conversation between a fellow subaltern and the divisional provost officer, described as 'a Guards officer of the Teutonic variety' and 'ideally suited to his work':

'Do you really shoot spies?' asked Stimpson, assuming a proper air of awe.
  'Of course,' said the provost officer.
'And do you do it entirely on your own? I mean the trial and that sort of thing.'
  'Of course.'
'But I suppose you take very good care that they really are spies, don't you? I mean – it's a sort of absolute power of attorney, isn't it?'
  'It's absolute, all right,' he said, grinning.

There is anecdotal evidence that some BEF units were given orders to take no prisoners save for interrogation. Indeed at Arras orders were even issued to shoot stray dogs, following reports that they were being used to convey messages. Several books about the campaign published later in 1940, such as those by James Hodson, Douglas Williams and Bernard Gray, make a virtue of what amount to war crimes, with frequent references to supposed spies 'shot there and then', 'shot right away' and 'summarily dealt with'. The unpalatable conclusion is that British units were uniformly trigger-happy around alleged spies, and that the numbers of innocent people executed in France, Belgium and elsewhere probably ran into the low thousands. There is a sad irony in this grim statistic, given that the death of 5,000 civilians as the Kaiser's army marched through Belgium in 1914 led to the demonisation of the Hun as a barbaric, baby-spitting horde for the better part of half a century.

Subsequent reports even had the mythical fifth column operating within the Dunkirk perimeter. The *War Diary* of the Royal Warwickshires records on 29 May, en route to Bray Dunes:

> On march passed thousands of lorries and guns lining the roadside, all abandoned and put out of action . . . Some were smouldering having been set alight, it is thought, by Fifth Columnists, because they lit up the countryside, and on a clear night made the marching personnel an excellent target from the air.

Similar tales from the beaches smack of pure invention, for example this extract from *The Epic of Dunkirk*, a work of patriotic eyewash written by E. Keble Chatterton:

> Waiting on Dunkirk beach for a boat was a party of 25 French soldiers, to whom a civilian approached and began making a pleasant conversation. Having ingratiated himself and aroused no suspicion, suddenly he whipped out a 'Tommy' gun and began filling the Frenchmen with lead. All except four. These were quick enough on the uptake to use the same tactics and shoot life out of him.

Elsewhere Chatterton offers another equally tall story, again involving the favoured weapon of the gangster:

> You never knew friend from foe in those dizzy days. One small British steamer had taken on board a full complement of passengers, principally wounded French troops, but among these were a dozen strangers who mingled with the crowd and seemed ordinary enough. Actually they were Germans disguised in French uniforms. Barely had the ship cleared the roadstead and gained the open sea than this bunch of gangsters produced twelve automatic pistols, aimed at the bridge and shot the captain . . . Simultaneously they shot the signaller, who showed himself a brave and resourceful sailor. Dragging himself painfully to the speaking tube, he whispered below to where seven of the crew happened to be . . . The sound of heavy treads indicated that seven men were racing to their shipmates' assistance. Their fury and indignation at such treachery composed one dominating passion and they killed the Nazis forthwith. Meanwhile the ship carried on towards England.

Back in Britain, the evacuation was not announced officially until the evening of 30 May, leading to a run of lurid rumours in the vicinity of ports such as

Dover. Stokers were said to have run amok, only to be hauled from their engine rooms laced into straitjackets. A sailor in the know had presented his wife with a revolver and two rounds of ammunition, while it was whispered darkly that other women were carrying poison capsules, that one old soldier had already committed suicide, and that vast communal graves were being prepared. Oblivious to these dangers, another unknown (but evidently more life-affirming) rumour drew prostitutes to Dover from all over the country, keeping the constabulary fully occupied.

Central to the myth of the BEF's glorious deliverance from Dunkirk are reports of sky-high morale. Apocryphal stories of British units drilling on the streets and beaches, as though on a parade ground, are legion. For example:

> Not many regiments of the BEF marched along the Mole at Dunkirk in threes . . . But 30 or 40 men of the Black Watch did it on June 1st. And they raised their voices in the din, and they sang . . . And they added in a shout, being British and given to irony, 'Up the pole!'

James Hodson tells of the stoic return of men of the Duke of Wellington's Regiment:

> One lad carried his heavy [Boys] anti-tank rifle to Halifax, delivered it to the Quartermaster saying, 'here it is, and I'd like a receipt for it.' That was typical of 'the Dukes' to the end, Yorkshire and humorous and tough.

Press and radio reports described the troops as little more than tired and dishevelled. At an unidentified port on the south coast, a *Daily Telegraph* correspondent watched as men 'from a famous Guards regiment' disembarked:

> They looked clean and smart, many had shaved, some had even found time to polish their boots. They carried their heads high and it was plain that events of the past week had in no way diminished their fighting spirit.

Writing in 1959, Dunkirk veteran David Divine had this to say about tales of chaos on the beaches:

> One of the minor but persistent myths of Dunkirk makes serious charges as to the morale of the BEF. In the early stages of the evacuation . . . there was unquestionably disorder and indiscipline on the beaches. Boats were rushed, and on occasion sunk under the weight of men or overturned in the surf. This was the period of the 'useless mouths' and of the base troops, and of small units that had been ordered to get back to Dunkirk under their own steam . . . But this was a temporary phase and at most it led only to local difficulties. The morale of the fighting army when it reached the beaches and the Mole matched the very highest traditions of the Service – it did more, it added to them.

However, Divine surely overstates his case. On the London–Dover railway line one police inspector noted with alarm the 'whirling flurry of sparks' as demoralised men pitched their rifles from carriage windows. Clearly none had heard the rumour that pay would be docked for items of equipment left in France. In Kent several units of the newly formed Local Defence Volunteers (later the Home Guard) were able to arm themselves with rifles and even Bren guns abandoned on the quays, together with substantial amounts of ammunition. When Anthony Eden addressed troops at Aldershot on 2 June he was hooted and jeered. Even by 30 May, Mass Observers were noting that troops lately back from Dunkirk were 'talking freely about their experiences, particularly in pubs' and that the effect of this was 'not good'.

Indeed not. Writing in his diary on 18 June, London schoolboy Colin Perry recorded:

> Today I heard a story from one of the lads in the gallant BEF. His officers – mainly, I take it, who had bought their commissions in peacetime – deserted their men when their ship was sunk by German dive-bombers. Terrible! Our army has something radically wrong with its organisation, whereas our navy and air force are superb.

Cecil King, a director of the *Daily Mirror* and *Sunday Pictorial*, records a meeting with Thomas Horabin, the Liberal MP for North Cornwall, on 21 June. According to Horabin, during a secret parliamentary session:

> Several people . . . referred to stories of officers running away at Dunkirk. It does appear that there were a lot of cases of officers who pushed in front of their men, or who deserted their men in order to get an earlier boat home.

Later King was told by Eric Fraser, Director of Statistics at the War Office, that

> The Dunkirk episode was far worse than was ever realised in Fleet Street. The men on getting back to England were so demoralised they threw their rifles and equipment out of railway-carriage windows. Some sent for their wives with their civilian clothes, changed into these, and walked home.

Conversely, many returning troops quickly came to appreciate – and exploit – their status as Dunkirk veterans. Peter Hadley noted:

> In the circumstances it was hardly surprising that a large number of soldiers suddenly became aware that they were heroes, and many heads were sadly turned by the enthusiasm of the welcome prepared. The rejoicing which sprang from relief at the miraculous escape was misconstrued as an expression of congratulation upon victory; and many who only a few hours before had succumbed to panic or who felt the chill of fear now wrote the letters 'BEF' on their tin hats and shoulder straps, and stepped forth

straightaway in the guise of heroes, accepting unquestioningly the homage paid to them by an adoring public, whether it took the form of admiring glances or manifested itself more practically in the shape of free drinks.

Montgomery, who quickly banned all such unofficial insignia, voiced much the same sentiment in his *Memoirs*:

> The fact that the BEF had escaped through Dunkirk was considered by many to be a great victory for British arms. I remember the disgust of many like myself when we saw British soldiers walking about in London and elsewhere with a coloured embroidered flash on their sleeve with the title 'Dunkirk.' They thought they were heroes, and the civilian public thought so too. It was not understood that the British Army had suffered a crushing defeat at Dunkirk and that our island home was now in grave danger. There was no sense of urgency.

The Dunkirk evacuation is often remembered as the triumph of the legendary Little Ships, an impression reinforced by J.B. Priestley's celebrated BBC news postcript broadcast on 5 June. Several books published later in 1940 stoked this particular myth, with stirring tales of 'heroes in jerseys and sweaters and old rubber boots' whose rag-tag flotilla 'went in, a line of cheeky arrogant little boats to sit like wrens on the edge of the battlefield'. In truth the contribution made by the armada of small vessels was not especially significant in terms of numbers: two-thirds of the men evacuated during Operation Dynamo were lifted from the Mole, and just 26,000 (8 per cent of the total) by the Little Ships from the beaches. However, the smaller vessels did give sterling assistance in carrying vital rations and ammunition ashore, and provided British propaganda agencies with solid gold copy.

A darker aspect of the legend of Dunkirk remained unexamined until forty years later, and the relevant official files at the PRO remain sealed. Crews aboard several boats which had already crossed the Channel to France displayed a marked reluctance to return, and on some Navy vessels the situation bordered on mutiny. Problems began as early as 28 May, when the steamer *Canterbury* refused to sail, after which a naval party was put aboard to stiffen the resolve of the crew. The following day *St Seiriol* and *Ngaroma* left port only after an armed guard was placed on each vessel, while the tug *Contest* was deliberately run aground by her crew. Once the boat had been refloated, the engineer still refused to cross to Dunkirk, claiming that his filters would become blocked by sand. On the evening of 1 June three passenger steamers, *Malines*, *Tynewald* and *Ben-My-Chree* refused to sail, and appeared to be acting in concert. Indeed the master of the *Malines*, George Mallory, defied orders by leaving Folkestone and returning to his home port, Southampton. He later explained:

> Seven of our consorts were sunk in the vicinity and the weakening morale of my crew was badly shaken. The wireless operator, purser, three engineers

and several other hands were already in a state of nervous debility and unfit for duty, while many of the crew were not to be depended upon in an emergency. I considered that the odds against a successful prosecution of another voyage were too enormous and the outcome too unprofitable to risk the ship.

Several naval ships also succumbed to collapses in morale. The destroyer *Verity* was ordered to remain in Dover harbour after twelve men jumped ship on 30 May, while no fewer than 28 on board the minesweeper *Hebe* had succumbed to fits, convulsions and panic attacks by 1 June.

More infamous was the behaviour of several RNLI crews. On arriving at Dover the coxswain of the Hythe boat, 'Buller' Griggs, refused to accept instructions to run his boat ashore at Dunkirk, take on troops, and float free at high tide. Griggs argued that his boat was too heavy, and sought written assurances about pensions in the event of his crew being killed. When these were refused, Griggs persuaded his colleagues from Walmer and Dungeness not to put to sea. In these circumstances, the Navy had no option but to commandeer the entire RNLI fleet, although to their great credit the boats at Margate and Ramsgate had already sailed with their own crews. Three weeks later both Griggs and his brother, the boat's mechanic, were dismissed from the service, after an RNLI inquiry found that 'failure to perform their duty at a time of great national emergency' reflected discredit on the lifeboat service 'and can in no way be excused'.

Just as the role of the Little Ships was less crucial than legend insists, the alleged absence of the Royal Air Force in the skies above Dunkirk is also a distortion. Between 10 May and the fall of France the RAF lost 959 aircraft, 453 of them precious fighters. During the nine days of Operation Dynamo alone the RAF lost 145 machines, 99 of them from Fighter Command, including 42 Spitfires. Churchill claimed that four times as many *Luftwaffe* machines were destroyed during the same period, although actual German losses totalled 132. This net loss for the RAF is partly explicable by the fact that British army and navy gunners blazed indiscriminately at anything which flew overhead. As one man on the Thames paddle wheeler *Golden Eagle* admitted:

Every time a Hurricane or Spitfire came low over the beach we opened fire because we had heard some had been captured by the Germans and were firing on the squaddies.

Despite the fact that the French prime minister, Paul Reynaud, had warned Churchill that the battle was lost as early as 16 May, poor strategy continued to dog the BEF during and after the Dunkirk evacuation. Historians remain divided on the role of the miracle of Dunkirk played by the stonewall defence of Calais, 25 miles to the west. The orthodox view was spelt out by Keble Chatterton in *The Epic of Dunkirk*, published in 1940:

A new and more wonderful story was to be written on stones already greyed by time's events. Nearly six centuries ago Calais was captured by the bravery of English soldiers. In May 1940 it was defended by English warriors, who bled and died with a self-sacrifice that would have been the admiration of their medieval ancestors . . . Let it be appreciated that on this Calais effort depended the possibility of Dunkirk's evacuation: any withdrawal of the beleaguered BEF a few miles further up the coast, pivoted on what could be accomplished in that gateway to France through which unthinking tourists used to make for Paris . . . Not one man around Calais had perished in vain.

A good deal of bad poetry about Calais was published in *The Times*, and by 1941 the defence of the port had been recast as a pivotal rearguard action which held the Germans back from Dunkirk for two vital days. According to a popular account written by Erik Linklater in 1941:

> The Fury of the death struggle engaged, during four vital days, the whole strength of at least two Panzer divisions that might otherwise have cut our retreating army's road to the sea . . . The scythe-like sweep of the German divisions stopped with a jerk at Calais. The tip of the scythe had met a stone.

While the tremendous bravery of the 3,000 strong Territorial garrison at Calais is beyond question, the plain fact is that their sacrifice was useless. Although reinforced by 30 Brigade, together with a battalion of 48 tanks, these fresh troops were landed with only half their stores and vehicles, and the enlarged force was still badly overstretched. Most of the tanks were quickly squandered in piecemeal engagements with German armour, while others were destroyed prematurely to prevent them falling into enemy hands. On the evening of 24 May the commander of the British garrison, Brigadier Claude Nicholson, received an order from the War Office to stay put 'for the sake of Allied Solidarity', and hold on to a harbour 'being at present of no importance to BEF'. Enraged by the 'defeatist' and 'lukewarm' tone of the order as drafted, Churchill sent one of his own devising on the afternoon of 25 May:

> Defence of Calais to the utmost is of highest importance to our country as symbolising our continued cooperation with France. The eyes of the Empire are on the defence of Calais, and HM Government are confident you and your gallant regiments will perform an exploit worthy of the British name.

Only on the night of 26 May was Nicholson told that the defence of Calais was required to buy time at Dunkirk, and exhorted that 'every hour you continue to exist is of greatest help to BEF'. In his memoirs, Churchill was adamant that this stand alone paved the way for the whole of Operation Dynamo:

> It was painful thus to sacrifice these splendid, trained troops, of which we had so few, for the doubtful advantage of gaining two or three days . . .

Calais was the crux. Many other causes might have prevented the deliverance of Dunkirk, but it is certain that the three days gained by the defence of Calais enabled the Gravelines waterline to be held, and that without this, even in spite of Hitler's vacillations and Rundstedt's orders, all would have been cut off and lost.

Yet this is untrue. The Germans committed just one armoured division out of seven against Calais, 10 Panzer, which had trailed behind other formations, and could not have reached the Dunkirk perimeter line along the Aa Canal before Hitler issued his infamous halt order at 11.24 am on 24 May. The German attack was not resumed until the morning of 27 May, by which time Calais had fallen, while even then 10 Panzer were sent in the opposite direction, to guard the coast between Calais and Audresselles. By the time Guderian decided to send 10 Panzer east towards Dunkirk, the port had been encircled by six other German armoured divisions. Nicholson died while a prisoner of war, haunted by a mistaken belief that he had failed his country. Yet as Guderian confirmed in his memoir *Panzer Leader*:

As the commander on the spot I am able definitely to state that the heroic defence of Calais, although worthy of the highest praise, had no influence on the development of events outside Dunkirk.

In some respects, the needless sacrifice of the garrison at Calais palls beside the almost total loss of the 51st (Highland) Division sixteen days later. As part of IX Corps under General Victor Fortune, the Division was initially sent to man French defences on the Maginot Line, and subsequently found itself cut off from the rest of the BEF by the rapid German advance. After being placed under direct French command the 51st was committed to the defence of the line of the River Somme, but as the situation deteriorated found itself trapped. Although the Division could have escaped by making for Le Havre or Dieppe, Fortune was denied permission by the French commander, Weygand, and finally found himself hemmed into the small harbour of St Valéry-en-Caux. According to Churchill, the loss of the 51st was down to 'gross mis-management' by the French:

I was vexed that the French had not allowed our Division to retire on Rouen in good time, but had kept it waiting till it could neither reach Havre nor retreat southward, and thus forced it to surrender with their own troops. The fate of the Highland Division was hard, but in after years not unavenged by these Scots who filled their places, recreated the division by merging it with the 9th Scottish, and marched across all the battlefields from Alamein to final victory beyond the Rhine.

This interpretation is highly ingenuous. By 8 June the position of the Highland Division had become so precarious that senior British commanders suggested to Churchill that it should operate independently. Instead, as with the garrison at Calais, the Division was deliberately sacrificed by Churchill in furtherance of a misguided policy of being seen to support France come what may. More than 10,000 troops marched into captivity from St Valéry on 12 June, together with another 1,000 taken on the Somme and in the Saar. From his prison camp, Major Wattie McCulloch offered this appraisal:

> At this time France was on the verge of collapse and every effort was being made to keep her in the war. It was no doubt thought that the desertion by the Division at this point of its French comrades would be fatal to the negotiations. One is forced to conclude that it was deliberately sacrificed as a political pawn. Whether this sacrifice was worthwhile is not for me to say. In the light of after events, it seems not.

A second BEF comprising of the 52nd (Lowland) Division and the 1st Canadian Division had been landed in France a week earlier, on 12 June, and the leading brigade also placed under French command. After just two days its reluctant commander, General Brooke, was informed by Weygand that the French were 'no longer capable of armed resistance'. Only on 16 June did Churchill finally allow Brooke to begin re-embarking his troops, the last of them leaving only after the new French government had set about negotiating an armistice. A farcical suggestion that British troops assist in holding a 'redoubt' in the Brittany peninsula thankfully came to nothing, despite Churchill's enthusiastic support.

It is well known that the initial campaign in France and Flanders resulted in an almost total loss of British equipment: 82,000 vehicles, 2,472 guns, 8,000 Bren guns, 76,000 tons of ammunition, and almost half a million tons of stores and supplies. Astonishingly, the second BEF also managed to leave behind a vast amount of stores, including 24,000 tons of munitions. The report of the Howard Committee, delivered several months later, determined that myth and rumour had been partly responsible:

> There was a tendency, both at Headquarters and at the ports, to pay too much regard to unauthenticated reports and rumours . . . A robust determination not to be stampeded by unverified reports and hypothetical fears of disaster would have allowed more time for an orderly and successful evacuation.

Although some 144,000 British personnel (mostly comprising base troops and the reformed BEF) were evacuated from France in relatively good order after Dunkirk, disaster struck on 17 June when the liner *Lancastria*, containing up to 9,000 men, was bombed off St Nazaire. The ship sank within fifteen minutes, and upwards of half the men on board perished, many of them RAF personnel. News of the disaster was censored, as Churchill explained in his memoirs:

When this news came to me in the quiet Cabinet Room during the afternoon I forbade its publication, saying: 'The newspapers have got quite enough disaster for today at least.' I had intended to release the news a few days later, but events crowded upon us so black and so quickly that I forgot to lift the ban, and it was some time before the knowledge of this horror became public.

News of the loss of the *Lancastria* appeared in *The Times* only on 25 July, after American newspapers had covered the story, and like the miracle of Dunkirk was quickly mythologised. Churchill downplayed the numbers involved, estimating that only 5,000 had been on board, of whom 3,000 had perished. Whatever the true figures, at a stroke this catastrophe brought about the deaths of more than twice the estimated 2,000 fatalities caused by air attacks on shipping at Dunkirk.

In France, the evacuation of the BEF – from Dunkirk, and from ports further west – is still seen as a betrayal rather than a miracle. Yet the unpalatable truth is that the Battle of France was lost even before war broke out. France failed to construct the vaunted Maginot Line all the way to the sea, and as the German attack developed in May, her armies – static, and geared to a defensive war – failed to provide an adequate substitute for the missing fixed line. Thanks to flawed dispositions and an inadequate command system, General Gamelin was unable to field a reserve at the critical moment. As Churchill later recalled:

> I then asked: 'Where is the strategic reserve?' and, breaking into French, which I used indifferently (in every sense): 'Où est la masse de manoeuvre?' General Gamelin turned to me and, with a shake of his head and a shrug, said: 'Aucune.'

This passage may have given rise to a myth of its own, for in 1949 Gamelin claimed he had not answered 'There are none' but rather, 'There are no longer any'. Yet Gamelin had himself written of his own armies on 18 May:

> The regrettable instances of looting of which our troops have been guilty at numerous points on the front offer manifest proof of . . . this indiscipline . . . Too many failures to do their duty in battle have occurred, permitting the enemy to exploit local successes, to turn the flank of the most gallant defenders, to wreck the execution of the leaders' concept and know-how. The rupture of our dispositions has too often been the result of an every-man-for-himself attitude at key points, local at first, then quasi-general.

Churchill still harboured vain hopes of keeping the French, and their Fleet, in the war, and to this end was prepared to sacrifice the garrison at Calais and the Highland Division. Yet France had already lost the will to fight, and indeed among many in France the idea took root that Britain had dragged their nation into an unnecessary war, while providing inadequate and half-hearted military support. Early in July the future Vichy prime minister, Admiral Darlin, informed a group of French naval officers that the British had prepared for the withdrawal of the BEF in secret long before it became a military necessity, while the head of the French Mission to the BEF concluded that France had supported the wrong side. The French Government refused to continue the war in exile, no politician of note made their way to Britain, and thus early in July it was found necessary to disable the French fleet by force at Oran and elsewhere.

Against this background, charges of abandonment and betrayal appear churlish. No fewer than 123,000 French troops were evacuated to Britain from Dunkirk, and 47,000 from other Channel ports. The task was not made easier by the refusal of many French troops to embark unless fully equipped, and with the rest of their unit. In the aftermath of the evacuation rumours abounded in France of French troops being forced out of boats and off the Mole, but these owed less to fact than to crude but effective German propaganda. Many French personnel were trans-shipped straight back to ports in the west of France, in the hope that they would return to the battlefield. Few did, and as many simply bolted or waited to be captured. True, some French units fought hard and well, particularly during the closing stages of the battle in June, but these proved the exception rather than the rule, which was that the bulk of the French army had no taste for the fight.

Of those who reached Britain, few elected to remain to carry on the war. Indeed after General de Gaulle toured the vast camps at Trentham Park, Aintree, Haydock, St Albans and Harrow Park, just 7,000 officers and men rallied to the Free French cause by the end of July. Then with the Field Security Police, Malcolm Muggeridge later recalled:

> Some months later I had occasion to visit the French troops temporarily housed in Olympia. They still looked forlorn, despite a group of local girls who had gathered to stare appreciatively at them. I asked one or two about General de Gaulle, and whether they proposed to join the Free French, but they only shrugged and made non-committal remarks. Most of them, I heard later, opted for repatriation.

Many French historians have rationalised their nation's catastrophic defeat with tales of German tank armies opposed by riflemen alone, and swarms of unopposed Stukas diving mercilessly from the skies. Under closer scrutiny, however, each one of these myths evaporates. In 1939 France could field 2,342 tanks against Germany's 2,171, a formidable armoured force which included the fast, well-armed Somua S35 and Char B1 models that were superior to all British and most German types. The situation was broadly similar in the air. For the invasion of France the *Luftwaffe* fielded a total of 2,670 aircraft, of which 1,000 were fighters, against 3,289 modern aircraft of the Armée de l'Air, including no less than 2,122 fighter types. A subsequent claim by the French air chief, General Joseph Vuillemin, that 'our air force ran into an enemy that outnumbered it by five to one' is patent nonsense, particularly given that between 10 May and 12 June the French took delivery of 668 new fighters, so that their combat strength in the air actually increased during the battle. Although it is commonly alleged that the RAF did next to nothing during the Battle of France and over Dunkirk, its combat losses exceeded those of the French air force.

Why, then, did the Armée de l'Air prove so ineffective in May 1940? The simple answer is that less than a quarter of its strength was committed to the battle in the north-east. As for the remainder, early attacks by the *Luftwaffe* on French airfields led to undamaged aircraft being dispersed in haphazard fashion to civilian airports, reserve bases and training fields, without any proper record kept. Deliveries from factories were also diverted from front line units to areas of safety. And so it came to pass that 150 fighters could be seen parked at Tours while the battle raged 200 miles north-east, and that after the Armistice some 1,700 front line aircraft were discovered on airfields in the unoccupied zone. The Italian Control Commission, when reporting on North Africa in 1940, found no fewer than 2,648 modern French combat aircraft there, over 700 of them fighters, many brand new.

More astonishing still is the fact that little, if any, of this equipment was put beyond use. The result, by way of shameful example, was that many of the estimated 7,000 French 75 mm weapons captured intact by Germany would be used to deadly effect against the Allies in Normandy four years later.

CHAPTER FOUR

The Massacre That Never Was

Among the most shameful episodes to occur on the road to Dunkirk in May 1940 were the massacres of almost 200 British prisoners of war by troops of the *Waffen-SS*. At Le Paradis on 27 May, 97 men of the Royal Norfolk Regiment were machine-gunned in a meadow by infantry from the *Totenkopf* Division, while at Wormhoudt the following day some 80 men of the Royal Warwickshire and Cheshire Regiments were herded into a barn by a detachment of the *Leibstandarte* Adolf Hitler, and brutally dispatched with bullets and grenades. Despite initial disbelief, both atrocities were later established as fact, and the officer responsible at Le Paradis, Fritz Knochlein, convicted and hanged in January 1949.

Yet even these twin tragedies are tainted by myth. For in recent years a damaging falsehood has entered into circulation, namely that these massacres were provoked by the killing of a larger number of SS prisoners by men of the Durham Light Infantry near Arras several days earlier, on 21 May. The allegation, which if true would amount to a major war crime, was made by journalist Nicholas Harman in his book *Dunkirk – The Necessary Myth*, first published in 1980. According to Harman:

> The distasteful truth is that men of the Durham Light Infantry did murder an unknown number of Germans who had surrendered, and were legitimate prisoners of war. The DLI advanced, took prisoners and were then forced to retreat. They could not take the prisoners back with them, so they killed the SS men rather than set them free to fight again. That, at least, is how some of the surviving members of the DLI describe the event.

Harman went on to assert that other British army units 'paid the price in blood' for these 'previous murders' a few days later, when the *Totenkopf* and *Leibstandarte* units carried out the killings at Le Paradis and Wormhoudt. Although the central charge against the DLI failed to excite much interest when it first appeared in print, the fiftieth anniversary of Operation Dynamo saw it repeated unchecked by at least two other authors, as well as by Harman in the revised edition of his own book. In *Pillar of Fire – Dunkirk 1940* (1990), published in association with the Imperial War Museum, Ronald Atkin stated:

> What was presented to the world as 'the Arras counter-attack' had far reaching consequences . . . Anger and resentment among the SS at reported atrocities against their comrades taken prisoner was one of the main causes of two massacres of British captives at the end of the same week.

Atkin also referred elsewhere to 'rumours of ill-treatment of German prisoners' taken at Arras, although no sources were given. In his otherwise highly regarded study *The Myth of the Blitz* (1991), Angus Calder also repeated the allegation:

> While SS troops did cold-bloodedly murder 170 British prisoners in two separate incidents, this was after men of the Durham Light Infantry had killed a great many (perhaps 400) SS men who were legitimate prisoners of war.

A later essay by Brian Bond, *The British Field Army in France and Belgium 1939–40*, refuted Harman's main allegation, yet still managed to lend the myth a measure of weight:

> The excuse of the SS units involved was that they were retaliating for British massacres of German prisoners during the fighting round Arras on 21 May.

The charge levelled by Nicholas Harman is a grave one. Yet the simple fact is that no such massacre took place in the vicinity of Arras on 21 May, either by the DLI or by any other British unit. As we shall see, at their highest Harman's allegations were based on hearsay, coincidence and slight historical research, while sailing perilously close to the law of libel. They also stand as a textbook example of the way in which mere speculation can become 'fact' by virtue of simple repetition. In order to understand the origin of this myth more fully, a brief summary of the historical background is required.

Having attacked France and the Low Countries on 10 May, German forces crossed the River Meuse at Sedan and Dinant on the 14th and 15th, and then advanced rapidly westwards. By 20 May they had reached Amiens, and also Abbeville on the Channel coast. The speed of this advance created a long and perilously narrow corridor, however, which was vulnerable to attack. Against his better judgement, Lord Gort succumbed to Churchill's demand for a counter-attack at Arras, the traditional rallying point for the British army in France, to be carried out by the BEF's sole tank brigade together with a mixed force of gunners, motorcycle scouts, and two Territorial battalions of the DLI. There were also elements of a depleted French light mechanised division with about 60 Somua tanks. Facing this inadequate force were elements of three German divisions: 7th Panzer, commanded by Major-General Erwin Rommel,

8th Panzer and the motorised SS-*Totenkopf*. Due to a total lack of air reconnaissance the strength and dispositions of the enemy were unknown to the Allies, and from the outset the Arras attack was a typically forlorn BEF venture. Both the tanks and the DLI were obliged to travel great distances to reach the start line, and arrived late and exhausted. Maps were scarce, artillery support delayed, and radio contact between units poor where it even existed. Nonetheless, at 2 pm on 21 May the mixed British force began to move south in two columns, initially on roads about three miles apart.

The left-hand column, consisting of 6 DLI, 4 RTR and assorted anti-tank units and motorcycle scouts, set out towards Hénin via Ecurie, Achicourt, Dainville and Beaurains. The column on the right, comprising 8 DLI, 7 RTR and similar anti-tank and recce support, followed a route which wheeled round the west of Arras through Maroeuil, Warlus and Vailly to Boisleux-au-Mont. 9 DLI followed both columns as a reserve. The RTR's total strength was some 75 tanks, although of these only 16 were heavy Mk II Matildas armed with two-pounder guns, the remainder being obsolete Mk Is armed with machine-guns, and a scattering of other light tanks. Nevertheless, on both flanks the tanks met with initial success against surprised German infantry and gunners, and in the evening held their own against 7 Panzer in a tank battle which began at about 7 pm. It was at this stage that the inexperienced infantry of *Totenkopf* are said to have panicked and fled from the field in large numbers, although these reports have been overplayed.

Convinced that hundreds of British tanks were advancing, Rommel took personal control of his gun batteries and succeeded in checking the British armour around Beaurains and Wailly, some three miles short of its objective. Indeed this action itself gave rise to the myth that the future Desert Fox saved the day at Arras by employing the deadly 88 mm anti-aircraft gun in an improvised anti-tank role. This is clearly false, since even these powerful guns would have been largely useless against tanks unless they had already been issued with armour-piercing shells. With the attack halted by fierce anti-tank fire and unopposed dive bomber attacks, the British force was obliged to withdraw after a single day of fighting, having lost more than half their tanks and suffering perhaps 200 infantry casualties. More a swipe than a counter-attack, the loss of so much armour made the battle a disaster. But the counter-attack had at least served to dislocate and delay the German advance by 48 hours, inflicting considerable damage in the process, and allowing four British divisions and a large part of the French 1st Army to withdraw towards the Channel ports. In addition, it caused consternation among higher German commanders, Guderian and Rundstedt included, and may have contributed to the delay in the eventual attack on Dunkirk.

Harman's allegations concerning the massacre of an unknown – but apparently 'large' – number of German prisoners by both 6 and 8 DLI were based in part on 'personal interviews' with two former DLI men, one an officer and the other a warrant-officer. Neither has ever been identified, and in February 2002 Harman told this author that he had mislaid all relevant papers, and forgotten their names. Whether either man was an eyewitness is hard to tell, as the core of Harman's evidence was limited to this:

There followed some incidents for which there is no satisfactory explanation. The official history of the DLI has this to say, in its account of the advance of the 8th Battalion:
'C Company, in company with some French tanks, then attacked a cemetery near Duisans where some 100 Germans had taken refuge from the Royal Tank Regiment. When they occupied it, they found only 18 alive and the French stripped them down to the skin and made them lie face down on the road until it was time to take them away.'
The war diary of the First Army Tank Brigade (composed of the two RTR battalions) notes more vaguely: 'At one time a large number of prisoners were taken – these were handed over to the infantry.' The war diary of 6 DLI records that 'large numbers of prisoners were taken.' On the only surviving copy of this document, in the Public Record Office at Kew, the number of prisoners taken was recorded. In the process of clipping it into a file, the digit preceding the two zeros in the total has been cut out of the paper. Other sources, notably the semi-fictional *Return Via Dunkirk*, by Gun Buster, put the number of prisoners at 400. There is no subsequent trace of these prisoners.

Since the only specific location mentioned by Harman is Duisans, the action around the cemetery merits close examination. The 'official history' quoted was not official at all, but instead a book written in 1953 by David Rissik which borrowed heavily from an earlier study by two former DLI officers, Peter Lewis and Ian English. Indeed English, as the officer in charge of 8 DLI's carrier platoon, had himself taken part in the Arras attack. Their account records:

C Company was soon in action. Supported by a few French tanks they attacked a cemetery about half a mile to the west of Duisans where over a hundred Germans had taken refuge when the British armour had passed through the village. The French tanks raked the cemetery area with machine-gun fire and when the infantry advanced they found only 18 Germans alive. The remainder had been mown down by the French gunners. The survivors were handed over to the French who stripped them to the skin and forced them to lie face downwards in the road until it was time to take them away.

This account, published in 1949, makes clear that these luckless German troops had been bottled up in the cemetery and shot up by three French tanks, and the survivors then rounded up by C Company of 8 DLI at about 4.30 pm. According to one account, some of the Germans in Duisans were howitzer crews from 8 Panzer, while it seems a number of others managed to escape from the cemetery into nearby woods. The conduct of the French armoured unit involved is arguably questionable. Lieutenant Ian Pitt, the intelligence officer with 8 DLI, was present at the scene and recalled in 1989:

We came to the cemetery at Duisans just after some French tanks had attacked German motorized infantry along the adjacent Arras-St Pol road. There were many German vehicles on fire. One German sergeant in a pitiful condition with both legs severed looked up at me and said 'shoot me', but I could not do it.

Some Germans who had escaped the hail of French fire had run into the cemetery and were hiding among the gravestones. Our French liaison officer came up to me and said: 'Look, our tanks have got some Germans bottled up in the cemetery, but our men don't want to have to get out of their tanks to flush them out. Will your men come and get them out?' I went into the cemetery with a Frenchman. The First World War gravestones were freshly chipped with machine-gun bullets from the French tanks. There must have been 18 to 20 very frightened young Germans lying there. Brandishing my revolver, I shouted: 'Heraus! Heraus!'

The Germans scrambled up with their hands above their heads. 'You English?' one man asked me. After the hammering they had taken from the French, they seemed relieved to see an English soldier. We marched them out. A French sergeant appeared and we handed the prisoners over to him. He started to push them around a bit, and made them strip to their underpants and lie down on the road. I thought all this was a bit unnecessary, though, of course, we were in the middle of a fluid battle situation and this was an effective way of making PoWs immobile. These Germans were, I believe, then passed to the rear under escort.

Another dozen or so Germans were captured by B Company in a wooded area closer to Duisans. A larger number of prisoners were taken by 4 RTR and 6 DLI on the left flank, while advancing towards Agny and Achicourt. Most of these men were from the 6th and 7th Rifle Regiments of 7 Panzer. According to Lieutenant-Colonel Harry Miller, commanding the left-hand column, the morale of these troops 'was low and they seemed always to be quite ready to be taken prisoner'. Second Lieutenant Tom Allison, a platoon commander in C Company 6 DLI, also noted:

My platoon went after about 50 Germans hiding in a summer house. They all came out with their hands up. A sergeant and some men captured another 50 or so nearby, so in all we had about 100 prisoners. At this stage some Stukas started to make things unpleasant. It was decided that we had better get the prisoners well to the rear. I was ordered to take charge of a ten-soldier escort. The prisoners were quite cheerful, certainly in better shape than we were, and some of them said they were Austrians. We gave the prisoners cigarettes, and quite a bit of talk took place between the escort and the prisoners.

> At Battalion HQ we were told to get them back to 151 Brigade HQ. This
> was at a place north of Arras [Vimy], about two hours' march away. I shared
> a motorcycle with another man and we rode up and down the column
> keeping it on the move. The only hint of trouble came when passing through
> the French villages, where civilians shouted insults at the 'Boche.'

Other prisoners were taken by 6 DLI, including several German anti-tank
gunners in the vicinity of Beaurains, and all were under guard by about 4
pm. In addition, motorcycle scouts from the Royal Northumberland Fusiliers
also took another 40 prisoners at Dainville. Their numbers were further
swelled by the 30 or so captured by 8 DLI on the right flank, so that the
total number was probably between 150 and 200. These men were
captured many hours before the Allied force was obliged to retire, and
Harman was quite wrong to infer that they were executed as part of a
hurried retreat by their DLI captors. Indeed en route to 151 Brigade HQ at
Vimy the prisoner column was apparently seen by a Royal Artillery officer
from the 368th Field Battery, Captain R.C. Austin, who published the
fictionalised memoir *Return Via Dunkirk* later in 1940 under the pseudonym
Gun Buster. By his account, at an unspecified 'small hamlet' just outside
Achicourt on the afternoon of 21 May:

> Suddenly round the corner of the road, marching in fours, appeared a
> column of German infantry. Prisoners. A Tommy with fixed bayonet
> marched in front. There were about 400 of them, a good bag for the
> Blankshires. They were a fine-looking lot of fellows, bronzed, fair-haired,
> clean shaven – in fact so fresh and clean-looking that they couldn't have
> done much fighting. Probably they had been brought right up to the front
> line in vehicles and captured almost immediately they alighted. The bulk
> of them were between twenty-five and thirty, and they looked so smart in
> their slate-blue uniforms, their blue helmets with the gold eagle on the
> side, and their new black jack-boots, that they suggested the parade
> ground rather than the battlefield. They were headed by a short, weedy-
> looking German officer with a face like Goebbels. He strode along in an
> arrogant swagger, and was a bit of a blemish on the otherwise
> satisfactory procession.

Austin records that he encountered the same column again the following
morning immediately south of Lens, some five to seven miles north of
Achicourt. If his account is reliable, it contradicts Harman's claim that there
exists 'no further trace' of the DLI's prisoners after 21 May:

> After crossing the Lens-Arras road, whom should I come across but the 400
> German prisoners I had seen brought into Achicourt the previous afternoon.
> They had been marched all the way back and were now lying asleep, dead
> beat, in a ditch, guarded by a few Tommies with fixed bayonets. Little groups

of refugees were prowling round with decidedly hostile intentions, trying to get at the prisoners . . . But the Tommies guarded their prisoners like diamonds. It was a whiff of sane old England to hear one calling out:

'Pass along, please, pass along,' just as coolly as a London policeman breaking up a crowd after a street disturbance.

Another account published in 1950, by Lieutenant-Colonel Ewan Butler and Major Selby Bradford, purports to record the subsequent progress of the PoW column. The figure of 400 was quoted once more, as it would be again in the *Official History* published in 1953. According to Butler and Bradford, in *The Story of Dunkirk*:

They were captured on 21 May, a few miles south-east of Arras, and at last the captives were marched back through the single escape corridor when Frankforce was forced to withdraw. Back went the luckless 400, as footsore as their captors, through Ypres to Furnes, on the Dunkirk perimeter. When three days later, the 50th [Division] moved across the beaches to queue up for a trip home, they still escorted their prisoners, who were now in a very depressed frame of mind. They did not like dive-bombing, and they resented long forced marches. In this their jailers fully agreed with them, but they looked at the problem from a somewhat different viewpoint.

No source for this information about their journey to the coast is given, or for the passage that followed:

As they stood in the water, waiting for a ship, General Martel remarked to one of the guards: 'You seem very keen to get these Huns home – why is it?'

'Awa' man, and use your nut,' the soldier replied, with deplorable lack of respect, 'we're takin' them back to Newcassel an' we'll have them marched behind us in chains up Grainger Street.'

When at last the remnants of 50th Division brought their prisoners safely back to England there was blue murder in many a northern heart as trim Military Police swept forward to convey the captives to prisoner-of-war camps. The Roman Triumph, which was to have electrified Tyneside, was indefinitely postponed.

Although both these sources were available to Harman in 1980, Gun Buster's second sighting on 22 May was glossed over. In fairness, it should be pointed out that Austin's account is heavily fictionalised, while the legend of Martel's encounter on the beach is almost certainly an invention. Certainly Martel made no mention of it in his memoirs, published in 1949. Whatever the truth of the so-called Roman Triumph scenario on Tyneside, subsequent sworn statements by DLI personnel make clear that in reality the 6th and 8th Battalions parted company with their PoWs long before, during the early hours of 22 May.

In May 1940 Captain Harry Sell was the DLI's brigade transport officer. Sell records that while he was at Brigade Headquarters at Vimy at about midnight on 21 May:

I was asked by the staff captain if transport was available for evacuation of prisoners. I advised no . . . The prisoners [later] being reported on the main road, I went at once and found them halted in close formation guarded by a few soldiers, who had slung rifles and no automatic weapons. The Corps of Military Police were all present and in charge. I understood that the prisoners were an amalgamation of those taken by both the 6th and 8th DLI. It was my job to see them off to 50 Division HQ, and I was advised that Captain Buckmaster, the Divisional intelligence officer, would be interrogating a selection of them.

As I walked down the column I did not hear any protest or see any signs of distress. No comments, gestures or demonstrations were made by or to them during their halt at Vimy. I explained the transport position to an NCO in charge, and he reported the prisoners all fit to march. A detachment of military police then took charge of the prisoners and I watched them march off well clear of the Brigade area. That was the end of the matter of the prisoners as far as the Brigade was concerned.

I would quote an entry from the Brigade HQ war Diary:

'May 22nd 01.00 hours – some prisoners were brought back from 6 and 8 DLI. These were sent on to the Divisional HQ escorted by Military Police.'

This is broadly confirmed by Maurice Buckmaster, better known as the chief of SOE's French Section from September 1941, but in May 1940 an army captain and intelligence officer for 50 Division. Buckmaster records that about 4 pm on 22 May, in the 'area' of Arras, he examined fourteen German prisoners from 7 Panzer, including three from the motorised 8th Rifle Regiment captured near Maroeuil, and one man from the 6th Regiment probably taken near Dainville:

They were all communicative and answered questions without reluctance. Morale seemed fairly good. There was no vindictiveness shown against England or France or resentment at being captured. The men were mostly very young . . . Talk of a massacre by the Durhams is nonsense.

If the account given by Austin (as Gun Buster) is truthful, he must have seen the prisoners for the first time late in the afternoon of 21 May near Achicourt, and then again the following morning outside Lens, several miles further north. Unless the column turned on its heel and retraced its steps south, it seems unlikely that at 4 pm on 22 May Buckmaster can have interrogated his fourteen prisoners anywhere very near Arras, but intelligence officers are mobile creatures, and this detail unimportant.

An obvious refutation of Harman's allegations is to be found in verifiable German casualty lists for 21 May. The battle cost 7 Panzer 89 killed, 116 wounded and 173 missing, while the *Totenkopf* Division lost 19 killed, 27 wounded and 2 missing. These figures, drawn from contemporary German military records, were published in Britain as early as 1966, but were not consulted by Harman. Many of the 173 listed as missing from 7 Panzer were undoubtedly taken prisoner by 6 DLI on the left flank. If dozens, let alone hundreds, of prisoners from *Totenkopf* were murdered in cold blood after capture, as is alleged, it is difficult to understand how they came to be absent from their unit casualty returns. Indeed no authoritative history of the *Waffen-SS* makes any mention of an alleged massacre anywhere in May, including Charles Sydnor's definitive 1977 study of *Totenkopf, Soldiers of Destruction.* Such a massacre is also absent from the published memoirs of at least two SS generals, Felix Steiner and Paul Hausser, and was never exploited for propaganda purposes by Germany during the war years. It is also surely significant that the supposed Arras massacre was not raised by Fritz Knochlein as part of his defence at his trial for the atrocity committed at Le Paradis.

Due to the chaos prevailing in late May 1940 there are no precise figures for enemy captives returned through Dunkirk. Indeed it had never been envisaged that prisoners taken by the BEF would be sent to Britain. The figure was probably less than 100, *Luftwaffe* personnel included. Twelve hundred elite German paratroopers captured in Holland had already arrived in Britain in mid-May, and by the end of July most had been shipped overseas to Canada, due to fears that they might break out and link up with the dreaded fifth column. A photograph of a glum-looking party of *Wehrmacht* captives at Dover railway station was published by *The Times* on 3 June, while eyewitness accounts make clear that their presence on boats and trains was less than welcome. If some or all of the DLI's prisoners never reached British ports from the battleground south of Arras, it is because they were handed over to the French, or simply released unharmed.

The account given by Charles Sydnor of the treatment of three *Totenkopf* privates taken prisoner four days later, on 25 May, bears repetition here:

The German prisoners were transferred immediately to a compound near the Channel coast . . . At the rear-area compound, the SS prisoners were interrogated by a German-speaking captain. They were given clean clothes, a warm meal, and cigarettes. During the last days of the fighting in northern France, these men were shuttled around behind the front. According to their own version of the captivity, they were not mistreated by the British. At one point, British soldiers even saved the prisoners from a French mob that tried to lynch them after the *Luftwaffe* had destroyed a small village and killed several civilians. Thereafter they were dressed in British greatcoats and helmets so as not to attract the attention of the French population. The SS men finally escaped when the British soldiers guarding them simply walked away in the confusion to join the last units being evacuated from Dunkirk.

The lack of any corresponding German allegation cannot be underestimated. Hauptman Hans Ulrich Schroeder, then adjutant with the 65th tank battalion of 7 Panzer, recalled the British attack at Arras in the following terms:

> We suffered some very heavy casualties before we were able to stop the British on 21st May. Our infantry on lorries and some of our tanks were hit very hard by British tanks. But a massacre of Germans after surrender? I never heard of such a terrible thing. There was no bad behaviour of that kind in this engagement. I was, of course, talking quite a lot with General Rommel that day and afterwards, and he never made any complaint about the way the British fought the battle, except that they fought rather well.
>
> We occupied the battlefield afterwards and made no discovery of Germans perhaps shot down after surrendering. Our wounded whom we recovered made no complaint. My impression – and that of General Rommel himself – was that the British in 1940 were honourable fighters.

In addition to the episode at Duisans cemetery, Harman relied on the testimony of a Royal Tank Regiment officer to support his contention that DLI troops dispatched German prisoners:

> An officer of 7 RTR on a scouting mission captured a German non-commissioned officer, and carried him back for interrogation. 'I continued into Dainville and handed over the prisoner to a Captain of the DLI for conveyance to Provost personnel. The troops displayed great animosity towards the prisoner, and I was compelled to draw my revolver and order them off before I could reach their officer.' This officer's report is quoted in the Official History of the war in France and Flanders; the passage here extracted was, understandably, omitted by the official historian.
>
> If the Germans had to rely on the Durhams' officers for their protection they were out of luck. By the evening of May 21st most of the DLI officers were dead, and every single one of their eight companies present was commanded by a second lieutenant.

The RTR officer in question was Lieutenant Thomas Hepple, who clarified details of his encounter with troops of 6 DLI in a letter to journalist Laurence Turner in 1981:

> I produced the German from inside the tank and enquired politely: 'Have you any means of dealing with this prisoner?' I was greeted with some remarks indicating that they had plenty of means of dealing with a '******* German.' I then clambered down with my prisoner to look for a Durhams officer. One or two soldiers laid hands on the German's shoulders and I didn't like that, so I pulled my revolver half out of its holster and spoke to them sharply, ordering them to calm down.

The Durhams then stepped aside and allowed me to reach one of their officers. He took charge of my prisoner quite happily, called over an NCO and instructed him to take the German back down the column to headquarters. This NCO was also quite correct in his attitude, and I was satisfied that the German was in safe hands.

Hepple's experience at Dainville hardly amounts to a massacre, and instead describes a tense but commonplace battlefield encounter. What, then, gave rise to the massacre myth? The incident described to Harman, probably at second or third hand, was eventually disclosed by George Self, who in May 1940 was a corporal with 8 DLI and present at Duisans. Although Self omitted the incident from his affidavit sworn on September 1989, the previous year he had volunteered the following information in a taped interview made for the Imperial War Museum. Following the French tank action at the cemetery:

The three French tanks cleared them out of the cemetery, shot them up. Then some of our lads followed in behind and went round to see if there were any prisoners. They passed some Germans that were lying dead. There were about six of them, all lying there wounded or dead. The last boy was shot in the back by one of these Germans that was supposed to be dead. I suppose they just lost their heads and opened up. If there was anybody else alive besides the one that shot our lad, they weren't alive very long . . . They shot everything.

Regrettable perhaps, but scarcely a war crime. As evening fell on 21 May the Territorials of the DLI had just fought their first battle, leaving some so exhausted they had to be kicked to their feet on their way back to Vimy. Many were close to the end of their tether, but even the shooting at Duisans described by George Self does nothing to support the allegation that the officers and men of both battalions of the Durham Light Infantry were complicit in mass murder. Elsewhere in his book Harman asserts that all BEF 'fighting units' had orders to take no prisoners, save for interrogation, but surviving DLI veterans are adamant that no such instruction was received by them at any time during the campaign.

Harman's flawed account of the DLI in combat at Arras contains a host of other, lesser errors. The regiment, apparently, accepted no recruits taller than 5 feet 2, never 'seriously expected' to have to fight in France, had few sergeants, Bren guns or radios, lost almost all its officers in the attack, and was described as 'practically untrained' – none of which is true. But these falsehoods pale beside the murder charge, and also beside the potential danger raised by allegations of this kind. In 1988 it was hinted that a former commander of the *Leibstandarte*, the infamous Wilhelm Mohnke, might yet stand trial for the massacre at Wormhoudt, news which triggered renewed public debate over the accusations levelled by Harman against the DLI. Concerned that the issue might be raised by the defence in any future trial, several former officers and men of the DLI felt obliged to swear formal affidavits which set out the entirely correct manner in which their prisoners were taken and treated at Arras on 21 May 1940. Mohnke never did stand trial, after a German prosecutor concluded there was insufficient evidence, thus removing the risk of the DLI's reputation being smeared in court. Nevertheless, this sorry tale stands as a stark illustration of just how damaging false 'history' can be.

CHAPTER FIVE

Myths of the Blitz

Prior to the outbreak of the Second World War, the threat of aerial bombardment of towns and cities was viewed with the same degree of terror as that stirred by nuclear war two decades later. Although bombing raids against Britain by Zeppelins, Gothas and Giants during the First World War caused little substantial damage, by 1923 the military theorist J.F.C. Fuller had conjured a nightmare scenario of London under fire:

> Picture if you can what the results will be: London for a few days will be one vast raving Bedlam, the hospitals will be stormed, traffic will cease, the homeless will shriek for peace, the City will be in pandemonium. What of the government at Westminster? It will be swept away by an avalanche of terror. The enemy will dictate his terms which will be grasped like a straw by a drowning man.

The following year the Air Staff estimated that every ton of bombs dropped on a city would cause 50 casualties, a third of them fatal. At this time the French were reckoned to be the only potential aggressor, and were credited with the ability to inflict 5,000 casualties on the first day. Based on the same ratio of casualties per ton, the Anderson Committee later predicted 2,000 tons of bombs during the first 24 hours, and a death toll of 28,000 within a month.

In November 1931 the Conservative leader Stanley Baldwin famously predicted that 'the bomber will always get through', while three years later Churchill prophesied 'tens of thousands of mangled people' in London, a city he described as 'the greatest target in the world – a kind of tremendous, fat, valuable cow, fed up to attract beasts of prey'. By 1938, with Germany identified as the probable enemy, the Air Staff had upwardly revised their estimates. The Germans were now credited with the ability to deliver as much high explosive in 24 hours as during the whole of the First World War. Three and a half tons of vastly more powerful bombs would be dropped on the first day, and thereafter 700 tons daily, causing 175,000 casualties a week. Many, including the Committee of Imperial Defence, anticipated that the maintenance of public order would pose the greatest problem. In January 1938 the Cabinet decreed that a large part of the Territorial Army should not be sent abroad in the event of war, but instead held in reserve to preserve law and order at home. Indeed throughout the Blitz of 1940/41 troops were retained in London with this very contingency in mind. Even the Mental Health Emergency Committee agreed, reporting in 1939 that psychiatric casualties were likely to exceed physical injuries by three to one, while three or four million hapless souls would succumb to hysteria.

Reputable scientists offered alarming statistics. In his book *ARP*, dating from 1938, Professor J.B.S. Haldane warned that the sound wave from a bomb was 'like that of the last trumpet, which literally flattens out everything in front'. Those within range not immediately killed would be permanently disabled, their eardrums burst inward and 'deafened for life'. The same gloomy result was predicted in the event of sustained anti-aircraft fire from guns positioned within London. Chemical warfare was also seen as inevitable, with London enveloped in deadly clouds of gas within hours of the outbreak of war. Lord Halsbury, for instance, forecast that a single gas bomb dropped in Piccadilly would dispatch everyone between the Serpentine and the Thames. *The Gas War of 1940*, a novel published in 1931 by the pseudonymous Miles, reflected (and no doubt increased) the fears of many:

In the dark streets the burned and wounded, bewildered and panic-stricken, fought and struggled like beasts, scrambling over the dead and dying alike, until they fell and were in turn trodden underfoot . . . In a dozen parts of London that night people died in their homes with the familiar walls crashing about them in flames; thousands rushed into the streets to be met by blasts of flame and explosion and were blown to rags.

In similar vein, the science-fiction of H.G. Wells offered countless depictions of great cities wiped out by a single raid, and large tracts of land poisoned for decades. After 1936, the expanding Wellsian mythology of bombs, blast, gas and pandemonium was given sharper focus by Alexander Korda's film adaptation of *Things to Come*, which depicted the destruction of Everytown by aerial bombardment and a troglodyte existence for the unlucky survivors. The devastation of the Spanish town of Guernica in April 1937, as depicted in cinema newsreels and books such as *Air Raid* (1938), also did much to confirm these apocalyptic fears. An example of a related hearsay arose in the wake of the Munich crisis in September 1938:

It has long been rumoured that the reason for Chamberlain's panic in Munich was a threat made by Göring to Neville Henderson. Göring is supposed to have told the British Ambassador at Berlin that he was quite prepared to destroy London if the negotiations fell through. He backed up his threat by having 1,400 Messerschmitts drawn up on the airport at

Munich when Mr Chamberlain came along with his umbrella to talk things over.

In some areas open trenches were dug in preparation for mass burials, and large numbers of cardboard coffins stockpiled. Indeed London County Council even envisaged dumping the dead in lime pits, or from hoppers into the Channel. The reality, when eventually it came, was very different. Between 1939 and 1945 the German air force dropped an estimated 64,393 tons of bombs on Britain, killing 51,509 and injuring approximately 211,000. In the heaviest raid on Coventry, discussed in greater detail below, 500 tons of bombs and 9,000 incendiary canisters combined to kill 544 and injure another 865. Overall, air raids on Britain signally failed to live up to pre-war expectation, with each ton of bombs killing or injuring an average of four and a half people.

On the morning of Sunday 3 September 1939, just 27 minutes after the declaration of war, the dread wail of air raid sirens across London announced that a raid was imminent. The alarm proved false, and was later attributed to a lone French aircraft which had strayed into British airspace. Nevertheless the phantom raid probably did much to fuel widespread rumours of mass devastation across the country, and on the east coast in particular. *War Begins at Home*, a Mass Observation anthology published the following year, records that

> In the absence of any official explanation of the supposed raids – the first real impact of war – people simply invented the news they were not given, in the image of the war that had for so long been looming in their nightmares and daydreams. The result was an astonishing proliferation of rumour . . . Nearly every town of importance was rumoured to have been bombed to ruins during the early days of the war. Planes had been seen by hundreds of eyewitnesses falling in flames. The fantasy situation was further reflected in the fact that on at least two occasions anti-aircraft units opened fire on our own planes.

Mass Observation collected literally hundreds of outlandish rumours at this time, including tales that a German aircraft shot down was found to have been disguised as a British machine, and that a Zeppelin was brought down in Essex. Each wailing siren was followed by almost gleeful rumours, reported as fact, of the destruction wrought on some distant location. Even before war was officially declared, two girl evacuees from Bradford were told by the daughter of their host that their home town had been flattened by a secret weapon, while another common evacuation rumour told of billeting families infected with venereal disease by evacuees. Rumours of mass destruction continued into the Blitz proper, as the following 11 Corps summary of 'Rumours and Indiscreet Talk' dated 25 September 1940 illustrates:

> One Division reports that troops returning from leave have sometimes brought back exaggerated stories of the horrible effect of aerial

bombardment in the neighbourhood of their homes. There is a similar tendency among civilians to make fantastic estimates of the damage done.

A 'widespread and persistent' (yet false) belief arose that the destruction of domestic animals had been made compulsory. This led to a veritable pet holocaust during the first week of the war, in which some two million cats and dogs were put down in Greater London alone, many by their owners. If truth is indeed the first casualty in every war, then in 1939 many of man's best friends ran it a close second.

When eventually the bombers arrived in force a number of myths quickly spread, most allied to the various signalling scares discussed in Chapter One. During the Blitz it was widely believed that German aircraft circled above British cities for hours prior to dropping their payload, patiently waiting for agents below to indicate targets. There were even isolated prosecutions for alleged signalling, including a German-Swiss resident of Kensington arrested after dark with a large cigar. According to one witness, a porter: 'He was puffing hard to make a big light and pointing it at the sky.'

As we saw in Chapter Two, the campaign in Flanders fed back several false reports of downed *Luftwaffe* bombers flown by female aircrew. During the Blitz, one of the best, and silliest, falsehoods held that many German airmen were rouged nancy boys. According to the *Daily Mirror* on 16 April 1941:

Officers of the German air force in a prisoner-of-war camp in England spend part of their pay on face creams. Two shot down had waved hair, rouged cheeks, painted lips and enamelled fingernails and toenails. The medical profession has a word for men of this type. It classifies them as moral deviates, a class with curious tendencies, including outbursts of emotional violence admirably suited to the ruthless tactics of the *Luftwaffe*.

Sir James Purves-Stewart, celebrated neurologist, discovered this abnormal German desire for face cream when he was inspecting what was at that time the only prison camp for German officers in this country. 'These young men, every one of whom was wearing at least one Iron Cross, were ill-mannered, aggressive and supercilious . . . This particular form of perversion happens to flourish most vigorously in Germany, and particularly in Berlin, where it receives open encouragement . . . Some time after visiting this camp I was on an official mission in Spain and was given corroboration of this state of affairs by a reliable medical colleague. During the Spanish war he had personally seen a German officer shot down. This airman had waved hair, rouged cheeks, painted lips and enamelled finger and toenails. A Scots acquaintance told me that a German officer with precisely similar make-up had been shot down in Scotland.'

The same story is echoed in a memoir by the official censor, Admiral George Thomson, who recalled that Rudolph Hess was found to have 'polished toenails' when he parachuted into Scotland in May 1941. Another story ran that arrogant enemy aircrew believed part of the British Isles to be in German hands already. According to American observer Harvey Klemmer:

> Several pilots, upon landing, have demanded to be taken to German officials in occupied territory. One lad, told that the nearest German officials would be found on the other side of the Channel, replied: 'They are at Reading. It is useless to lie to me. I know all about it.' Other captured fliers seem to have the impression that Scotland and Ireland have been occupied and that the British fleet has been sunk. Several of them have had German-English dictionaries among their effects.

One oft-repeated myth concerned an apocryphal German pilot who baled out of his aircraft over London, only to land in the blitzed East End, where he was promptly torn to pieces by an angry crowd before the police could intervene. One variant cast the pilot as an unfortunate Pole whose poor English proved his downfall, although neither incident has any basis in fact. Yet another tale told of special Gestapo aircrew, whose viciousness knew no bounds. Klemmer again:

> A young pilot was brought down at Folkestone. He had been machine-gunning women and children on the sea front. It turned out that he was an old Cantab and spoke English well.
>
> 'What kind of a soldier are you,' asked a British officer, 'machine-gunning women and children?'
>
> The German replied: 'I have got just as bad an opinion of that sort of warfare as you, but I am just the pilot. When I am told to come down to 20 metres, I come down to 20 metres. I don't know my navigator or my rear-gunner. The chances are there is a Gestapo man in the plane. Therefore, I obey orders.'

Inaccurate reports about enemy aircrew numbers also gave rise to parachutist scares. Schoolboy diarist Colin Perry recorded on 14 August:

> There was a report in the *Evening Standard* yesterday that twelve airmen had baled out of a bomber we had shot down. It appears as if a sprinkling of Nazi parachutists are already entering our island.

Similar scares arose after 17 parachutes were discovered in the Midlands on 13 August, some decorated with large eagles, and another 59 over a wider area the following day. The mystery drop triggered a massive search by police, troops and the Home Guard. As well as sabotage paraphernalia, maps, pack saddles, wireless sets and lists of targets were also found, although the dummy drop was apparently made by the *Luftwaffe* with the object of undermining British morale.

Few, if any, listeners attached much credibility to New British Broadcasting Station broadcasts by Lord Haw Haw, commonly supposed to have been

William Joyce, a British citizen of Irish-American birth. Many broadcasts by NBBS personalities other than Joyce were incorrectly attributed to him, and at the height of Haw Haw's popularity during the first two months of 1940 any number of traitors, Quislings and Nazis were 'unmasked' by British newspapers as the real Lord. The popular legend that Joyce correctly identified the clock on a certain church (the given location varied infinitely) as running ten minutes slow appears to have been entirely false. Indeed an investigation by the Ministry of Information in January 1941 established 'no case in which Haw Haw or any German wireless made predictions regarding a specific place or announced any detailed facts which . . . could not have been obtained through an explicable channel.' Another Haw Haw story ran that whenever the German wireless warned of a raid on a specific target, bombers turned up on the dot. Yet another rumour local to Winchester was noted by Naomi Royde Smith in September 1940:

> Weeks ago there was a rumour nobody believed though everybody spoke of it, to the effect that Winchester Cathedral was not to be bombed because Hitler meant to be crowned there. It was said to be one of Haw Haw's efforts and some people added the rider that the broadcaster was an Old Wykehamist and had made special arrangements with Field-Marshal Göring to spare his beloved school. Nobody had actually heard Haw Haw say this, and as any Coronation dream would obviously have Westminster Abbey as its centre, the tale died down.

In fact it persisted, for shortly afterwards Royde Smith was obliged to report:

> Another dead rumour has done the phoenix act. The nanny of a friend of mine has been told by her brother in law, who heard it on his wireless, that Haw Haw has cast aside all his old school ties and has consented to allow Göring to order bombs to be dropped on Winchester.

It was popularly supposed that Göring flew over London in person during the Battle of Britain. The story, often repeated throughout the war, stemmed from a false German news agency report, in which it was claimed that the *Luftwaffe* commander-in-chief had piloted a Junkers 88 over the capital on 15 September, escorted by two fighter bombers. By 1942 some in Plymouth claimed to be able to identify Göring's aircraft by virtue of its distinctive engine note. One elderly workman in Plymouth even confided that he had met Göring in an air raid shelter. This tall tale was told to André Savignon, a displaced French writer living in the city:

> Three weeks earlier, during a night raid, he had gone to a shelter – which he pointed out to me – at the other end of the park. His electric torch showed him one other occupant, a very fat man seated on a bench and who was struggling to unknot a bootlace. He crossed over and, without a by your

leave, did the job for the stranger; noting meanwhile that these were knee-high boots such as airmen wear, and they looked to be of foreign make. The two men started to chat. My interlocutor, who admitted he was trembling, for the raids frightened him, prophesied gloomily: 'And they'll soon come back.'

'No,' the other responded, 'No, they will not come back, be-cause their work is done. I can give you the cer-tain-ty of that, my friend.'

The old workman stared at the stranger, who, in addition to his foreign accent, had a singular air. He suddenly thought: 'I've seen that face in the newspapers.' Could it be . . . Yes! Herman Göring! Parachuted down to take stock of the damage wrought! 'Then I got up and ran. And believe me, a devilish laugh rang out after me.'

There were also innumerable variations on a theme encountered in the First World War, involving a chance encounter with a former German friend or fiancé, usually in Piccadilly, Mayfair or the Army and Navy Stores. Updated two decades on, one from the Lancashire town of Leyland told how an enemy pilot had flown above the rooftops at such a low altitude that he was recognised as a former apprentice at the Leyland Motor Works. Another told of a tradesman who called at a newly let house to solicit orders, only to find the door opened by the brutal Prussian who had commanded the camp in which he had spent the previous World War as a prisoner.

Rumours of new and secret German weapons were never in short supply, as this selection illustrates. An American correspondent in Germany reported that the *Luftwaffe* were constructing 200 giant tank-carrying aircraft for use in the invasion of Britain, each capable of lifting a 30-ton tank. The tanks, it was said, would be lowered through a trapdoor and let loose on the English countryside. A machine for generating earthquakes was feared, as was a cross-Channel tunnel from which torpedoes would be launched against Dover, as well as giant German guns mounted on the Brocken which could, in half an hour, demolish London. The giant gun scare, backed up by overt German threats, appears to have been taken quite seriously, as Klemmer records:

It was freely rumoured in London in September 1940 that projectiles resembling cannon shells had been found in the city. The rumours gained added credence from the occasional dropping of bombs when airplanes were not known to be over the capital.

The same rumour was updated in 1944 during the so-called Little Blitz, when it was feared that London might be bombarded with a rocket gun, and even said that rockets had fallen on Park Lane. Another rumour at this time told of a 400-ton bomb built in the form of a glider, which would be towed across the Channel by a fleet of German aircraft. Remarkably, warnings of 'flying bombs' and 'robot aircraft' had appeared in American newspapers as early as 1940, four years ahead of the arrival of V1s and V2s.

Foreign objects thought to have been dropped from enemy aircraft triggered countless scares. In September 1940 considerable anxiety was caused in various parts of the country by the discovery of mysterious white threads in fields. After officials were sent to investigate, it was established that the threads were nothing more or less than spider webs, and in other cases slime trails left by slugs and snails. In the same vein, it is also reported that some had followed trails of sky-blue wool laid, so they believed, to guide parachutists across the country.

White powder scares attracted far greater attention. The occasional discovery of a patch of white powder in a street or field caused a number of poison alerts, often in the mistaken belief that the mysterious substance was an arsenical compound, which on contact with rain, mist or fog could generate a deadly gas capable of wiping out entire areas. Investigators usually found the powders to be harmless flour or cement, or – as in Newport in September 1940 – a mixture of rice and tapioca. A typical case is described by Klemmer:

In W--, one day, a citizen reported breathlessly to the local ARP that there was a pile of mysterious powder in the roadway. The neighbourhood warden refused to have anything to do with it, insisting on calling in his chief. The chief in turn notified the police. By this time a crowd was collecting. The word got round that the powder was believed to be arsine, the gas which would go directly into the blood stream and cause instant death.

The gas squad were notified. They came with steel cylinders and took samples of the powder. Then the decontamination squad arrived, all rigged out in oil-skins, boots, rubber mittens and gas masks. Aided by the fire department, they scrubbed down the pavement, sprinkled it with lime and pronounced the street safe for traffic. The sample, meanwhile, was being analysed by a local chemist. He reported that it consisted mainly of starch.

The ARP people went to Brighton to another chemist. After exhaustive research . . . he announced to a breathless audience that Hitler's secret weapon, in this case at least, consisted of Benger's baby food. The most amusing part of the whole affair was that the woman who had been responsible for the excitement was there all the time . . . By the time the woman discovered her loss, the village was in an uproar and the poor woman was afraid to confess her part in the affair.

In May 1940 rumours about 'arsine' reached fever pitch, among them a story that the deadly chemical smoke was able to penetrate existing gas masks with ease. As a result, within two months every respirator in the country was fitted with an additional 'contex' filter, fastened on with adhesive tape. In Southampton a fire at a local pickle factory in September 1940 triggered a full-scale gas alert, after 'onions and vinegar frying and boiling together produced a miasma blown by the wind'. Other rumours told of gases intended to lull the population into a state of pliable quiescence, induce vomiting inside respirators, or cause everyone within a two-mile radius to burst. Gas also played a part in the revival of a popular First World War myth first spread in 1915, which held that some unknown but deadly horror would befall users of the London Underground. The warning was supposed to have been given to a kindly nurse by a wounded German officer, brought back from death's door. In 1940 the revived legend had changed little:

> The German pilot is supposed to have become very fond of his nurse in the English hospital to which he was taken after being shot down. When it came time for him to be taken away, he is reported to have told the girl: 'You have been very nice to me here. I don't know how to repay you. The only thing I can do now is to warn you – never go out without your gas mask after September 15th.'

To this Klemmer adds:

> I have been told that German prisoners, of whom there are some thousands in camps scattered all over the country, seem to be very worried about gas. They are very careful of their respirators, and, it is said, grab them with something approaching panic whenever the alarm goes.

The corollary was a panoply of fantastical countermeasures. One camouflage enthusiast suggested that a gigantic canvas, painted to look like the countryside, might be suspended over London. A related proposal was a scale reproduction of the entire British Isles, to be positioned elsewhere as a decoy. A businessman suggested building a roof over Oxford Street so that stores would not have to fret about the black-out. An American newspaper report announced a device which shot large steel nets high into the air, preventing raiders from penetrating beyond the coast. Another man proposed shells loaded with coiled springs. One optimist proposed that clouds should be frozen so that anti-aircraft guns could be mounted on them; another that a helicopter powered by a 'perpetual motion engine' could carry guns, searchlights and men to colossal heights. Often no details were given at all, beyond the sure fact that the 'secret anti-raid weapon' would soon be brought to bear on the enemy air force. Conversely, in October 1940 it was whispered that the most effective bombs dropped by the *Luftwaffe* were British, part of the loot from the lost campaign in France and Flanders.

A persistent myth told of the existence of fantastical death rays, both British and German, said to be able to stop engines from a distance and cause enemy raiders to crash. The story was common to the locality surrounding every Chain Home RDF station in Britain, whose true purpose – radar – remained as secret as the presence of four 360 ft steel transmitter masts allowed. At Bawdsey, in Suffolk, it was said that the engines of cars and even light aircraft had been jammed:

> Pre-war motorists in the area recall 'authentic rumours', never first-hand but always from reliable sources, of cars whose engines for some

unaccountable reason refused to function in spite of every effort on the part of their drivers to rectify faults. The usual story was that an RAF officer would come along the road and ask if the motorist was in trouble and, on receiving the usual answer, would inform the perplexed driver that at such and such a time all would be restored to working order. As in all such stories, this is just what happened, and so the story spread far and wide that the tall towers could inhibit the ignition of car engines.

The death ray story continued to be believed right up until the true nature of radar was revealed to the public towards the end of the war. In fact the Air Ministry had displayed an active interest in destructive rays since 1935. The idea was to generate a beam of electromagnetic waves of sufficient strength to heat living tissue to boiling point, and cause bombs to explode spontaneously. Although it was soon concluded that the power required was beyond current technology, this research did lead to the invention of radar, while the Secret Intelligence Service (MI6) continued to fund death ray research by a Dutch charlatan. As R.V. Jones records:

Invariably he had an excuse for the apparatus not working, right up to the outbreak of war. At last, when it was clear that the SIS was not being fooled any longer, and would therefore give him no more money, his final report stated that although the apparatus had been a failure as a death ray, he had discovered that it had remarkable properties as a fruit preserver.

A typical secret weapon-cum-ray rumour, from early October 1940, was described by Colin Perry:

There is now cheering news of a new weapon; a sort of rainbow, apparently – seen over France and here. A ray? Trust the British to invent something.

Rumours of a German death ray surfaced again in London early in 1944, this time in the form of a 'supersonic beam' directed from distant aircraft, said to be capable of shrivelling up acres of the city in a matter of seconds.

Several myths surround genuine countermeasures that were actually deployed. During the first year of the war anti-aircraft gunners claimed to have destroyed 444 hostile aircraft, although the true figure was a fraction of this total. During night raids in 1940 Britain was virtually defenceless, since both gun-laying and airborne interception radar remained ineffective, while it was quickly established that searchlights were more helpful in guiding *Luftwaffe* crews towards vital areas than in spotting bombers for the guns below. On 10 September, after several days' unopposed pounding of London, large numbers of guns were called into the London area to shoot blind at their maximum rate of fire across 200 square miles of sky. This move was chiefly intended to improve low civilian morale by giving an impression of defence, although it did force the *Luftwaffe* to fly higher. During September alone, AA batteries fired

260,000 rounds of heavy ammunition, yet brought down only one aircraft for every 30,000 shells fired. By January 1941 radar and experience had reduced this figure to 4,000, although official claims that 45 per cent of raiders approaching London were forced to turn back by anti-aircraft fire were never accurate.

Worse still, on occasion the barrage above London was so intense that as many civilians were killed and injured by shrapnel and unexploded shells as by enemy action. During the first serious raid on London in 1943, on the night of 17/18 January, a survey of friendly fire damage revealed the following catalogue: six killed by shell splinters; four wounded by a shell in Enfield; a sailor severely injured by a shell splinter in Gipsy Hill; two civilians killed by another shell elsewhere; one man killed and two injured by a shell which hit a wall in Battersea; and two more killed in like fashion in Tooting. The danger was increased by the introduction of 'Z' batteries in 1941, which fired salvos of 100 rocket projectiles at a time, these accelerating to 1,000 mph in under two seconds before detonating simultaneously. The din was likened to 'an express train passing through the living room, before crashing in the back garden'. On 3 March 1943, a new Z battery positioned in Victoria Park, Hackney, may have triggered the Bethnal Green tube disaster, when 178 were crushed or suffocated following a panic on a stairwell. Other sensational rumours attached to this tragedy, including reports of a fifth column agent who shouted aloud that an oil-bomb had fallen in the street outside.

The record for Balloon Command was no less chequered. During six years of war balloon barrages brought down approximately 100 aircraft, yet three-quarters of these were Allied planes. Just 24 German aircraft are known to have fallen victim to the blimps, whereas in June 1940 the Harwich barrage alone managed to account for two RAF Hampden bombers in a fortnight. True, they undoubtedly boosted civilian morale, and would later bring down no fewer than 278 V1 flying bombs, but like AA fire they could also be dangerous for those on the ground. On 13 June a Heinkel 111 of KG 27 struck a balloon cable over Newport, Monmouthshire, and plunged into a built-up area, killing two children. In October an exploding barrage balloon fell on the Dover Castle pub in Lambeth, killing two firemen. The cable had trailed across railway tracks near Waterloo Station and stopped all traffic for an hour.

In 1940 the popular Korda film *The Lion Has Wings* offered the stirring vision of a German raid panicked and scattered by the sight of a balloon barrage, and despondently turning for home. The reality was that during *Luftwaffe* 'turkey shoots' of blimps above Dover that summer, spectators on the ground actually applauded each time a balloon was shot down in flames. Several balloon rumours were highly imaginative. One held that the mooring cables were electrified, so that enemy aircrew would be fried on contact. Another claimed that the cables acted as a magnet: 'bombs are attracted to the cord and slither down harmlessly.'

The legend of the 'Blitz spirit', by which citizens of every creed and class, galvanised by crisis, were united as never before, to share a strong bond of equality of sacrifice, has a far more limited basis in fact. Since the end of the war, popular myth has greatly inflated the extent to which the British Public smiled on through adversity. Over 5,000 people fled Britain during the last two days in August 1939, and by July 1940 no fewer than three sitting MPs had absconded abroad. Among those who stayed behind instances of minor discord were not uncommon. Writing in *Crime in Wartime*, Edward Smithies records that common flashpoints among civilians during the war years were the ubiquitous queues, whether at shops, or for trains and buses, or outside air raid shelters, and even inside them. If court records are a reliable barometer, altercations between customers and shopkeepers were also not unknown.

The Stygian black-out facilitated crime generally, although at the outset a few optimists had predicted burglars would be 'forced out of business' by the 'perpetual fear of opening a blackened window to find a family party in progress'. The facts failed to match the dream, as Hermann Mannheim noted in *War and Crime*, published in 1941:

> It is not only the burglar who profits from the black-out. According to newspaper reports, larcenies from telephone boxes, thieving from the docks, bag-snatching, assaults on police or on women, and other forms of hooliganism seem to be of fairly frequent occurrence . . . The criminal courts have, from the beginning, paid particular attention to crimes of this kind by imposing severer sentences, though they avoid entirely such savageries as are reported from certain countries abroad.

More serious was the extent to which civil defence personnel seized opportunities to steal and loot from bombed houses. Indeed almost half the arrests made by police for this type of offence were civil defence workers. A Mass Observation reporter recorded in 1941 that some Heavy Rescue and demolition men took up their posts with this very object in mind.

> Some men come on the jobs in the hope of picking up loot. Even most of those who are not primarily concerned with what they can find are not averse to taking something when it turns up. The press campaign and the heavy sentences for looters don't seem to worry them. In fact, they are stupidly and foolishly open about it, and will often scramble for bluey in full view of passers-by . . .
>
> Condan found a suitcase and opened it. The foreman pounced on him immediately. He warned us not to open a case if we found it. He picked up a handbag and took out a purse which was empty. Then he turned to us and said, 'It's the funniest bloody bomb I ever came across. I been all through the last war and I done several jobs in this, but I never come across a bomb like it. It's blown every bag open and knocked the money out, it's even knocked the money out of the gas meters, yet it didn't break the electric light bulb in the basement!'

Looting was often from the rubble of bombed houses, although empty properties were also vulnerable. Some seem to have considered that the goods taken were a form of reward for dangerous rescue work, or that loot from commercial premises was fair game. In London a squad of special plain clothes anti-looting detectives was formed by Scotland Yard, who mingled with civil defence workers to catch offenders red-handed, while in 1941 police in Birmingham went so far as to warn the public that firewatchers were responsible for a substantial proportion of the increase in cases of larceny. In some towns, such as Portsmouth and Liverpool, troops even stood guard after raids to deter looters. Probably the most infamous case was the aftermath of the bombing of the exclusive Café de Paris in London on the night of 8/9 March 1941, when a single bomb plunged through the roof to the dancefloor, killing 34 revellers (including the band leader Ken 'Snake Hips' Johnson) and injuring 80 more. The immediate aftermath was witnessed by the novelist Nicholas Monsarrat:

> The first thing which the rescue squads and the firemen saw, as their torches poked through the gloom and the smoke . . . was a frieze of other shadowy men, night-creatures who had scuttled within as soon as the echoes ceased, crouching over any dead or wounded woman, and soigné corpse they could find, and ripping off its necklace, or earrings, or brooch; rifling its handbag, scooping up its loose change.

As the historian Philip Ziegler noted, like the sinking of the *Titanic* several decades earlier, at the Café de Paris it was the instant transition from opulence and glitter to appalling destruction which captured public imagination, and further sensationalised the gruesome stories of quick-witted looters tearing open handbags, and stripping rings from the fingers of the dead and wounded. In truth, the devastation and theft at the scene was little different to any number of other incidents in cities across Britain. In the opinion of Barbara Nixon, an ARP worker in Finsbury:

> It was a gory incident, but the same week another dance hall a mile to the east of us was hit and there were nearly 200 casualties. This time there were only 10/6d frocks, and a few lines in the paper followed by, 'It is feared there were several casualties.' Local feeling was rather bitter.

The defiant sentiment that 'Britain can take it' was often found to be wanting in heavily bombed areas. Official reactions in many cities visited frequently by the *Luftwaffe* give a consistent picture far removed from the myth of modern memory. Unity of purpose and high morale often gave way to boredom, apathy and pessimism, as we see from this appraisal from the Ministry of Information:

> Coventry: There was great depression, a widespread feeling of impotence and many open signs of hysteria . . . Terror, neurosis . . . Women were seen to cry in the street, to attack a fireman and so on. (November 1940)

Bristol: Much talk of having been let down by the Government, and of the possibility of a negotiated peace. (December 1940)

Portsmouth: On all sides we hear that looting and wanton destruction had reached alarming proportions. The police seem unable to exercise control . . . The effect on morale is bad and there is a general feeling of desperation . . . Their nerve had gone. (May 1941)

Outside London, where there was no Tube in which to seek refuge, many towns were depopulated after dark, after residents decamped to the countryside to sleep rough. In Portsmouth some 90,000 people left the city each night during the heavy bombing of the 'May Blitz' of 1941, while in Belfast 100,000 fled to the countryside after the first major raid in April. In Liverpool the figure for 'trekking' was 50,000, and in Clydebank the overnight population fell from 50,000 to 2,000 after the first attack in March. Previously many in Clydebank had imagined themselves immune from bombing, on the false premise that Germans were not antagonistic to the Scots, and because magnetic fields in the surrounding mountains would dislocate aircraft engines. In the aftermath of the heavy raid on Liverpool on 7 May, there arose the enduring legend of mass peace demonstrations and martial law, described as 'one of the great rumours of the war' by Tom Harrisson, the director of Mass Observation. The myth took in food riots, summary shooting of defeatists, Irish troublemakers stirring panic, homeless marchers with white flags and the removal of trainloads of unidentified corpses for mass burial. According to Harrisson:

The Liverpool rumour of martial law was encouraged by the police and army temporarily closing the city centre to cars and persons without special business, in order to ease congestion and enable surface debris and unexploded bombs to be cleared. There was no public explanation for this necessary measure. Some of the victims jumped to conclusions.

The Liverpool myth was slow to fade, outlasting an earlier rumour popular in the north-west that bowed and bloodied East Enders in London had petitioned Churchill to end the war. A year earlier, in May 1940, a rumour swept the country that the royal family were set to leave for Canada, that a shadow government had already been formed on the far side of the Atlantic, and that the War Cabinet was also preparing to pack its bags as soon as the invasion began. In recent years some historians have sought to challenge the myth of the Blitz by citing the fact that various dignitaries, usually Royals, were on occasion jeered and hissed during visits to blitzed areas. But in Southampton, according to a Mass Observer, the underlying cause was trekking by local civic leaders:

After the big raid, when Southampton's High Street was left in ruins, and most of the centre of the town, the King and Queen came on a flying visit.

As they went down the High Street, people booed. But we were not booing the king and queen. It was all the town's top brass who were with them. Everybody knew that they got out of Southampton every night, and only came back to meet the King and Queen.

Among the most enduring memories of 1940 are the stirring speeches made by Winston Churchill, although even here not all was as it seemed. On 13 May Churchill made his first speech as Prime Minister, in which he famously stated that he had promised nothing but 'blood, toil, tears and sweat'. However, this speech was made to the House of Commons alone, and for the BBC broadcast his words were simply read aloud by a newsreader. In fact Churchill himself did not record it for posterity until November 1942. His first broadcast speech, on 19 May, is little quoted today, and instead the next memorable phrase came on 4 June, when Britons were exhorted to fight the enemy on the beaches. That evening Churchill refused to repeat the speech for the BBC, and with no recording from the Commons available, an actor named Norman Shelley was substituted. Shelley, who played Larry the Lamb for Children's Hour, repeated the deception on 18 June, for the speech which ended with the immortal phrase: 'This was their Finest Hour.' On 20 August Churchill famously informed the Commons that 'never in the field of human conflict was so much owed by so many to so few.' However, the BBC did not broadcast this speech, and the prime minister addressed the nation just once more in 1940, on 11 September. There followed an elongated gap of five months, unbroken until Churchill broadcast again on 9 February 1941.

Another radio myth concerns BBC newsreaders, who in June 1940 broke with tradition and began each bulletin by giving their names. According to the *BBC Handbook* of 1941:

> The reason for this is not a hankering after self-advertisement – although at first some listeners unfairly took this to be so; in wartime listeners must be able to recognise instantly the voice of British broadcasting and then, in any possible emergency, they will be on their guard against some lying imitation by the voice of the enemy.

In fact, self-promotion was precisely the motive, as the celebrated newsreader John Snagge revealed in 1972:

> I said to Lotbiniere one day [in 1940], 'It seems to me ridiculous that if Outside Broadcast people can get their names mentioned, why shouldn't the announcers chosen to read the news also give their names?' To my surprise the powers that be accepted it . . . When it came out afterwards, and a reason was asked for it, Lotbiniere and I said it was for security reasons. After the invasion of Poland there had been a number of false announcers put up by the Germans . . . But it was in fact I, not normally the inventive type, who first suggested it, for a different reason.

Two of the most enduring myths of the Blitz arose long after the war had ended. In 1977 the author Len Deighton published *Fighter*, a highly readable account of the Battle of Britain, in which he claimed that sustained heavy bombing of Manston airfield in August 1940 resulted in a mutiny among ground crew. By this account, airmen refused to leave the shelters for days on end, pilots had to rearm and refuel their own aircraft, and local civilians took the opportunity to loot the damaged buildings for tools and spares. The situation deteriorated so far, so it was said, that the station chaplain was obliged to disarm one officer who threatened to kill everyone else in the mess. On the basis of Deighton's account, the same allegations were repeated by Angus Calder in *The Myth of the Blitz*, yet this alleged mutiny is neither confirmed nor denied by official documents. The station record book briefly states that:

> Later it was decided to evacuate permanently all administrative personnel and those not required in connection with station defence and servicing of aircraft. Accommodation for evacuated personnel was found in Westgate.

Although between 28 August and 5 September the Operations Record Book is blank, there is no evidence that pages have been removed from the original now lodged with the Public Record Office. Rocky Stockman, the author of the *History of RAF Manston*, has failed to locate any reliable evidence which backs up Deighton's claim, and despite interviewing many of those present at Manston in 1940 unearthed nothing beyond 'vague mentions of shadowy stories at fourth or fifth hand'. Deighton has not revealed his original source, and as Stockman rightly points out:

> There were a number of administrative and other non-combatant personnel at Manston at the time and they were at the station mainly because it provided service office and living accommodation. There were also some newly-arrived recruits. They were most likely to have been the ones in the shelters. That is where they should have been during the raids. They would not have known what to do in 'turning round' the fighters, and would have impeded the others had they tried. They were later evacuated to Westgate and other places.

It is clear from the example of certain ships during the Dunkirk evacuation that morale can rapidly fail under sustained attack, and that fear can be contagious. However the notion that the entire station at Manston refused to obey orders is difficult to credit, and it is more likely instead that the actions of a few dazed, fatigued and shell-shocked personnel have been magnified to become the so-called mutiny. The same form of numerical exaggeration is a hallmark of the military myth, and can be seen in the case of the massacre that never was at Arras, where the killing of perhaps half a dozen German prisoners became the calculated murder of 400.

Another Blitz myth surfaced in 1974, in the wake of the publication of *The Ultra Secret* by Frederick Winterbotham. A wartime Group Captain with SIS, Winterbotham was in charge of security and communication of decrypted Enigma signals at Bletchley Park, and did history no less a service by breaking the 30-year silence surrounding Ultra with his unauthorised book. Because he had no official sanction, however, Winterbotham was not allowed access to classified material, and instead had to rely on memory alone. This led to a number of errors in *The Ultra Secret*, the most significant of which concerned the devastating German air raid on Coventry on 14 November 1940. Of this Winterbotham wrote:

> At about 3 pm on November 14th someone must have made a slip up and instead of a city with a code-name, Coventry was spelt out . . . There were, perhaps, four or five hours before the attack would arrive . . . I asked [Churchill's] personal secretary if he would be good enough to ring me back when the decision had been taken, because if Churchill decided to evacuate Coventry, the press, and indeed everybody, would know we had pre-knowledge of the raid and some counter-measure might be necessary to protect the source.
>
> In the event, it was decided only to alert all the services, the fire, the ambulance, the police, the wardens, and to get everything ready to light the decoy fires. This is the sort of terrible decision that has to be made on the highest levels in war. It was unquestionably the right one, but I am glad it was not I who had to take it.

The ten-hour raid code-named Moonlight Sonata duly took place, and resulted in unprecedented civilian losses: 550 killed and 1,000 seriously injured. A total of 50,749 houses were destroyed or damaged, and the attack even gave rise to a new verb for urban devastation: to Coventrate. Rumours in circulation during the immediate aftermath included news that a man had been shot while signalling with a night light, and that prior to the raid a swastika of smoke appeared in the sky as a warning to fifth columnists to evacuate the city. The inference from Winterbotham was that the scale of the tragedy might have been greatly reduced if the city had been evacuated, but that Churchill decided against this in order to preserve the security of Ultra. Subsequently several other authors repeated the claim that the city had been martyred, including Anthony Cave Brown in *Bodyguard of Lies* (1976):

> Should not the population of the inner city, together with the aged, the young, and those in hospitals who could be moved, be evacuated? To all these propositions, Churchill said no; there must be no evacuations and no warnings.

Cave Brown stated that Ultra had provided Churchill and his advisors 'at least 48, possibly 60 hours' warning' of the raid, a claim repeated by William

Stevenson in *A Man Called Intrepid* (also 1976): 'The name of the target was in Churchill's hands within minutes of Hitler's decision . . . If the citizens were not warned, thousands would die or suffer.'

Although the sacrifice of Coventry was quickly accepted by many as a harsh but necessary reality of war, in fact the story is pure myth. The official history of British Intelligence in the Second World War by F.H. Hinsley, published in 1979, clearly states that no decrypts on 14 November alerted Bletchley Park, Downing Street or the Air Intelligence branch to the possibility of an imminent raid, let alone identified Coventry as a target. Instead, as the scientist R.V. Jones disclosed in 1977, the destruction of Coventry was the result of a technical error. In the summer of 1940 British scientists discovered that the *Luftwaffe* had developed a system of radio beam guidance to enable aircraft to bomb targets 'blind', in particular at night. Based on the pre-war Lorenz blind-landing apparatus, the new system was code-named *Knickebein* (Crooked Leg). The pilot listened for a continuous signal from the transmitter in France to check that his course was correct. If he veered to the left, the signal broke into morse dots, and dashes if he veered to the right. A second beam intersected over the target, and told the bomb-aimer when to release the payload. A later development, X-Gerät, provided even greater accuracy, and was also operational by November 1940. The weakness of both systems was their simplicity, and by September a unit designated 80 Wing RAF had developed a method of jamming and deflecting the beams by means of customised medical electro-diathermy sets, as well as existing Lorenz equipment.

In the meantime, intelligence gleaned from downed enemy flyers had indicated that a massive raid on Coventry and Birmingham was scheduled between 15 and 20 November. In addition, an Ultra decrypt from Bletchley indicated a major night raid was scheduled for 15 November, code-named Moonlight Sonata, but with no specified target. On the morning of 14 November the Air Staff informed Churchill that the target was probably in the Greater London area, with the caveat that 'if further information indicates Coventry, Birmingham or elsewhere, we hope to get instructions out in time'. When German test transmissions began just after 1 pm on the same day the target was confirmed as Coventry, and by 3 pm the RAF jammers were ready to deploy electronic counter-measures, code-named Cold Water. It was then that disaster struck. Due to what R.V. Jones described as a 'lack of attention to a seemingly trivial detail', 80 Wing set their transmitters to the wrong frequency, and thus had no impact on the German beams. Jones went further in his condemnation of the error:

> Whoever had determined the modulation note had either been tone deaf or completely careless, and no-one had ever thought of checking his measurements. I was so indignant that I said that whoever had made such an error ought to have been shot.

It is therefore nonsense to suggest that Winston Churchill knowingly permitted the destruction of Coventry. No evacuation was ordered simply because those in the know had good reason to believe that effective counter-measures were in place, which would result in German bombs falling in empty fields. Furthermore no Ultra decrypt had mentioned Coventry by name, and instead the information passed to Churchill by Winterbotham at 3 pm on the afternoon of 14 November was the product of (correct) calculations by the RAF interception unit at Kingsdown, identifying Coventry as the target. It can only be assumed that after a gap of 34 years, and with no official papers to hand, Winterbotham was simply mistaken about the source of the information he passed to Churchill at 3 pm, and unaware of Cold Water.

In the event, the decision to allow the bombing of civilians in known areas was postponed for four years, until the arrival of V1 flying bombs over London in June 1944. In order to minimise damage to the centre of the city, the Chiefs of Staff proposed to allow Double Cross agents to exaggerate the number of rockets falling on the north and west of London, thus encouraging the Germans to shorten their range and hit less important districts to the south, such as Croydon and Wandsworth. Initially the Cabinet rejected the idea, on the premise that:

It would be a serious matter to assume any direct degree of responsibility for action which would affect the areas against which flying bombs were aimed.

By mid-August, however, the plan stood approved, and would soon be applied to V2 rockets as well. The result was that in addition to the havoc wrought along 'Bomb Alley' in Kent, Sussex and Surrey, the London suburb of Croydon went on to receive a total of 142 doodlebugs, while Wandsworth trailed only slightly with 124. In these districts, at least, the legend that for each V1 fired the Germans lost six men killed by engine blast must have given little comfort.

CHAPTER SIX

The Invasion That Never Was

In the middle of August 1940 an invasion alarm was triggered in the North of England following the arrival of almost 100 'phantom parachutists', whose canopies and equipment were dropped by the *Luftwaffe* as part of a baffling ruse. Another feverish rumour held that the Isle of Wight had been occupied by enemy troops. By the middle of September it was widely reported that a German landing attempt had been repulsed with devastating losses, and that the Channel was white with corpses, hundreds of which had been washed ashore along the southern and eastern coasts of Britain.

By December, American reports pegged the German losses at no less than 80,000, all of whom had perished in the course of two attempts to cross the Channel. Hospitals in occupied France were said to be filled to overflowing with invasion troops, all suffering from severe burns, and the whole army set to mutiny if a third attempt were ordered. So widespread were these rumours in Britain that the chief press censor, Rear-Admiral George Thomson, was forced to admit:

> In the whole course of the war there was no story which gave me so much trouble as this one of the attempted German invasion, flaming oil on the water and 30,000 burned Germans.

It is established historical fact that Operation Sealion, the planned German invasion of the British Isles, never weighed anchor, and by October had been postponed until the following spring. What, then, was the truth behind the rumours of countless bodies washed ashore that autumn, and the invasion that failed?

Following the fall of France in June, the first serious invasion alert came on the night of 31 August, when an RAF reconnaissance patrol sighted a large German convoy off the Dutch coast. At a time when many defence planners were fearful of a landing on the east coast, this intelligence caused considerable alarm in London, as Churchill's private secretary, John Colville, recalled in his diary:

After dinner the First Lord rang up from Brighton to say that enemy ships were steering westwards from Terschelling. The invasion may be pending (though I'll lay 10–1 against!) and all HM Forces are taking up their positions. If these German ships came on they would reach the coast of Norfolk tomorrow morning.

Thus alarmed, the Admiralty hurriedly ordered a unit already at sea, the Immingham-based 20th Destroyer Flotilla, to investigate. The result was a disaster. On making to intercept the enemy force with instructions 'not to lack daring', the five lightly armed fast minelaying destroyers ran into an uncharted minefield 40 miles north-west of the Texel. Both the *Esk* and *Ivanhoe* were sunk, the *Express* seriously damaged, and the Flotilla commander, Lieutenant-Commander Crouch, fatally injured. Almost 300 men were killed, and the total casualty figure (including wounded and missing) closer to 400. Only during the Dunkirk evacuation had the Nore Command suffered worse casualties in a single day.

Over the course of the next few days the survivors were landed at several east coast ports, including Great Yarmouth, from where some were transported inland to Norwich. In September 1940 Pat Barnes was a schoolgirl living on a poultry farm in Spixworth, north-east of the town, and recalls of that month:

> For two days a convoy of army ambulances occupied Crostwick Lane, travelling slowly, the drivers very grim-faced. We used to get lots of army traffic through the lane but nothing like this. Occasionally an army lorry would stop for eggs or apples, and so the next time my mother asked what was going on two weeks before. She was told that they contained the dead bodies of Germans washed up on the beach, as an invasion had been attempted. But that was all we were told.

Instead of revealing to inquisitive civilians that a substantial number of their own side had become casualties of a false alarm, it was judged far better to spread word that the mysterious convoy carried the remnants of a thwarted German invasion force. It is significant that this explanation was given two weeks afterwards, for rumours of a Channel battle and bodies on beaches first surfaced in strength in the wake of the Cromwell alarm on 7 September, a Saturday, although at this stage none spoke of charred bodies or burning seas.

According to Admiral Thomson, the rumour first began to circulate on the south coast. One such told of a landing in Sandwich Bay, where the inshore waters were said to be 'black' with German dead, later buried secretly in the sand dunes. A diarist named John Allpress in the Suffolk town of Bury St Edmunds recorded the corpse rumour as early as 12 September:

> Tales begin to come through about an attempted invasion last Saturday evening. All LDVs called out. Tales of how the enemy got to within six miles of our coast and were then sunk. Dead bodies on the beaches reported.

Similarly, Ipswich air raid warden Richard Brown noted the following day:

> What is the secret of last Saturday's affair? New York now has rumours that
> Jerry corpses were being washed up on the Yarmouth beaches in quantities.
> Green says 30,000 of them, but I should have thought they'd be too weighty
> with equipment to do anything but sink.

Indeed the rumour seems to have been particularly strong in Suffolk. On 14
September the diary of London schoolboy Colin Perry, later published as *Boy in
the Blitz*, recorded:

> I hear from Lancaster in the flats, who has just been to Wickham Market in
> Suffolk, that on Saturday night and again on Tuesday invasion was
> attempted. Not one Nazi returned. Their bodies are still being washed up
> along our shores. That is the end of all Nazis who seek to molest our
> freedom – death.

On 15 September warden Richard Brown also recorded rumours of attacks
on the west coast of England, and in Scotland too. In Kent and Sussex there
were even rumours of a thwarted parachute landing, as recorded in Chapter
Eleven. The regular military also noted reports of bodies on beaches. An
11 Corps summary of 'rumours and indiscreet talk' dated 25 September
revealed:

> 15 Division report the currency in their area of a rumour that the bodies of
> thousands of German soldiers have been washed up on the beach at Clacton.
> The source of this cannot at present be traced.

In the same sector of north Essex, an intelligence summary from the 45th
Infantry Brigade reported:

> Rumours of a spectacular nature have been very widespread. The following
> were the principal ones noted:
> (i)   nearly all troops in the Sub Area have heard the rumour that
>   thousands of bodies of German troops were washed up on the south
>   coast of England in the early part of the month.
> (ii)   another rumour, not so widespread, is that an invasion by sea was
>   started but was destroyed before reaching this country.

In his account of 'authentic conversations' heard in Kent at the end of
September, diarist James Hodson recorded the supposed remarks of an infantry
officer:

> I suppose you've heard the tale about all the dead Germans washed up on
> the beach after their invasion which failed? The latest addition is they were

tied up in bundles of three – they refused to go on board and were shot and disposed of in this way. Lots of funny stories go about.

Another diarist, Naomi Royde Smith, recorded of the rumour in September:

It began with a reported tocsin in Cornwall, spreading to Hampshire, heard by many . . . The Germans had landed somewhere in Dorset; in Kent; in Lincolnshire. This was officially denied. Then a whisper started that the corpses of German soldiers, in full battle dress, had been washed up all round the coast. Presently the horrid detail that each corpse had its hands tied behind its back was added . . . Then the tale grew into patent absurdity. The whole of the Channel from Weymouth to Devonport was covered with the corpses of stricken armies . . . The entire population of the Reich must have perished.

At Southend, it was whispered, the enemy remains were collected in corporation dustcarts, while in Southampton the wreckage from the barges was said to have solved the local fuel shortage. One man told a reporter:

The fact is that the whole coastline is in the occupation of the military authorities. If they thought it was necessary to conceal the dead bodies of Germans they would have no difficulty. For myself, it is enough that closed lorries going to and from the beach at one point and mysterious ambulances at another, are indications that out of the ordinary things have been happening.

If the great invasion rumour was soft-pedalled and censored at home, British deception agencies were enthusiastic in spreading the story abroad, as is clear from the numerous foreign newspaper reports played back by the British press. At first glance, it might seem curious that the rumour was not exploited more fully as propaganda on the Home Front. According to Thomson, this was because it might spread 'alarm and despondency' in 'ticklish circumstances', but in fact the opposite held true. Throughout this period Churchill was keen to keep both the military and the civilian population at a high state of alert to repel invasion. In addition there was a difficult balance to strike. Although in 1914, a similar end had been achieved by the spreading of false reports of the shooting of army sentries by spies, the LDV had already shot and wounded too many motorists for this to be a sensible option in the summer of 1940. The rumours of bodies on beaches provided a more subtle hint of the ongoing enemy threat, while at the same time painting a macabre but pleasing picture which boosted morale. It also played well in America, giving the impression that Britain was by no means a lost cause, yet still imperilled and deserving of military aid.

The failed invasion myth can thus be seen to have been a valuable export during Britain's hour of need. Precisely which agency originated the rumour is difficult to establish with certainly, given the paucity of available documents on intelligence and deception operations, but the channels through which it passed are easier to identify. In *The Big Lie*, published in 1955, a former major named John Baker White claimed some credit, having served in a small sub-section of the Directorate of Military Intelligence (DMI) charged with the delivery of propaganda and disinformation to enemy troops. Although White did not say so, his post evidently involved liaison with similar departments in other organisations such as MI5, MI6 and SOE, as well as the Ministry of Information and the BBC:

> Our task was to create in the minds of the German High Command, and of Hitler himself, a completely fictitious picture of what they would have to face if they launched an invasion attempt. A picture of a powerfully armed Britain, and above all armed with new weapons of terrible destructive power. We had to put over the Big Lie.
>
> By methods that must remain forever secret, Britain supplied many of the rumours . . . I cannot say today, any more than I could have said at the time, how the thought and the wish became a rumour that was to go around the world . . . Before the rumour was fed into the pipeline that ran to the bar of the Grand Hotel in Stockholm, the Avenida in Lisbon, the Ritz in Madrid, and other places in Cairo, Istanbul, Ankara and elsewhere, not forgetting New York, it had to get over certain hurdles, including the committee that had to study all rumours before they were launched.

In addition to the DMI, those in the know must have included Department EH, an MI6 sub-section charged with the creation of propaganda for consumption by the enemy, and later absorbed into SOE, and also British Security Co-ordination (BSC), the MI6 station in New York code-named Intrepid. Later refinements of the great invasion rumour involving burning seas required input from the eccentric Petroleum Warfare Department (PWD), created in July 1940, and from Lord Maurice Hankey, secret service doyen and roving Minister Without Portfolio, who had conducted his own experiments with fuel on water during the First World War.

Prior to November 1940, the rumours fed into the pipeline concerned bodies alone. The following selection, from the BSC-friendly *New York Times*, and doubtless devised with no little merriment, are typical of those floated abroad, only to be repeated by British editors starved of more reliable sources closer to home.

> NAZI DEAD SAID TO HALT FISHING: A Scottish family received a letter today from a relative in Sweden reporting that fishermen were forced to abandon herring fisheries because the bodies of many German soldiers were floating in the waters off the southern coast of Sweden. The letter said that the German authorities had offered a reward of about 75 cents for each body recovered with the uniform intact.

NAZI LOSSES SEEN IN INVASION DRILLS: The Germans have suffered severe losses in exercises and manoeuvres in the English Channel preparatory to an invasion attempt, according to passengers who arrived [from Lisbon] on the *Exeter*. One estimate was that 10,000 men had been lost. 'The German soldiers,' said one passenger, who refused to give his name because he has relatives living in Holland, 'were heavily armed and weighted down with full equipment. They were taken a mile or so to sea off the Netherlands coast aboard flat-bottomed boats. The boats would come toward shore and the men were forced to leap out and swim. We people living near the sea saw thousands of floating bodies in the water. Many soldiers rebelled and were chained and taken back to the interior of Germany to be punished for their insubordination.'

LETTER TO THE EDITOR FROM NORWAY: In Oslo truckloads of German soldiers – tied and bound – pass in the streets on their way to Fort Akershus, where they would rather be shot than drowned. The reason being that they refuse to invade England in the little boats much too small to cross the North Sea . . . They have received a severe handling by the RAF. German losses in Cherbourg are estimated at between 40,000 and 50,000 killed and wounded. Almost every civil and military hospital from the Belgian to the Spanish frontier has been requisitioned.

Innumerable variants were in also circulation in France, and were recorded by Marie Bonaparte in her excellent book *Myths of War*. Moreover it is clear that several passengers arriving in New York from Lisbon on liners such as the *Exeter* were primed by British intelligence. On 21 September the *New York Times* reported:

Robert Solborg, returning with his wife and daughter after 20 years of residence in France, said the Germans were holding invasion practice off the French coast also . . . and that British bombers had taken a heavy toll. Mr Solberg added that he had definite information that the Germans have attempted no actual invasion of England. He said the British, tipped off by the Dutch and French, waited for the barges with planes and submarines and that 'thousands of Germans have been lost in this fashion.' Mr Solborg said he recently visited a French Channel port where bodies of German troops were being washed ashore daily.

On the same date, a *Daily Mail* correspondent in New York teased further details from Mr Solborg, described as the vice-president of a steel company:

The British sent submarines and planes and sank the barges. It is estimated that at least 10,000 Germans lost their lives. Many of the German troops are refusing to continue the practice and hundreds are being transported back to Germany with their hands tied behind their backs.

In fact, Solborg was no ordinary refugee. A former Tsarist cavalry officer who fled the Bolshevik revolution in 1917, Solberg (the correct spelling) had already acquired American citizenship prior to the outbreak of the Second World War, and in December 1940 was recruited by American military intelligence. In October 1941 he was posted to London to liaise with SOE, reporting directly to Colonel William Donovan, the OSS chief whose own role in promoting the invasion that never was is examined below. However, Solberg was clearly already well acquainted with British intelligence. Hints about information passed back by Dutch and French patriots was simply a cover for Enigma decrypts, although Solberg would hardly have been privy to the Ultra secret.

To be completely effective, a rumour requires some foundation in fact, and so it was with the legend of the bodies on the beaches. Late in September 1940 Gunner William Robinson, stationed at Herne Bay with 333 Coastal Artillery Battery, was dispatched to Folkestone to take part in a macabre detail. Together with half a dozen others, he was instructed to search the beach between Hythe and St Mary's Bay for dead Germans. On the first day two corpses were located, together with seven or eight more over the following two days. All were taken by truck to a field west of New Romney, where they were unloaded behind a canvas screen. An NCO checked the bodies for identity discs and paybooks, which were then handed over to the supervising officer. Robinson recognised the dead men as German soldiers, rather than airmen or naval personnel, by their field grey uniforms. All appeared to have been in the water for some time. By way of a reward for this unpleasant fatigue, Robinson and his colleagues drew a daily ration of twenty Woodbines, and additional daily pay of two shillings.

The bodies kept on coming. On 20 October the corpse of a German anti-tank gunner, Heinrich Poncke, was recovered from the beach at Littlestone-on-Sea, near Dungeness. According to the brief report in *The Times*:

> He was wearing the uniform of a German infantry regiment and appeared to be about 28. The body had been in the sea for several weeks and death is believed to have been due to drowning.

Like the bodies recovered by Gunner Robinson, this single body was removed to New Romney for burial. Unlike the others, Poncke's arrival was reported openly in local and national papers, and even announced by the BBC. It is unlikely that he perished while attempting to invade Britain. More probably, he was a casualty of a 'cutting out' operation against German flak trawlers in the Channel on 11 October, when three Felixstowe-based motor torpedo boats sank two such trawlers north of Calais and captured 34 crewmen, several others being drowned. These prisoners were seen passing through a London railway station, thus fuelling speculation. Over the next few weeks Poncke's body, like others, was carried by the tide, with the result that small numbers were washed ashore on both sides of the Channel. This tends to confirm the truth of

The fiction: how German propaganda depicted Dunkirk to the French. (*Author's collection*)

The fact: some of the 170,000 French troops evacuated to Britain. (*Author's collection*)

A British soldier wearing a 'trophied' *Waffen-SS* steel helmet. (*Author's collection*)

Disconsolate German prisoners at Dover in May 1940, having crossed from Dunkirk. (*Author's collection*)

A stereotypically 'Germanic' fifth-columnist in French hands. (*Author's collection*)

Another alleged fifth-columnist in French custody, soon to be 'rendered harmless for good' according to the original caption. (*Author's collection*)

A rare photograph of German Brandenburg troops in action in May 1940, masquerading as Dutch military police to capture a canal bridge at Roosteren. (*After the Battle*)

The *Lancastria* goes down off the French coast, 17 June 1940. (*After the Battle*)

An armed guard to prevent looting, Birkenhead, March 1941. (*Author's collection*)

WARNING!

LOOTING

LOOTING FROM PREMISES WHICH HAVE BEEN DAMAGED BY, OR VACATED BY REASON OF, WAR OPERATIONS IS PUNISHABLE BY DEATH OR PENAL SERVITUDE FOR LIFE.

Warning to looters, 1940. Although no looters were executed, the maximum penalty on summary conviction was increased from six months to one year. (*Author's collection*)

'Trekkers' from Southampton, December 1940. (*Author's collection*)

First World War atrocity propaganda is echoed in this British magazine cover from May 1940. (*Author's collection*)

Rudolf Hess pictured at home (left) (© *Wolf Rudiger Hess*) in 1939/40 and at Nuremberg in 1946 (*After the Battle*). Even allowing for five years in captivity it is hard to believe that the later photograph is of a different man.

This Heinkel III brought down in Dorset in May 1941 is equipped with a cumbersome balloon fender. In fact four times as many Allied aircraft fell victim to barrage balloons than did German. (*After the Battle*).

A cloth swastika laid out by German paratroops near the Moerdijk Bridge in Holland, 10 May 1940. Markers of this kind were mistakenly identified as the work of the fifth column. (*Author's collection*)

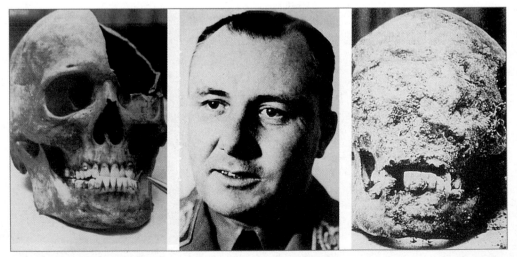

The two skulls found in Berlin in December 1972. The more photogenic 'Bormann skull' on the left is in fact that of Dr Ludwig Stumpfegger, Hitler's doctor. (*After the Battle*).

an official statement made to the House of Commons by Clement Attlee in November 1946, which estimated that 'about 36' German soldiers had been washed ashore at scattered points between Cornwall and Great Yarmouth over a period of several weeks.

At the same time that rumours of bodies, rewards, mutinies and overflowing hospitals were circulating abroad, a quite separate deception was being fed to the enemy. The idea of augmenting conventional coastal defences by burning fuel on the surface of the sea had been investigated as early as 1937 by a team of Royal Engineers at Christchurch, while an Admiralty proposal to attack enemy harbours with fire ships was tested in May 1939, eventually leading to the abortive Operation Lucid in the autumn of 1940. By May of that year, surplus fuel stocks in Britain had reached such a level that it was decided by Lord Hankey and Geoffrey Lloyd, the Secretary for Petroleum, to test ways and means of exploiting it for defensive purposes. A number of uncoordinated and largely unsuccessful experiments were unified at the beginning of July under the auspices of the Petroleum Warfare Department, at first little more than a miscellany of displaced sappers, oilmen and Post Office electrical engineers.

As well as flooding inshore waters with fuel from bulk storage on land, the PWD also devised roadside flame traps and the so-called Flame Fougasse, a 40-gallon drum filled with gun cotton, petrol and gas oil. These proved so effective that by June 1941 some 7,000 flame traps and 12,000 fougasses had been installed, chiefly in southern England, where they were manned by the Home Guard. Experiments at setting the sea on fire took longer to perfect, with the first trial at Dumpton near Margate on 3 July an ignominious failure. According to the unofficial history of the PWD, *Flame Over Britain*, published by its wartime director Sir Donald Banks in 1946, the first success was at Titchfield on the Solent on 24 August, when pipes from ten Scammel tankers were rigged to deliver twelve tons of fuel an hour onto relatively calm water. According to Banks, both trials were interrupted by air raids, and observed by inquisitive enemy aircraft. However it is more probable that the Germans first learned of British flame warfare defences by virtue of one of the 'methods that must remain forever secret' alluded to by John Baker White.

The remarkable truth is that German intelligence were aware of the PWD's sea-fire research as early as 10 August. The revelation that Sealion's first wave might encounter burning oil off the landing beaches greatly concerned the German High Command, and spurred prompt investigation of counter-measures. At Wilhelmshaven on 18 August the German navy carried out tests using 100 tons of a petrol–oil mixture, and found that in calm conditions it burned for almost 20 minutes, generating a great deal of smoke and heat. It was decided to counter this threat with pump and fire-fighting vessels, depth charges and booms fashioned from log chains. However, the fact that a German trial was apparently staged six days before the first successful British test of a sea flame barrage leads to the inevitable conclusion that details of this untested (and ultimately ineffective) weapon had been planted on German intelligence by the beginning of August, and that subsequent British trials in

1940 were little more than window dressing, deliberately staged in full view of the enemy.

From November 1940 onwards, rumours of a failed invasion attempt leaving thousands of German bodies floating in the Channel were deliberately co-mingled with the falsehood that Britain could set fire to the sea. The first variant, launched in September, held that British submarines had spread oil on the water. A 'Short Invasion Phrasebook' dropped in large quantities by the RAF over the enemy coast in late September made explicit reference to seas of petrol and burning comrades, while the BBC's German service offered similarly mordant language lessons on the radio. Then, in November, the *War Illustrated* ran an article which suggested that the Sealion armada had set sail on 16 September, largely on the strength of several imaginative American stories, such as that run by the *New York Sun*:

> The carnage was reported to have been terrific; neutral observers stated that the number of killed, drowned and wounded were to be counted in tens of thousands. All available hospital accommodation in and around the Channel ports had to be commandeered for the German wounded, and one report quoted a French doctor who said he had seen several thousand severely burned German soldiers in hospitals in occupied France; they had been, said the doctor, on board transports and barges preparing for the invasion of England when they were caught by British oil bombs, and the flaming oil on the surface of the water burned the troops as they leapt into the sea.

A French variant, noted by Marie Bonaparte in early October, stretched credulity to breaking point:

> 350,000 men were burnt alive by fuel oil spread on the sea. The British collected the corpses, identified them by their identity discs, loaded them in planes and dropped each corpse in its own village to strike terror into their families and undermine German morale . . . From Calais to Honfleur, the German soldiers could be seen swimming ashore upright. It was an army of the drowned. Their heavy equipment had slipped to their feet and so they were kept upright . . . The Germans are in such terror of embarking for England that they have to be driven aboard with machine-guns at their backs and their hands tied, to prevent them committing suicide.

By December, the burning sea story had expanded to include two thwarted invasion attempts. According to a report in the *New York Times* by one Boris Nikolayevsky, no doubt issued from the BSC office on Rockefeller Plaza:

> 'We were caught like fish in a frying pan,' was the way a German soldier who escaped from the débâcle described it to a French nurse. Only a few thousand Germans succeeded in reaching the French coast. The others perished in the sea or were burned to death. The Germans tried again in

September, over another route, and suffered a similar fate. People in the occupied French ports estimate that perhaps as many as 80,000 German troops perished in the two attempts. The fact is that hospitals in occupied France are filled with Nazi soldiers, all of them suffering from severe burns. Thousands of dead Germans have been washed ashore.

A string of official denials from Berlin from 25 September onwards had little impact, and in due course the great invasion rumour took on a life of its own. Several books published in Britain in 1941 helped to perpetuate the myth, including *The Battle of Britain* by James Spaight, who wrote of a 'mid-September mystery' in which 'a large number of German troops were burned severely' by oil bombs, and bodies washed ashore'. An American writer, Lars Moen, had been trapped by the German attack in May, and was unable to leave Europe until late October. Moen devoted no little space to the invasion rumour in his book *Under the Iron Heel*, which he acknowledged was largely cobbled together from reports told by others on board the *Exeter* en route from Lisbon. 16 September was again identified as Der Tag, on which 'a considerable force of towed triple-barges' on exercise were cut off by British destroyers, and their human cargo roasted after RAF bombers dropped vast quantities of oil drums and incendiary bombs. Moen added:

I first learned of the burned patients from a Belgian nurse working in an Antwerp hospital; Americans living near Ostend confirmed reports of the bodies being washed ashore . . . It was extremely significant that reports from the most widely scattered sources were unanimous on one point: that a considerable number of German soldiers had been badly burned.

These various suggestions that oil-filled bombs and torpedoes could wreak such havoc are plainly nonsensical, for no bomber or submarine then in service was capable of carrying a payload of oil sufficient to kill 80 men, let alone 80,000. Instead, a more subtle account aroused greater interest, this time by the celebrated commentator William Shirer, then a journalist with Columbia Broadcasting. In his *Berlin Diary* for 18 September, Shirer recorded an incident at the Potsdamer Bahnhof:

I noticed several lightly wounded soldiers, mostly airmen, getting off a special car which had been attached to our train. From their bandages their wounds looked like burns. I noticed also the longest Red Cross train I've ever seen. It stretched from the station for half a mile . . . I wondered where so many wounded could have come from, as the armies in the west stopped fighting three months ago. As there were only a few porters I had to wait some time on the platform and picked up a conversation with a railway workman. He said most of the men taken from the hospital train were suffering from burns.

The following day, Shirer claimed to have observed another long Red Cross train unloading wounded and received word of two more at Charlottenburg. This contemporary account, by a highly reputable journalist, is not easily dismissed, although precisely what Shirer witnessed first-hand beyond 'several airmen' remains ambiguous. Shirer later concluded the men in Berlin were casualties of an exercise surprised by the RAF, but it should be borne in mind that he was actively pro-British, and was thanked by name in the official history of BSC in New York, written in 1945. The suspicion therefore remains that in 1941 Shirer deliberately exaggerated the hospital train story as a morale booster, at a time when the war was going particularly badly for Britain. Curiously, there exist apparently reliable reports of similar trains seen at the Gare du Nord in Brussels at about the same time. Yet even the most hardened conspiracy theorist must baulk at the notion that, in the years since 1945, all mention of a large-scale amphibious disaster to rival the Dieppe raid in 1942 can have been expunged from every memoir, unit history and official file.

Where some spread the invasion myth as part of the war effort, or were merely gullible, others simply lied in pursuit of personal gain. In April 1942 an American journalist named Charles Barbe gave a talk at the Royal Institute of International Affairs at Chatham House, in which he claimed that 33,000 men from three fictive *Waffen-SS* divisions had perished in a sea of flame in September 1940, and that on the coast near Dieppe he had seen with his own eyes 'bodies on the shore like driftwood [and] blackened tree stumps'. The lecture was duly reported in the British press, but Barbe's mooted book, *None So Blind*, failed to find a publisher. Three years later another man finagled his name into print with a claim that he had watched the invasion attempt one weekend in September from a spot on the Sussex coast near Bognor, and saw hundreds of bodies washed ashore.

Following Barbe's lecture at Chatham House the invasion myth was largely absent from the press until October 1944, although in the interim fact and fiction began to blur. Graham Greene had published his short story 'The Lieutenant Died Last' in 1940, but this story of a thwarted German fifth column and parachute attack proved more popular as a film, *Went the Day Well?*, released in November 1942, and which went on to inspire *The Eagle Has Landed*, the postwar thriller by Jack Higgins. Greene's original story also informed *When the Bells Rang*, an anonymous book from May 1943 in which the Kentish town of Russocks is occupied by jackbooted Nazi thugs. None of these books mentioned burning oil and charred bodies, but a popular Will Hay comedy feature from 1942, *The Goose Steps Out*, includes a pointed reference to visiting Germans receiving the 'warmest welcome' of their lives. Indeed *Went the Day Well?* referred to an invasion attempt which 'went up in smoke'. Evelyn Waugh also noted the rumour in his 1952 novel *Men At Arms*, which spoke of troops being consoled in September 1940 'by a rumour, quite baseless, which was travelling the whole world in an untraceable manner, that the invasion had sailed and been defeated, and that the whole Channel was full of charred German corpses'.

In August 1944 the existence of the PWD was revealed to the public for the first time, after Geoffrey Lloyd held a press conference and released details of assorted petroleum weapons. The rapid Allied advance across north-west Europe following D-Day brought correspondents into contact with liberated civilians, some of whom resurrected the mid-September mystery. After speaking with a nurse in Brussels, John Parris of British United Press claimed to have uncovered 'final details' of Hitler's 'calamitous attempt to invade Britain on September 16th 1940.' By this account, printed in the *News of the World*:

> Thousands of German soldiers – 50,000 so it is said – were burned to death or maimed for life on that September day. 'A nightmare in hell' was how German soldiers described it after the RAF, catching the Nazi fleet in mid-Channel, dumped oil on the water and set fire to it with incendiary bullets . . .

The nurse claimed to have treated German casualties at a Brussels railway station on 17 September, and that Red Cross trains had passed through for three days after. Of one wounded soldier, said to have been burned about the head and shoulders:

> He said they had been told they were going to invade Britain, that nothing was going to stop them, that it was just a matter of getting into boats and crossing the Channel. He told me: 'It was horrible. The sea was ablaze. The British bombed and machine-gunned us. Hell couldn't be worse.' Then he died, there on the stretcher. We looked after more than 500 soldiers as best we could. Many of them died in Brussels railway station, others in our hospitals.

Many still believed that the mid-September mystery was the 'biggest secret' of the war, and several questions raised in the House of Commons had drawn only evasive answers. One of the most persistent inquirers was the Conservative MP, Major Vivyan Adams, whose wife Mary was the director of Home Intelligence at the Ministry of Information. Thus in June 1945 Geoffrey Lloyd, by then the Minister for Information, held a second press call on the subject, which became front page news on both sides of the Atlantic. In it Lloyd revealed for the first time that British intelligence agencies had fostered the burning sea rumour overseas, albeit in an unlikely manner:

> It always seemed to happen that when we were conducting full-scale experiments and making a tremendous blaze there was a German aeroplane about. On many occasions it came and bombed us. In this way the Germans must have known what we were doing, and in fact they showed us they expected us to use flames as a defence, for they carried out experiments with asbestos suits.
>
> And the Germans killed thousands of their own troops in an effort to restore confidence where terror of the fire weapon spread fastest – through

the ranks of the *Wehrmacht*. They arranged a great demonstration to show that specially equipped troops could pass unscathed even if the sea was on fire. Thousands of asbestos suits were made, and each man of the troops to take part in the demonstration wore one (10,000 asbestos suits were ordered in Paris alone).

Huge quantities of oil were spread off the French coast and set on fire. The trial armada set out – to disaster. A large number of the headpieces of the suits were defective and the men inside were roasted to death. For weeks afterwards the burnt bodies of German soldiers were being washed up on the south coast. Meanwhile, by pamphlets dropped by planes, radio, and whispering campaigns, stories of Britain's terrifying fire defences were being spread.

In November 1946 the new Prime Minister, Clement Attlee, gave a written answer to the Commons on the subject of the 1940 invasion scare, in which the figure of 'about 36' was offered in relation to German army corpses washed ashore. This estimate was endorsed by Churchill in *Their Finest Hour*, who added a little spin of his own:

We took no steps to contradict such tales, which spread freely through the occupied countries in a wildly exaggerated form, and gave much encouragement to the oppressed populations. In Brussels, for instance, a shop exhibited men's bathing suits marked 'For Channel Swimming.'

Against this background it is curious that two other semi-official accounts published soon after the war sought to deny the story. Guy Gibson, the celebrated leader in 617 Squadron for the raid on the Ruhr dams in 1943, had been killed in action the following year, and his ghost-written memoir *Enemy Coast Ahead* shelved until 1946. In it Gibson dismissed as fictitious rumours that 'thousands of German soldiers were buried on the east coast of England', while concluding that 'no-one will ever know anyone who saw a dead German soldier, although many a man will claim to know someone else who knows someone else who buried one.' Eleven years later, in his otherwise excellent book *Invasion 1940*, Peter Fleming too dismissed the rumours of bodies on beaches out of hand, although inadequate research meant that Fleming was unaware of earlier books by Thomson, Bonaparte and Baker White, or even the arrival of the corpse of Heinrich Poncke at Littlestone in October 1940, which had been reported in the press and by the BBC.

In November 1957 Fleming took part in a BBC television programme, *The Finest Hour*, in which the invasion myth was discussed in detail. William Robinson also appeared on the programme, and told of the part he had played in the recovery of bodies at St Mary's Bay. Faced with this testimony Fleming was stumped, although despite the fact that Fleming served with both MI(R) and SOE during the war, it is unlikely that his botched debunking of the great invasion rumour formed part of any official cover-up. Indeed his book had drawn attention to an otherwise obscure German film biography of Admiral

Wilhelm Canaris, whose legendary career is examined in detail in Chapter Ten. Produced in 1954, *Canaris* offered up a liberal account of the wartime activities of the German chief of intelligence who acted, albeit sporadically, as an Allied informant. During scenes concerning Operation Sealion, an *Abwehr* agent is seen to remove a canister of secret film from a Whitehall office, which in Berlin is found to contain graphic footage of flamethrowers, fougasses and sea flame barrages. In fact these clips are genuine PWD footage, shot at Studland Bay and Moody Down Farm on 1941, and first shown in public in 1945 by Geoffrey Lloyd. In the 1954 movie, a detailed scale model of a sea flame barrage at Hastings is unveiled, and Canaris has only to exhibit these several 'beast eating' devices to the German High Command to secure the cancellation of Sealion as 'suicidal'.

It is unclear on which sources screenwriter Erich Ebermeyer based this fictionalised version of history, but the scenario is less far-fetched than it might seem. The fact that German counter-measures were tested before the first successful British trial is clear evidence that specific disinformation was fed to German intelligence, and the cover subsequently offered by Banks and Lloyd – that inquisitive German aircraft overflew Dumpton and Titchfield – rings hollow. It is less likely that any *Abwehr* spies obtained film from Whitehall, or that Sealion was postponed and later cancelled solely on the basis of the threat posed by flame warfare. Nonetheless, on this reading Sefton Delmer of the Political Warfare Executive was probably not guilty of exaggeration when he wrote of his radio broadcasts in September 1940 that:

> The line about burning in the Channel fitted in perfectly, as of course it was intended to do, with the information which our deception services had planted on Admiral Canaris . . . Our rumour agencies, too, had been busy spreading it everywhere. The mean murderous British, it was said, had apparatus in readiness in which they were going to set the Channel and the beaches on fire at such time as Hitler launched his boats. This was a lie. But it went over so well that it is believed by many Germans to this day.

Today, the dual invasion myths of floating bodies and burning seas are less well remembered, having been displaced by the more trivial legend of spies dressed as nuns. In fact, the rumour of the invasion that never was represents Britain's first substantial deception and propaganda victory of the Second World War, at a time when Britain's finest hour was fast becoming her darkest. The fact that much of it relied upon secret channels and unavowable black propaganda meant that the truth of the matter was never disclosed, and that even as late as 1992 an identical set of rumours and falsehoods would become attached to supposed wartime events at the village of Shingle Street on the Suffolk coast. If nothing else, the controversy surrounding Shingle Street disproves Sophocles' dictum that a lie never lives to be old.

In closing, another passage from John Baker White's *The Big Lie* deserves mention, for – if correct – it would do much to explain the genuine mystery surrounding the bodies recovered by Gunner Robinson's party. By the time the invasion rumour swept the country after 7 September the Battle of Britain was already over. Nonetheless, according to White:

> When we engaged upon building up the Burning Sea deception we considered a hundred and one ways of adding substance to it. One ingenious plan involved the use of human bodies . . . Our scheme was to take the charred bodies of *Luftwaffe* men shot down in the Battle of Britain, dress them in the burnt uniforms of German infantry soldiers and float them ashore on the tide at various points along the invasion coast . . . So far as I know, it was never put into operation, but it had a much more important counterpart later in the war.

True or not, the counterpart referred to by White is the case of The Man Who Never Was, examined in Chapter Nine. Given that corpse deceptions had been a feature of British military planning since the First World War, White's suggestion might not be as fanciful as it seems. It might be argued that his broad hint, if true, would hardly have been cleared for publication under the D notice procedure. Or could it be, as the diplomat Sir Lewis Namier once observed, that 'a great many profound secrets are somewhere in print, but are most easily detected when one knows what to seek'?

CHAPTER SEVEN

Hitler Myths

Given that Adolf Hitler was regularly reported as having been killed, it is ironic that in the wake of his suicide in Berlin on 30 April 1945, few were prepared to believe he was dead. The myth of a still-living Hitler in hiding is just one of countless Führer legends to have emerged during and after the Second World War, the most popular of which are examined below.

Rumours that the German Chancellor had 'gone off with a gun and shot himself' circulated in Britain during the first week of the war in September 1939, and were followed by regular reports of his death or disappearance. In the run-up to D-Day in May 1944 a rumour circulated among British troops that Hitler had been assassinated, and word that he was 'dead and buried' was still current in American units at the end of the same year. According to the text of a popular US army talk from February 1945, warning against 'the Rumor Racket' (see Appendix Two): 'Wishful thinking gave that one wide acceptance. Legal minds assembled a lot of evidence that seemed to substantiate the Dictator's demise. His absence from the German scene could be explained in no other way. It was welcome news. Unfortunately it wasn't true.'

After the war the reverse held sway. As we saw in Chapter Two, a notable feature of life in postwar Germany was an abundance of rumours that deceased military and party figures were still alive, including Gunter Prien, Martin Bormann, Wilhelm Canaris and Adolf Hitler. A poll taken in Berlin in April 1946 revealed that fewer than 10 per cent of German civilians believed Hitler was dead. Following the German surrender in May 1945 there were any number of dubious sightings, setting a pattern which would become familiar over the next four decades. Hitler was variously seen living as a hermit in a cave near Lake Garda in northern Italy, as a monk in St Gallen, as a shepherd in the Swiss Alps, and working as a casino croupier in the French resort of Evian. Other newspaper stories maintained that he was working as a fisherman in the Baltic, or on a boat off the west coast of Ireland, and reported sightings in Grenoble and Albania. In July 1945 the US Office of Censorship intercepted a letter written to a Chicago newspaper, claiming that Hitler was living in a German-owned hacienda 450 miles from Buenos Aires, protected by two doubles and an underground hideout, from which he was hatching plans for long-range robot bombs. This intelligence was treated seriously by the FBI, although enquiries made via the American embassy in Argentina led nowhere.

The first falsehood about Hitler's demise had been promulgated by Admiral Karl Dönitz, the German military commander in northern Germany and Hitler's designated successor. When Dönitz announced Hitler's death by radio at 10.20 pm on 1 May, the German public was told he had been killed in action that same afternoon, fighting 'at the head of his troops in Berlin'. In fact Hitler had committed suicide a day earlier, by shooting himself through the mouth in his subterranean bunker, while his new bride, Eva Braun, took cyanide. The falsehood of a hero's death was intended to bolster the shattered morale of the German armed forces, yet it was not the only confusing announcement made. On 9 June the Russian commander Marshal Georgi Zhukov announced to the world that Hitler's corpse had not been identified, that the circumstances were 'very mysterious' and that the German leader 'could have flown away' from Berlin 'at the very last moment'. Zhukov's statement informed a subsequent announcement by General Eisenhower, who voiced doubts about Hitler's death at a press conference in Paris on 16 June. At the Potsdam Conference on 16 July the Soviet General Secretary told President Truman that Hitler was thought to be living in Spain or Argentina, while that same month the Russian newspaper *Izvestiia* carried a mischievous report that Hitler and Eva Braun were alive and well and living in a moated castle in Westphalia, which lay in the British zone of occupation. British intelligence were not amused, and in September ordered a young major named Hugh Trevor-Roper to conduct an official enquiry, code-named Operation Nursery. The results were published two years later as *The Last Days of Hitler*, although the book was banned behind the Iron Curtain.

An official Soviet statement released in September 1945 muddied the waters further still:

No trace of the bodies of Hitler or Eva Braun has been discovered . . . It is established that Hitler, by means of false testimony, sought to hide his traces. Irrefutable proof exists that a small airplane left the Tiergarten at dawn on 30 April flying in the direction of Hamburg. Three men and a woman are known to have been on board. It has also been established that a large submarine left Hamburg before the arrival of the British forces. Mysterious persons were on board the submarine, among them a woman.

Meanwhile the bizarre rumours continued to multiply. In August an American lawyer informed the FBI that Hitler was living as Gerhardt Weithaupt in Innsbruck, together with Alfred Jodl. In 1946 he was sighted in a coffee room in Amsterdam, having developed a very long body and arms, and was also reported as leading a wolfpack of rogue U-boats, albeit suffering badly from seasickness. The FBI received thousands of letters alleging that Hitler was living in America, having purchased land in Colorado, or riding the subway in New York. Another submarine story arose following the discovery of a message in a bottle, which claimed that Hitler had escaped from Berlin only to sink with the U-boat *Nauecilus*. Another South American report had him living on a farm at La Falda in Argentina, disguised by plastic surgery performed on board the boat which had smuggled him across the Atlantic. A rival story placed him in Zurich, where he had aged dreadfully and affected a demeanour 'similar to that of a pensioned official'. The motive behind at least some of these reports is hinted at by Hugh Trevor-Roper:

> Throughout the summer and autumn of 1945 many resourceful journalists had been pursuing phantoms of Hitler with energy and enthusiasm, and the pleasant lakes of the Swiss frontier and the romantic Tyrolean Alps and the comfortable resorts of Upper Austria were frequently visited by devoted investigators whose scrupulous consciences forbade them to ignore even the most inconsiderable clue. In the course of these researches many engaging theories were propounded; but as winter drew near, and personal excursions became less attractive the consensus of opinion began to allow that Hitler had really remained in Berlin, and the mystery of his fate was one that could best be solved not by strenuous travel in an inclement season, but by ingenious meditation in well-heated saloon bars.

Some of the hoaxes were probably delusional. In December 1947 a German airman calling himself Baumgart claimed he had flown Hitler and Braun to Denmark on 28 April 1945, although the witness afterwards retired to a mental hospital in Poland. Another false report came from a northerly region of Sweden. According to the author of an anonymous letter posted to the American embassy in Stockholm:

> If you look in the Bauerska mountains you will find a long cave about 466 metres or maybe even longer, with about 92 doors well camouflaged. Hitler has here a room 30 by 30 metres, with electrical stoves, one big, one small. There is food there, cans of all kinds for several years ahead and lots of money of all kinds of currencies. There is also a pipe from the top of the mountain in which food can be dropped down. Those who bring food there are called 'Ravens'. Those who built this in the mountains have been killed long ago so it would not be discovered. When you have found it, I demand one sixth of what is there and a jeep and a tractor. You will know my name when you have found him.

Phantom sightings of the erstwhile Führer continued up until 1992, when a Canadian paper reported that Hitler had finally passed away in South America. Even as late as 1980 the author of *Hitler's Secret Life* was prepared to treat seriously claims that Hitler escaped from Berlin in a float plane at the last minute, and that four Americans arrested in Brazil in 1966 on smuggling charges were actually detained 'because they saw an old man near the landing strip at Tres Marias whom Brazilian officials feared they recognised'.

But that is to jump ahead. Back in 1945, in the wake of Russian claims about moated castles and large submarines, the mystery surrounding Hitler's death was compounded by inconsistencies in the accounts given by bunker survivors, some of whom were released from Soviet jails in 1955. Thirteen years later a licensed Russian journalist named Lev Bezymenski published *The Death of Adolf Hitler: Unknown Documents from the Soviet Archives*, which admitted for the first time that Soviet troops found Hitler's remains in a shell crater in the Chancellery garden on 3 May 1945. Bezymenski also revealed that an autopsy was carried out in the Berlin suburb of Buch on 8 May, which concluded that Hitler had chosen poison over a bullet. The author continued that the corpses of Hitler and Braun, as well as the Goebbels family, were afterwards burned completely and 'strewn to the wind'.

The poison revelation came as a bombshell in 1968. A decade later, in 1979, an American author named James O'Donnell published *The Berlin Bunker*, a meticulously researched account in which a third scenario was offered, combining poisoning and shooting, with Hitler squeezing the trigger of his pistol while simultaneously biting down on a cyanide capsule. The truth emerged only in 1992, when Russian journalist Ada Petrova discovered a series of six previously classified files in a Moscow archive, referenced as I-G-23. These revealed that the Buch autopsy in May 1945 had been flawed, and that a year later further bone fragments were recovered from the shell crater in the Chancellery garden. These included charred sections of skull with an outgoing bullet hole, fired at point-blank range. However, these fresh findings were kept secret since Moscow preferred to hold out that Hitler chose a coward's death, and to hide the embarrassing mistakes made at Buch. Knowingly or not, Bezymenski had been misled, and Hugh Trevor-Roper had been substantially correct all along. It was a great shame that Trevor-Roper proved less erudite in 1983, when, as Lord Dacre and a former Regius Professor of History at Oxford, he unwisely endorsed the forged 'Hitler Diaries' as genuine.

The true fate of Hitler's corpse was revealed in 1995 in *The Death of Adolf Hitler* by Ada Petrova and British journalist Peter Watson. After the autopsy, the remains of Hitler, Braun and the entire Goebbels family (as well as General Hans Krebs and two dogs) were buried in wooden boxes at Finow, 30 miles from Berlin. On 3 June 1945 the boxes were moved and re-buried in an isolated forest area near Ratenow, then moved again on 23 February 1946, to a courtyard in Magdeburg. With these premises due to be returned to East German control in 1970, the remains were again exhumed in April of that year and found to consist of a 'jellied mass'. This grisly consignment was conveyed to an area of waste ground near Schonebeck, burned thoroughly, and the ashes dumped into a tributary of the Elbe. Only two groups of Hitler remains were retained in Russian archives: four parts of the skull in the State Archive of the Russian Federation, and his jawbone in the KGB Archive.

The publication of *The Death of Adolf Hitler* should stand as the last word on the circumstances surrounding the Führer's demise. Before it reached print, however, the controversial Hess historian Dr Hugh Thomas advanced another of the imaginative 'double' theories on which his reputation is based. In *Doppelgänger: The Truth About the Bodies in the Berlin Bunker*, Thomas asserted that the bodies burned and buried in the Chancellery garden were not those of Hitler and Braun, but instead substitutes which formed part of a complicated forensic fraud. The main evidence on which Thomas relied was a supposed poor match between dental records and the (few) teeth left in the corpses found, and inconsistencies arising from blood stains and types. By this hypothesis, Hitler was strangled by an aide rather than shot or poisoned, and a female corpse substituted to allow Braun to escape from Berlin. As Thomas is forced to admit, however, his alternative scenario is nothing more than 'relatively uninformed speculation', which calls to mind the question of why the author chose to commit it to print.

In 2001 Hugh Thomas turned his attention to the 'untimely' death of the *Reichsführer-SS* in his book *SS-1*, in which the indefatigable doctor yet again postulated the existence of a double in relation to a leading Nazi. According to Thomas, the circumstances of the capture of Himmler at Bremervoerde by Intelligence Corps personnel on 22 May 1945 were suspicious, in that his unwieldy party of a dozen or so men were too conspicuous, their forged papers too poor, and that Himmler's answers under interrogation were inaccurate. Thomas also cited supposed medical anomalies, including an absent duelling scar on the left cheek, oddly muscular legs and a nasal deformity which the real Himmler never had. None of the evidence is particularly compelling, and Thomas himself was only able to offer that the man who swallowed cyanide at Luneburg was 'perhaps' not Heinrich Himmler, but a double intended to assist in the escape of the real *Reichsführer*. As with the Hess theory, it is hard to believe that any such double could have been found, let alone persuaded to commit suicide. And if the British authorities were really so unsure about the identity of the corpse that photographs were taken from deliberately obscure angles, as Thomas suggests, why allow a death mask to be cast, and preserved as an exhibit at the Royal Army Dental Corps Museum in Aldershot?

Besides Hitler, the other leading undead Nazi was Martin Bormann. Although Hitler Youth Leader Artur Axmann claimed to have seen Bormann's corpse near the Weidendammer Bridge on the night of 1/2 May, a widespread belief persisted that Hitler's deputy escaped to South America. In 1945 Stalin informed Harry Hopkins that Bormann had escaped from Hamburg in a submarine, and in October 1946 the former *Reichsleiter* was sentenced in absentia at Nuremberg. In 1965 the Soviet journalist Lev Bezymenski claimed Bormann had escaped to South America to serve 'US imperialism' during the Cold War, while the South American connection was restated three years later in a Bormann biography by James McGovern. In 1967 a hapless peasant was arrested in Guatemala, followed several years later by a 72-year-old German expatriate living in Colombia. In his book *Aftermath: Martin Bormann and the*

Fourth Reich, the American writer Ladislas Farago claimed to have run Bormann to ground in the hospital of a Redemptorist convent in Bolivia. By way of contrast, the former German intelligence chief Reinhardt Gehlen asserted that Bormann had acted as a Soviet spy, and in May 1945 sought and found refuge in Moscow.

A year after this unverifiable revelation, in December 1972, two sets of human remains were unearthed on waste ground near the Invalidenstrasse in West Berlin and identified as those of Bormann and Hitler's doctor, Ludwig Stumpfegger. Despite the fact that their identities were confirmed by the renowned American forensic odontologist Dr Reidar Sognnaes, and a DNA match established, the myth that Bormann had survived persisted. In 1981 the case for South America was pressed again in *Nazi in Exile* by Paul Manning, which suggested that Bormann was responsible for Germany's economic rebirth in the years following the war, while the Moscow connection was repeated by Hugo Beer in 1983, and by J.O.E.O. Mahrke in 1992. Two recent variations are more ridiculous still. In 1995 the *News of the World* claimed that Bormann had been living as Peter Broderick-Hartley in Reigate, Surrey, having undergone plastic surgery. The following year saw the publication of *Op JB* by Christopher Creighton, which offered a fantastical tale in which Bormann was smuggled out of Berlin by a team of British commandos, selected by Churchill, with the object of accessing Nazi currency reserves secreted in Swiss bank accounts. Creighton's incredible tale, which involved a double and Bormann later running a riding school in the English countryside, has since been demolished by the intelligence historian Nigel West in his study *Counterfeit Spies*.

Another Bormann falsehood revolves around the celebrated photograph of the skulls discovered in 1972, as Dr Sognnaes explained some time later:

> The 'Bormann skull', which a few years ago was so prominently displayed in the world press, was none other than Bormann's post-mortem companion, Stumpfegger. The photographic mix-up of the two skulls may have been purely accidental. Perhaps the Stumpfegger skull was simply chosen as the better looking one by the competing photographers, whereas what later turned out to be the Bormann skull at first appeared like a toothless blob of dirt.

Despite this clarification, the image of the more photogenic Stumpfegger skull is still routinely captioned as that of Bormann, even in minutely researched accounts such as *Berlin Then and Now* by Tony Le Tissier (1992) and *The Death of Adolf Hitler* by Pedrova and Watson (1995).

Probably the most enduring Hitler myth is the canard that the Führer possessed only one testicle. While there can be little doubt that the tale was both current and popular in Britain during the Second World War, contemporary mores on taste and decency prevented it being recorded in print. Nevertheless this infamous lyric proved cheering when sung to the tune of Alford's deathless *Colonel Bogey March*:

Hitler has only got one ball
Göring has two, but very small
Himmler has something similar
But poor old Goebbels has no balls at all.

Spy Mysteries Unveiled, an espionage potboiler written by Vernon Hinchley in 1963, further explored the theme:

Hitler's abnormal sex life was due to his freakishly under-developed genitals, and he never recovered from the sneers of fellow soldiers during the First World War. Thereafter he would never allow himself to be seen in a bathing costume. This meant that he could never bathe in the sea.

Hinchley went on to connect this phobia with Hitler's failure to cross the Channel in 1940. The testicle legend might well have been forgotten had it not been for the findings of the Buch autopsy, conducted in May 1945 but not made public in the West until 1968. The autopsy was carried out by a commission comprising five Soviet military doctors, the principal examiners being two Lieutenant-Colonels named Shkaravski and Krayevski. Their report stated:

The genital member is scorched. In the scrotum, which is singed but preserved, only the right testicle was found. The left testicle could not be found either in the scrotum or on the spermatic cord inside the inguinal canal, nor in the small pelvis.

We now know that the Buch autopsy was substantially flawed, and there is every reason to suspect that it was also incorrect in respect of the missing testicle. Indeed it is not unreasonable to suggest that data was deliberately falsified by the Soviets, who wished to present Hitler as a coward with a sexual defect. Certainly several Germans who were intimates of Hitler dismissed the allegation that he was a monorchid, including his valet Heinz Linge, who protested that he had seen his employer's intact testicles when once they had both urinated against a tree. Two Nazi doctors also stated they had observed no 'anomalies of the genitals' when examining Hitler, although some doubt has been cast on their testimony, particularly given that one of them, Dr Erwin Giesing, was an ear specialist. Conversely, in 1971 Hitler's company commander from the First World War wrote to *Die Zeit* to claim that he had indeed had only one testicle, a fact on which he was positive since the army had periodically conducted genital inspections for venereal disease. The legend that Hitler was impotent is probably a variation of the original testicular allegation, and at this remove is equally impossible to confirm or deny.

The allegation that Hitler was a homosexual, or at least displayed homosexual tendencies, was also widespread during the early war years. In 1934 one Ernst Hanfstaengl issued a libel writ after the *Daily Express* described him as 'Hitler's Putzy' and an 'intimate friend', although Beaverbrook indicated he would defend the charge and the case fizzled out. The diaries of Sir Harold Nicolson record a conversation with a Swiss aristocrat in October 1939, who revealed that Hitler was 'the most profoundly feminine man' he had ever met, and that there were 'moments when he becomes almost effeminate'. In February 1940 an article in *The Listener* concurred, making much of Hitler's supposed intellectual inferiority complex and 'effeminate mysticism'. The American journalist William Shirer watched Hitler closely one day in September 1938 as he left a hotel in Bad Godesberg, having met with Neville Chamberlain, and noted his 'very ladylike' walk and 'dainty little steps'. In 1940 a refugee German industrialist told Henry 'Chips' Channon that Hitler 'was certainly a homosexual' and that his failure to ascend to a rank higher than corporal in the First World War 'was due to his very pronounced perversion. In later years he reformed.' While it is famously hard to prove a negative, it is difficult to believe that such stories were anything more than crude propaganda, and certainly no serious biographer of Adolf Hitler has turned up anything that substantiates the claim. *The Hidden Hitler*, published by Lothar Machtan in 2001, remains the subject of fierce controversy.

Although there is little to choose between Hitler and Stalin as icons of evil, Hitler became the subject of a far greater number of unlikely (and unpleasant) rumours. Following the publication of *Mein Kampf*, in which Hitler referred to prostitution in Vienna and to venereal disease, some claimed he had contracted syphilis in a brothel on his seventeenth birthday, and that the condition continued to afflict him for the rest of his life. As well as the stock myths that Hitler was mad, it was variously said that he was an epileptic, a drug addict and a sexual pervert. A book published in New York in 1941 said to have been written by 'Hitler's psychiatrist, Kurt Kruger' repeated the allegation of homosexuality, and offered the distasteful falsehood that Hitler became anti-Semitic at the age of ten after watching the village grocer, a Jew, rape his mother. When his beloved cousin, Geli Raubal, committed suicide in September 1931, it was said that Hitler had her killed because she was pregnant by a Jewish lover. It was also whispered that Hitler had pulled the trigger himself. Later Hitler was widely rumoured to have sired a secret child with Eva Braun, said by some to have been born in Dresden in 1942. The Führer myth list is almost endless.

Several books written by or about Hitler's inner circle are completely fictional. In 1947 one Josef Greiner published a memoir in which he claimed to have been a close associate of the young Hitler in Vienna between 1907 and 1908, and again in Munich in 1913. According to Greiner, in Vienna Hitler was so filthy and impoverished that he was obliged to discard his underclothes because they were tattered and lice-ridden, and he faked antique oil paintings by roasting them in an oven. Greiner went on to attribute all manner of hetero- and homosexual exploits to Hitler, and rounded off his account with a predictable claim that his erstwhile friend was still alive, having flown out of Tempelhof on 30 April 1945 in a prototype Messerschmitt turbo-jet. The entire book was a tissue of lies, as were the supposed 'intimate notes and diaries of Eva Braun' published as *The Private Life of Adolf Hitler* in 1949. As well as peddling several hoary old tales about syphilis and astrology, the fraudulent Braun diaries also hinted at incest, group sex and other 'sexual riddles' which 'cannot be reproduced because of their obscenity'. According to the publisher's preface, Braun had entrusted the diary to her friend Luis Trenker, described as 'a well-known Austrian writer, film director and film star', following a meeting at the ski resort of Kitzbuhel in the winter of 1944–5. In fact they were fiction.

Another unreliable memoir, never actually published, led subsequent historians to perpetuate the myth that between November 1912 and April 1913 Hitler lived with relatives in Liverpool. The source of the story is an undated typescript written in about 1940 by Brigid Dowling-Hitler, titled *My Brother-in-Law Adolf*. The author was the Irish wife of Hitler's half-brother, Alois Hitler Jnr, an itinerant waiter and razor blade salesman. After a somewhat mundane account of the future Führer's sojourn in Toxteth, Dowling went on to describe her subsequent adventures inside the Third Reich while trying to rescue her son William Patrick from the clutches of the Gestapo, including lengthy meetings with Hess, Himmler and other Nazi leaders. In *The Life and Death of Adolf Hitler*, published in 1973, writer Robert Payne relied on the spurious Dowling memoir to support the notion that Hitler learned to respect the English people and the Royal Navy while in Britain, which informed his decision to spare the BEF at Dunkirk and seek a negotiated peace. However, contemporary police records reveal that Hitler was living in Vienna throughout this period, while Immigration Service files show no record of Hitler having visited Britain at this or any other time. The reason that Hitler never once mentioned his pre-war trip to England, either in print or in conversation, is because it never took place.

Popular in its day, *The Flying Visit* by Peter Fleming offered a satirical fantasy in which Hitler parachuted into England in a vain effort to broker peace, and which prefigured the arrival of Rudolf Hess in May 1941 by a full year. Stranger even than this fiction was the belief of some within the British intelligence community that Hitler might be kidnapped and flown to RAF Lympne in Kent – this on the hearsay that his private pilot, Hans Bauer, was dissatisfied with his employer's conduct of the war. This unlikely tip had been passed on by the British air attaché in Bulgaria, but apparently convinced Sir Arthur Harris (who had worked at the Air Ministry before taking over Bomber Command) to arrange a reception. Two platoons of troops were posted to Lympe to act as guards, and a possible arrival date pencilled in: 25 March 1941. It was anticipated that Hitler's personal aircraft, a four-engined Focke-Wulf Fw200, would approach the airfield with its wheels down, and even when the Kondor failed to arrive on the appointed day, the troops were kept in place until May. Details of this bizarre plan are preserved in an Air Ministry file deposited at the Public Record Office.

Although few today believe Adolf Hitler survived the holocaust of Berlin in May 1945, a steady flow of books and theories have sought to exaggerate his supposed interest in the occult. The subject of astrology seems first to have been raised in the minutes of a meeting of the Services Consultative Committee on 6 March 1940, when it was recorded:

> A large number of Germans are superstitious and it is believed that a good deal of interest is taken in astrology. There was a rumour that Hitler himself believes in astrology, and had employed the services of an astrologer. We suggest obtaining from a well-known astrologer a horoscope of Hitler predicting disaster for him and his country and putting it into Germany by secret channels.

However, the idea was overtaken by the Fall of France, and the subsequent invasion threat and attendant rumour-mongering discussed in Chapter Six. Nevertheless, as late as October 1940 the Joint Intelligence Committee were prepared to take some account of astrology in attempting to predict the date of a cross-Channel assault. For the period beginning 19 October their minutes record:

> The moon and tides were suitable, the incidence of fog likely, and Hitler's horoscope, a sign to which he was reported to pay considerable attention, was favourable during this period.

Anti-German astrological propaganda first emerged in the wake of the Hess affair in 1941, when it was hinted that the Deputy Führer had been misled by bogus astrological predictions, and when deception agencies began to circulate false horoscopes, as well as bogus quatrains by the sixteenth-century French seer Nostradamus. Although much of this British activity took the form of unavowable 'black' propaganda, and was therefore unknown to the public at large, a tour of America undertaken by a Hungarian astrologer known as Louis de Wohl did much to promote the myth that Hitler was reliant on the science of the stars. A great deal of nonsense has been written about de Wohl's American tour, and his contribution to the Allied war effort generally, including the false claim that de Wohl had once been Hitler's personal astrologer. In fact de Wohl had arrived in London as a refugee in 1935, and quickly developed a clientele as a professional astrologer. In his memoir *The Stars of War and Peace* (1952), de Wohl claimed that Hitler had been convinced of the value of astrology by Hess while the pair were imprisoned in Landsberg prison in 1923–24, and that in 1935 de Wohl himself had been invited to place his own expertise at the service of Germany and the Führer. Neither seems very likely.

After war broke out de Wohl offered his services to British intelligence, but was rebuffed until September 1940, when he was allowed to set up his own 'Psychological Research Bureau' in an unfurnished suite at the Grosvenor House hotel. It seems that few took seriously his claims to be able to 'predict the predictions' of Hitler's own tame astrologers, said to include Karl Ernst Krafft. However in May 1941 it was decided to send de Wohl on a tour of the

United States, in part because a number of American astrological journals had begun to carry articles and letters predicting a German victory. Initially the 'astro-philosopher' de Wohl made little headway, although a lecture to a convention of the American Federation of Scientific Astrologers in Ohio in August was apparently a success, and his comparisons between the horoscopes of Hitler and Napoleon enthusiastically received. In addition, arrangements were made for certain of de Wohl's predictions to be circulated around various English-language newspapers in Africa. Typical of those is an item credited to Sheikh Youssef Afifi, which appeared in a Cairo paper and promised:

> Four months hence a red planet will appear on the eastern horizon and will indicate that a dangerous evil-doer, who has drenched the world in blood, will pass away . . . This means that an uncrowned emperor will be killed, and that man is Hitler.

Harford Montgomery Hyde, who served on the staff of British Security Coordination in New York, confirms that steps were taken to ensure the story was picked up by American correspondents in Egypt. At the same time, correspondents in Nigeria filed a story based on a report from a remote district, which told of a vision seen by a priest called Ulokoigbe. In the priest's own words:

> In the light, I saw a group of five men on a rock. One was short, with long hair; the second was fat and shaped like the breadfruit; the third monkey-faced and crippled; the fourth had glass in his eyes like the District Officer; the fifth was leopard-faced. After a quarrel the fifth vanished. The cripple stabbed the breadfruit man in the back. The long-haired one cursed the glass-eyed one and pushed him from the rock. Then the cripple jumped from the rock leaving Long Hair alone. Long Hair seized the crown from the rock, but it did not fit his head and fell off. In a wild rage, Long Hair slipped from the rock and fell shrieking like a madman. The crown was left in its proper place in the middle of the rock.

This droll fable, which lampoons Hitler together with Göring, Goebbels, Himmler and Hess, was also reproduced in the United States. Elsewhere de Wohl predicted Germany would use Brazil as a stepping stone for hostilities against the USA, and attacked pro-German figures such as Henry Haye and Charles Lindbergh. Throughout the tour he was accompanied by a senior SOE secretary, and paid in cash each week by a BSC minion who was obliged to climb the fire escape of his modest Manhattan hotel. After returning to London in February 1942 de Wohl purchased the uniform of an army captain, and was observed 'walking down Piccadilly looking just like an unmade bed'. The masquerade proved short lived, and by the end of 1943 de Wohl had outlived his usefulness. By the end of the war he had returned to writing pulp fiction, delivering a derivative supernatural thriller titled *Strange Daughter*, revolving around black magic and attempts to birth a daughter of the devil. Even in his highly unreliable BSC history *A Man Called Intrepid*, William Stevenson was correct in describing de Wohl as a quack.

Allegations that Hitler and the Nazis were devotees of even darker arts were not common during the war years, a book from 1943 called *The Occult Causes of the Present War* proving the exception rather than the rule. According to author Lewis Spence, the marked 'Satanic element in Nazism' was the work of a 'mysterious and well-concealed body of Satanist or Luciferian origin' which had manifested itself in 'practically every European revolt since the beginning of the Christian era'. In relation to Hitler himself, the plainly conspiratorial Spence offered little beyond enigmatic statements that the Führer was a 'mystical mulatto' and 'the creature of shadowy people'. Despite claims to the contrary by later authors, it is most unlikely that the Allies considered the Nazi hierarchy to consist of a cabal of sinister pagan adepts, or that at Nuremberg evidence of ritualistic and occult practices was excluded for fear it would lead to acquittals on grounds of 'diminished responsibility' or insanity. This last allegation was made by Michael Bentine, supposedly on the word of Airey Neave, an IMT prosecutor, although Neave made no mention of the issue in his own memoir published in 1978. Why such an important disclosure should have been entrusted to Bentine, a former RAF intelligence officer turned comedian and parapsychologist, is obscure. In truth Bentine probably adapted it from a highly unreliable book called *The Spear of Destiny*, discussed below.

Today readers can choose from a whole raft of books which purport to establish intimate links between the Third Reich and the occult, including *Satan and Swastika*, *The Occult Reich*, *Hitler and the Occult* and *Hitler – Black Magician*. Among the themes customarily churned out are the Thule Society, the Ordo Templi Orientis, Wotanism, the influence of George Gurdjieff and Karl Haushofer, secret polar bases, and quests for ancient relics such as the Holy Grail, which in turn have informed Hollywood blockbusters such as the *Indiana Jones* series and *Seven Years in Tibet*. A detailed exploration lies beyond the scope of this study, and the curious are instead advised to begin their researches with *The Occult Roots of Nazism* by Dr Nicholas Goodrick-Clarke, who wrote cogently in 1985:

> Books written about Nazi occultism between 1960 and 1975 were typically sensational and under-researched. A complete ignorance of the primary sources are common to most authors, and inaccuracies and wild claims were repeated by each newcomer to the genre until an abundant literature existed, based on spurious 'facts' concerning the powerful Thule Society, the Nazi links with the East, and Hitler's supposed occult initiation . . . The modern mythology of Nazi occultism is scurrilous and absurd.

One of the best known, and most absurd, of these books is *The Spear of Destiny* by Trevor Ravenscroft, which first appeared in 1973. During the war, Ravenscroft was commissioned in the Royal Fusiliers, then served in a commando unit and took part in the abortive Keyes raid on Rommel's headquarters at Beda Littoria in Libya in November 1941. Ravenscroft was captured during this operation, and was held as a prisoner until 1945. After the war he became a journalist on the Beaverbrook press, and developed an interest in the occult and the supernatural, which in turn led to contact with an Austrian historian named Walter Johannes Stein. Stein was an expert on Grail Romances, as well as the so-called Spear of Destiny or Holy Lance, with which a Roman centurion named Longinus was said to have pierced Christ's side as he hung on the cross at Golgotha. According to Stein, the Spear was thus invested with great supernatural power, which enabled its owner to control the destiny of the world.

A shared interest in the Spear led Stein to a passing acquaintance with Adolf Hitler in Vienna between 1909 and 1913. According to Ravenscroft, Stein 'himself witnessed at this time how Hitler attained higher levels of consciousness by means of drugs and made a penetrating study of medieval occultism and ritual magic', and as a result 'knew more about the personal life of Adolf Hitler than any man alive'. A staunch opponent of Nazism, Stein fled to Britain in 1933, and during the war acted as 'a confidential advisor to Churchill regarding the minds and motivation of Adolf Hitler and the leading members of the Nazi Party'. Incredibly, Stein claimed to be able to capture lost moments in history through transcendental meditation or 'mind expansion', and in turn taught Ravenscroft this highly original research methodology after the pair met in 1948. In 1957 Stein was taken ill suddenly and died. According to Ravenscroft:

> Very considerable pressure was brought to bear to dissuade Dr Stein from revealing what is now presented as the content of this book . . . Sir Winston Churchill himself was insistent that the occultism of the Nazi Party should not under any circumstances be revealed to the general public. The failure of the Nuremberg Trials to identify the nature of the evil at work behind the outer facade of National Socialism convinced him that another three decades must pass before a large enough readership would be present to comprehend the initiation rites and black magic practices of the inner core of the Nazi leadership.

Ravenscroft eventually published *The Spear of Destiny* in 1973, and presented a novel case. The magical Spear was seized by Hitler as a 'talisman of power' following the *Anschluss* in 1938, having passed through the hands of Hereward the Wake, King Athelstan, Charlemagne and the Hohenstauffen dynasty. After standing in Nuremberg throughout the Blitzkrieg victories in Poland and the West, it was finally recovered by US forces in April 1945, whereupon General Patton became fascinated with the relic. Stein – or more probably Ravenscroft – appears to have recovered no end of lost moments. Having had his 'occult sight' opened by one Dietrich Eckhart, Hitler mastered the mysteries of Atlantis and The Secret Doctrine with the help of the Thule Society and Karl Haushofer. Meanwhile select members of the SS 'took oaths of irreversible allegiance to satanic powers' while Himmler was identified as a 'Planetary Doppelgänger' and an 'anti-human in a human body'.

Without exception, these claims are complete nonsense. Walter Johannes Stein certainly existed, but is not mentioned in any substantial biography of Hitler or Churchill, nor in Churchill's own war memoirs. The spear on display in the Hofburg Museum in Vienna is a medieval relic, and thus nowhere near as ancient as Ravenscroft would have readers believe. His method of 'mind expansion' was simply a device by which spurious history could be fabricated, rather than researched, while the circumstances of his supposed disclosures to Ravenscroft are highly dubious. Perhaps conveniently, Stein died long before Ravenscroft put pen to paper, and was thus unable to confirm any of the fantastical claims made on his behalf. Equally convenient was the fact that, during his long years of study with the sage Austrian doctor, Ravenscroft 'took no verbatim notes or tape recordings of Dr Stein's actual words'. *The Spear of Destiny* is nothing more than well-written mystical, neo-classical clap-trap, and seems only to have been taken seriously by virtue of the author's brief military career. A telling insight into Ravenscroft's bizarre state of mind came in 1979, when with scant moral justification he sued writer James Herbert for alleged plagiarism in his novel *The Spear*. As Herbert later recalled:

> One day we were in court and my QC said to Ravenscroft, 'You are saying terrible things about Mr Herbert, but you don't know him, you've never spoken to him.' And Ravenscroft turned round and said, 'I do know him' – and he thumped the witness stand in front of him – and said, 'I have met Herbert, I was there and he was there.' And the QC said, 'I'm sorry, where? Where were you both?' He was kind of bemused. Ravenscroft said: 'At the Crucifixion! I was on the right-hand side of Christ and Herbert was on the other side.'
>
> We showed in court that Ravenscroft himself had copied paragraph after paragraph from other historians like Hugh Trevor-Roper . . . Then we asked for Ravenscroft's notes, and would you believe they were all on a little sailing boat that he had, which got shipwrecked, and everything was so waterlogged it had to be thrown away. He didn't have one scrap.

Indeed, certain aspects of *The Spear of Destiny* are simply odious. In a chapter dealing with 'astrological pest control', Ravenscroft claims that in 1924 the anthroposophist Rudolf Steiner was able to rid a Silesian estate of rabbits by means of homeopathic 'potentisation' of traces of spleen, testes and skin. Two days after the ashes were cast to the wind, so it was said, the entire rabbit population panicked and fled north, their survival instinct fatally undermined. According to Ravenscroft:

> There was to be a sinister sequel to this astonishing demonstration . . . The Nazis repeated the experiment with the 'potentised' ashes of the testicles, spleens and portions of the skin of virile young Jews in an attempt to drive

the remnant of the Jewish population out of Germany for ever . . . The order to carry out this diabolical plan came from Hitler himself . . . Many rumours, later the subject of a number of black books, circulated in post-war Germany that the SS had scattered the ashes from the gas ovens in the concentration camps across the length and breadth of the Reich.

Once again, no historical foundation exists for this disturbing claim, and it is to be regretted that Ravenscroft chose to present these various myths and legends as fact, rather than the fictive fantasy they undoubtedly are. Ravenscroft returned to the fray with *The Cup of Destiny: The Quest for the Grail* in 1980, and died in 1989, the same year in which a sequel of sorts appeared in the form of *Secrets of the Holy Lance*. Written by 'Colonel Howard Buechner and Captain Wilhelm Bernhart', this claimed that the Spear was secretly taken to a base in Antarctica, and a replica placed in the Hofburg Museum. Secret Nazi treasure and U-boats ferrying wanted Nazis to South America also figure prominently in this account, about which readers will no doubt draw their own conclusions.

CHAPTER EIGHT

Hess and the Royals

The bizarre arrival of Rudolf Hess by parachute near Glasgow on the night of 10 May 1941 has given rise to more outlandish myths and legends than any other single event during the Second World War. Since 1946, more than twenty books dealing with the Deputy Führer's mysterious 'peace mission' have appeared in print, spawning a thriving worldwide Hess conspiracy industry to rival those surrounding Jack the Ripper and the Kennedy assassination. Among the many contentious issues are whether Hitler approved of the ill-starred plan, whether Hess was expected by a well-connected peace lobby in Britain, or else lured to Britain as part of an elaborate intelligence sting, whether the Allies replaced Hess with a double, and whether he was murdered at Spandau Prison in 1987, or died by his own hand. Although few if any of these questions are likely to be resolved to the satisfaction of every Hess investigator, some of the more outlandish theories can today be safely dismissed.

The established facts of the Hess affair run as follows. At 5.45 pm on Saturday 10 May Hess, a pilot for more than twenty years, took off from the Messerschmitt works airfield at Augsburg, Bavaria, in a twin-engined Bf 110 fighter-bomber. After a journey of almost 1,000 miles lasting four hours, Hess crossed the British coast over Alnwick in Northumberland, then flew on towards his objective, Dungavel House, eventually baling out at 11 pm to land near the village of Eaglesham. Detained by the local Home Guard, Hess gave his name as 'Alfred Horn' and asked to see the Duke of Hamilton, then a serving RAF officer. After being transferred into army custody Hess was unmasked, and explained to various interrogators that the purpose of his flying visit was to seek peace between Britain and Germany. In this he failed magnificently: Hitler quickly issued a statement which alleged that Hess was mentally disordered and 'a victim of hallucinations', while Hess was detained in Britain as a prisoner of state until his conviction for conspiracy and crimes against peace at Nuremberg in 1946. Thereafter Hess was held as a Prisoner No. 7 at Spandau Prison in Berlin, always denied parole, and died on 17 August 1987 at the age of ninety-three.

Myth and falsehood surround his epic flight even before Hess set foot on British soil. In his controversial account *The Murder of Rudolf Hess* (1979), Dr Hugh Thomas reproduced a series of photographs said to record Hess departing from Augsburg on 10 May. The Bf 110 shown was not equipped with long range drop-tanks, leading Thomas (and others) to surmise that the aircraft lacked sufficient fuel to reach Glasgow, and would therefore have had to land to refuel en route, or that two aircraft were involved. According to Thomas, Hess was shot down by the *Luftwaffe*, and replaced by a double for the flight to Scotland. However these various suppositions are based on careless research. Hess flew to Scotland in a Bf 110E, which with drop-tanks boasted a more than adequate range of 1,560 miles, and which bore the works number 3869 and the radio code VJ+OQ. The machine shown in the photographs carries the works number 3526, while Thomas managed to misquote the radio code as NJ+OQ. Although reports that a drop-tank was later recovered from the Clyde have never been verified, the simple fact is that the photographs were taken on one of the twenty-odd training flights Hess made from Augsburg before 10 May, using a completely different machine.

Some accounts offer that Hess must have landed and refuelled at an intermediate airfield such as Schiphol or Aalborg, but this would not have been necessary. Nor is it true that Hess flew from Calais, as reported from Sweden in 1943, or that for part of his flight Hess was escorted by no less a dignitary than the future SS Reichsprotektor of Bohemia, Reinhard Heydrich, in a Bf 109 fighter. A postwar claim by the *Luftwaffe* fighter ace Adolf Galland should also be treated with caution. In his memoir *The First and the Last* (1955), Galland claimed that 'early in the evening' of 10 May he received an agitated call from Göring, ordering his entire group into the air to bring down the Deputy Führer. A dubious Galland responded by sending up a token force. However, the claim is only credible if Göring and others had advance knowledge of the Hess flight, and opposed it, which raises the question of why Hess was allowed to take off from Augsburg in the first place. In the same vein, some have claimed that it would not have been possible for Hess to have flown over German territory without prior authorisation, but this is convincingly countered by Roy Nesbit and Georges Van Acker in their book *The Flight of Rudolf Hess* (1999). Suggestions by Richard Deacon that the Bf 110 flown by Hess was fitted with American parts are plainly nonsensical.

The account given by Hess of his route to Scotland is also suspect. Hess was said to have been very proud of his achievement in flying from Augsburg to Eaglesham, a distance of almost 1,000 miles, the last 400 over water and enemy territory. On a map drawn by Hess on 8 August 1941, while a prisoner, he claimed to have flown north-west from Augsburg to Den Helder in Holland, then north-east for 70 miles, and then north-west again to a point above the middle of the North Sea. Here, at 8.52 pm, he made another 90 degree turn to port in order to approach the British coastline from the east. Hess claimed he then realised he had an hour to kill, since at this more northerly latitude the sun set later than in southern Germany, whereas he wished to fly overland at dusk, and as a result executed several complicated zig-zag manoeuvres to kill time. But as Picknett, Prince and Prior argued in their highly detailed study *Double Standards* (2001), there is good reason to doubt this account. When Hess left Augsburg he was observed heading north, not north-west, while a part of his later zig-zag manoeuvres were carried out within range of British Chain Home radar, who instead recorded Hess (designated Raid 42J) as flying straight in from the east. Hess, at bottom an amateur pilot, claimed to have been navigating alone, which makes it highly unlikely that he could have followed such a complicated course over open water, yet still managed to land just eleven miles from his intended destination, Dungavel House. Given that Hess had been considering his mission since at least September 1940, and may have made several previous abortive attempts, it is unlikely he would have overlooked the fact that dusk fell later in the north. Instead, the authors of *Double Standards* guess that Hess made use of a then-secret German radio-navigational system, broadcast from the station at Kalundborg on the west coast of Zeeland in Denmark. Kalundborg lies precisely due north of Augsburg, and due east of Alnwick and Dungavel House, thus making Hess's journey far more simple, but 250 miles – and one tell-tale hour – longer.

It is abundantly clear from the timing of his flight that the Hess mission was closely linked to the impending German invasion of the Soviet Union, which was launched just six weeks later, on 22 June 1941. This much was confirmed by Lord Beaverbrook on several occasions after the war. The conquest of Russia by Germany, never viable under any circumstances, would certainly be made harder by fighting a war on two fronts. The Russian factor would also explain why Hitler might deny all knowledge of the mission if it failed, assuming he was privy to the plan from the outset. Had Stalin discovered that Germany wished to make peace with Britain, he would have deduced immediately that an attack on Russia was close at hand. Instead, Germany sought to lull her notional Soviet ally into a false sense of security by continuing to threaten Operation Sealion, the seaborne invasion of Britain. Furthermore Hitler might not have wanted his Axis partners, chiefly Mussolini, to think that he was negotiating behind their backs. While this hypothesis does nothing to prove Hitler knew and approved of the Hess peace mission, it does show that he would hardly have admitted so even if he did.

On being informed of the Hess flight, Hitler is reported by some (including Albert Speer) to have flown into a paroxysm of rage, although other accounts (Hess adjutant Karl-Heinz Pintsch) relate that he received the news calmly. Some are of the opinion that what followed was part of a German strategy of plausible denial. Surprisingly, the first public announcement about the affair came not from London but Berlin, in the form of a radio bulletin broadcast on 12 May at 8 pm:

A letter which he left behind unfortunately shows by its distractedness traces of a mental disorder, and it is feared he was a victim of hallucinations. The Führer at once ordered the arrest of the adjutants of party member Hess, who alone had any cognizance of these flights, and did not, contrary to the Führer's orders, of which they were fully aware, either prevent or report the flight. In these circumstances, it must be considered that party member Hess either jumped out of his plane or has met with an accident.

While it is true that his driver, bodyguard and two adjutants were arrested, little punitive action was taken against others close to Hess. Karl and Albrecht Haushofer, his trusted geopolitical advisors, were arrested and detained, but neither was ill-treated and both were released without penalty. The aircraft designer Dr Willi Messerschmitt was merely rebuked by Göring, and no action at all taken against his chief test pilot Helmut Kaden (who had given Hess intensive instruction), or against Ernst Bohle, the chief of Hess's own foreign intelligence bureau, the *Auslandorganisation*. His wife Ilse and son Wolf were allowed to remain in their villa in the Munich suburb of Harlaching, and awarded a pension. Had Hess really acted alone, and against the express wishes of Hitler and the party in general, one might have expected the outcome to have been very different.

It has often been claimed that Hess was deliberately lured to Britain as part of an elaborate intelligence sting. This theory has spawned a number of books in recent years, including *Hess: Flight for the Führer* by Peter Padfield (1991), *Ten Days That Saved the West* by John Costello (also 1991), *Churchill's Deception* by Louis Kilzer (1994) and *Hess: The British Conspiracy* by John Harris and M.J. Trow (1999). Certainly this chimes with the theory favoured by Stalin, who initially believed that Britain was in league with Germany to destroy the Soviet Union, and that the Hess mission was engineered by British intelligence with the Duke of Hamilton as a go-between. Moreover the Russians had some difficulty in understanding why Hess was not immediately prosecuted as a war criminal, and instead detained in comfortable quarters to await a postwar trial. In October 1942 the party newspaper *Pravda* (Truth) declared:

> It is no coincidence that Hess's wife has asked certain British representatives if she could join her husband. This could mean that she does not see her husband as a prisoner. It is high time we knew whether Hess is either a criminal or a plenipotentiary who represents the Nazi government in England.

Several days later *Pravda* published a photograph of 'Mrs Hess' giving a piano recital in London. However this turned out to be Myra Hess, the well-known pianist who boosted wartime morale in London by playing lunchtime concerts to packed houses at the National Gallery. Indeed Churchill and Stalin argued over the point when they met for the Moscow conference in October 1944. Churchill recorded in a later memorandum:

> The Russians are very suspicious of the Hess episode and I have had a lengthy argument with Marshal Stalin about it at Moscow in October, he

steadfastly maintaining that Hess had been invited over by our Secret Service. It is not in the public interest that the whole of this affair should be stirred at the present moment.

The intelligence sting theory is superficially attractive, if only because it would explain the dense veil of official secrecy which still surrounds much of the Hess affair. According to Padfield and Costello, MI5's Double Cross Committee masterminded the affair, while Harris and Trow favour the Special Operations Executive. Anthony Cave Brown concluded that the Secret Intelligence Service (MI6) was behind the trap, while it has been suggested by Philip Knightley that MI6 induced Hess to come to Britain as they too favoured a negotiated peace with Germany. According to KGB sources, the traitor Kim Philby later revealed that SIS lured Hess to Britain by means of forged letters from the Duke of Hamilton, although Philby made no mention of this in his memoir *My Secret War*.

The greatest problem with the sting theory is that it is not supported by the conduct of the British authorities after Hess landed at Eaglesham. Had Hess been expected by the intelligence services, and by extension the military, it seems unlikely he would have been detained in a number of scout huts by the Home Guard for four hours until transferred to Maryhill Barracks in Glasgow. Even if the confusion on the ground in Scotland is explicable in the fog of war, the fact remains that Britain did nothing to exploit the windfall as a political and propaganda coup, or announce to the world that Hitler was suing for peace. Instead the flight of the Deputy Führer to Scotland was announced to the world by Berlin, and only afterwards admitted by the British authorities on the most neutral terms. Far from being paraded before the world media, Hess was kept under close confinement for the next five years, and not seen in public until Nuremberg. If any photographs of Hess were taken between May 1941 and October 1945, not a single one has been released into the public domain. Even Joseph Goebbels, Hitler's propaganda minister, expressed his bafflement. Moreover Hess himself seems never to have indicated that he was lured to Britain.

Probably the most outlandish variation on this theme is the proposition that Hess was lured to Britain by bogus astrology. This fantastical notion was a favourite of spy writer Richard Deacon (alias Donald McCormick), who developed it at considerable length in books such as *British Secret Service* and *17F: The Life of Ian Fleming*, despite the fact that there is no verifiable (or even circumstantial) evidence to support it. According to Deacon, the luring of Hess was 'a brilliant coup' for which Fleming, the creator of James Bond, deserved full credit:

Hess, however, presented a somewhat easier target. Vanessa Hoffman's information convinced Fleming that while Canaris could not be won over by any faked horoscopes, Hess might well be exploited in this way . . . There was everything to be gained and nothing to be lost by planting faked horoscopes on Hess. Fleming had discovered through various of his occultist friends such as Aleister Crowley and Ellic Howe that Hess regularly consulted astrologers, and that one of these was Karl Ernst Krafft . . . Exactly how the bogus horoscopes were worded, or the advice they gave to Hess, remains a mystery.

According to Deacon, Fleming, in wartime a serving officer in the Naval Intelligence Division, was acquainted with infamous occultist Aleister Crowley, and with Dennis Wheatley became involved in a 'very hush-hush' assignment called Operation Mistletoe. This in turn involved nocturnal occult rituals staged in the Ashdown Forest, involving 'a dummy dressed in a Nazi uniform, sat on a throne-like chair', with the object of influencing Hess. Deacon also stated that after Hess arrived, Fleming suggested he be questioned by Crowley. Others have cited the involvement of Maxwell Knight, Tom Driberg and Louis de Wohl in this same astrological plot. Deacon quoted with approval a claim by Nicholas Campion, cited as 'one of the founders of the Institute for the Study of Cycles in World Affairs and a leading astrologer', who in 1984 advised Deacon that he had:

> Cast the horoscope for the time at which Hess took off from Germany. It was most inauspicious. It transpires that this is a most evil horoscope in any traditional sense, largely because six planets were in the house of death and two other points were strong: the fixed star Algol (which leads one to lose one's head) and the evil degree Serpentis, so called 'the accursed degree of the accursed sign.'

Aspects of this farrago of nonsense are repeated in books such as *The Man Who Was M* (Anthony Masters, 1984) and *The Occult Conspiracy* (Michael Howard, 1989). Yet in his own introduction Deacon had warned his readers that this tale of the luring of Rudolf Hess was 'far removed from reality' and 'totally bizarre'. In truth, the only contemporary references to Hess and astrology appeared in newspapers in London and Berlin on the same day, 14 May 1941. According to an article in the *Volkischer Beobachter*:

> As is well-known in Party circles, Rudolf Hess was in poor health for many years and latterly increasingly had recourse to hypnotists, astrologers and so on. The extent to which these people are responsible for the mental confusion that led him to his present step has still to be clarified.

In London *The Times* published some highly speculative information supposedly received from a correspondent in Switzerland:

> Certain of Hess's closest friends have thrown an interesting light on the affair. They say that Hess has always been Hitler's astrologer in secret. Up to last March he had consistently predicted good fortune and had always been

right. Since then, notwithstanding the victories Germany has won, he has declared that the stars showed that Hitler's meteoric career was approaching its climax.

The detail disclosed by *The Times* was almost certainly official disinformation, with both newspaper reports intended to discredit Hess as deluded or mentally unstable. Hitler's motive for a policy of plausible denial in relation to the Hess peace mission have already been discussed. In Britain, however, very different reasons may lie behind the official policy of silence and secrecy surrounding Hess.

There is a strong body of evidence, not all of it circumstantial, that Rudolf Hess came to Britain expecting to conclude ongoing peace negotiations with senior officials, and then to fly back to Germany from Dungavel. In their minutely researched account *Double Standards*, Picknett, Prince and Prior offer the following facts in support of this argument. By May 1941 Britain was losing the war: Greece had fallen, Rommel was winning in North Africa, U-boats were sinking a colossal tonnage of Allied shipping, and Britain's cities were being heavily bombed from the air. At this time Churchill was by no means as popular as postwar myth suggests, having endured a vote of confidence on 7 May. In Britain there remained a strong peace lobby, which included Lloyd George, Lord Halifax, Rab Butler, Lord Beaverbrook, Sir Nevile Henderson and Sir Samuel Hoare. It is also possible that senior figures within MI6, including Sir Stewart Menzies, favoured peace. Moreover other senior establishment figures had been pre-war members of the Anglo–German Fellowship, including the Duke of Hamilton. Hamilton later denied this, just as he denied meeting Hess at the Berlin Olympics in 1936, but in fact his own archives betray his membership of the Fellowship in 1936, while there is ample evidence of the meeting in Berlin from Henry Channon, Kenneth Lindsay and even Churchill. Hitler too wished to end the war in the west, as is clear from his 'last appeal to reason' of 19 July 1940, since the occupation and administration of Britain and the Empire would be a complicated task, and deplete those resources required for the planned attack on Russia. Against this background it seems more than likely that Hitler knew of, and endorsed, the Hess mission.

According to the authors of *Double Standards*, their research suggests that the proposed terms of the armistice included a 25-year alliance between Britain and Germany, and the adoption by Britain of an attitude of 'benevolent neutrality' towards Germany's forthcoming war on the Soviet Union. Britain would continue to rule her Empire, while Germany would govern Europe. It is also suggested that there were detailed proposals regarding other issues, such as a reduction in strength of the Royal Navy and RAF. The main obstacle to the plan was the staunchly anti-Nazi Churchill, as the prime minister himself admitted to the Commons on 27 January 1942:

When Rudolf Hess flew over here some months ago, he firmly believed that he had only to gain access to certain circles in this country for what he described as 'the Churchill clique' to be thrown out of power and for a government to be set up with which Hitler could negotiate a magnanimous peace.

Sir Patrick Dollan, a former editor of the *Glasgow Daily Herald* and the then Lord Provost of Glasgow, seems to have been privy to inside information which he felt strongly should be made public. During a series of lectures given around the city in June 1941, Dollan made revelations which were summarised by the *Bulletin and Scots Pictorial* on 20 June, clearly having been missed by the censor:

> Hess came here an unrepentant Nazi. He believed he could remain in Scotland for two days, discuss his peace proposals and be given petrol and maps to return to Germany.

The precise identity of those within the 'certain circles' to which Churchill alluded remains the subject of fierce debate, and is unlikely now to be established with any certainty. A wide-ranging study of pro-peace groupings in Britain before and during the Second World War can be found in *Profits of Peace* by Scott Newton, published in 1996. Some were pro-Hitler, but most appeasers simply wished to avoid another European war which would have a devastating effect on economic and social stability.

It is clear from a letter which the Duke of Hamilton published in *The Times* of 6 October 1939 that he too remained pro-peace even after the outbreak of war. The Hess affair caused the Duke of Hamilton a great deal of personal embarrassment, and led to his uttering a number of libel writs against journalists and Hess commentators until his death in 1973. It is only since then that historians have been able to publish detailed research. According to the authors of *Double Standards*, there is reason to believe that a reception committee awaited Hess at Dungavel House, which may have included the Duke of Kent and a Polish contingent, and that the mission went awry only after Hess failed to locate his destination and instead baled out over Eaglesham. Hamilton, then a serving Wing Commander stationed at RAF Turnhouse near Edinburgh, remained a Privy Councillor and a Keeper of the Royal Household. A former member of the Anglo–German Fellowship who had hoped to avoid war, he was also a friend and sponsor of Albrecht Haushofer, a close political advisor to Hess who had been privy to the flight from its inception.

On landing Hess asked to be taken to Hamilton, and although the official version holds that the Duke slept through the night and did not see 'Alfred Horn' until about 10 am the following day, at Maryhill Barracks, the evidence of his widow supports the theory that Hamilton in fact left his bed and went to meet Hess while the latter was being escorted to Maryhill. Indeed this was reported as fact by the *Glasgow Herald* on 16 May 1941, who added that 'representatives of the Intelligence Service and the Foreign Office were present'. Some have claimed that it would not have been possible for Hess to have landed his Bf 110 on the small grass airfield at Dungavel, but the strip was a designated Emergency Landing Ground and there is evidence that a comparable Bristol Beaufighter set down safely there the previous month.

What had initially been promoted as a crack in the Nazi regime was in danger of being recognised as a crack in the British hierarchy. Indeed rumours of collusion between Hess and people in high places, and whispers that Hamilton was a Quisling, quickly entered into circulation in Britain, raising the dread spectre of a Hidden Hand or fifth column. Although Churchill subsequently dismissed the Hess mission as merely an 'escapade', in truth he must have recognised it as a potential turning point in the war. In May 1941 the defeat of Germany hinged on two main factors: America joining the conflict, and Germany invading the Soviet Union, so that Stalin too would become a British ally. Little was revealed to the press about Hess, and Churchill made no statement to the Commons until January 1942. Rather than exploit Hess's arrival as propaganda for short-term gain, Churchill instead reversed the crisis to further his own ends. By accident or design, the truth slipped into print in America later in 1941, in the somewhat mystic book *That Day Alone* by the Canadian commentator Pierre van Paassen. According to van Paassen, Churchill pretended to negotiate with Hess in order to ensure that Hitler attacked the Soviet Union, to strengthen British ties with America, and to bring about the end of the Blitz. The book was published in abridged form in Britain in 1943, but with this passage deleted. It seems unlikely that van Paassen was privy to inside information. Nonetheless, the devastating night attack on London by 520 bombers on 10 May 1941 was the last significant German raid on the capital until the so-called Little Blitz early in 1944, which again suggests the complicity of Hitler in the Hess peace plan. In short, Churchill ruthlessly exploited the Hess affair to stifle the peace lobby, and those who wished to remove him from power.

Another persistent Hess legend is that the RAF did little or nothing to intercept Raid 42J, which in turn is offered as proof that Hess was expected and protected. Here the evidence is confusing. Three Spitfires from 72 Squadron based at Acklington attempted to intercept the Bf 110 as it crossed the Northumberland coast, and as it approached Glasgow an airborne Defiant night fighter from 141 Squadron at Ayr was alerted, although not scrambled as some accounts suggest. *In Ten Days That Saved the West* (1991), John Costello claimed that the Duke of Hamilton refused to allow fighters to attack Hess, and that anti-aircraft defences in the areas he overflew were ordered not to open fire. Both statements are incorrect. The sectors over which Hess passed were Ouston and Ayr, rather than Turnhouse, and both tried to shoot down the intruder. Moreover, for obvious reasons it was common practice for AA batteries to refrain from firing on enemy targets which were being pursued by the RAF, since this carried the risk of bringing down friendly aircraft. In 1999 it was claimed that two Czech Hurricane pilots from 245 Squadron, Vaclav Bauman and Leopold Srom, had been closing on Hess when their attack was inexplicably called off. Soon after returning to their base at Aldergrove in Northern Ireland, the two men were subjected to an intensive interrogation by

Gunther Prien dines with Hitler following the sinking of the *Royal Oak* at Scapa Flow in October 1939. (*After the Battle*).

A propulsion unit from one of Prien's torpedoes, recovered from the sea bed some years later. This relic disproves allegations that the *Royal Oak* was sabotaged, and that Prien never entered Scapa Flow. (*After the Battle*).

Police examine one of the bogus sabotage sets dropped over England in August 1940. (*Author's collection*)

The myth of Hitler's supposed doubles is reflected in this French newspaper clipping from 1944. (*Author's collection*)

C'est un faux HITLER
que la propagande nazie
photographie aujourd'hui

LE VRAI

Courbe au sillon très marqué

lobe inférieur large et court

Depuis de longues années, on assure périodiquement qu'Hitler a des sosies qui prennent parfois sa place. Aucun document sérieux n'avait jamais pu étayer cette légende. Or, voici que notre confrère le « Daily Express », de Londres, a eu l'idée de soumettre à des experts deux de photos du Führer, transmises à des époques différentes par les services du Dr. Goebbels : la première (celle de gauche) date du début de 1939. La seconde (celle de droite) a été transmise le 16 novembre dernier à Stockholm et représente, dit la légende officielle, « Hitler conférant, à son quartier général, le 25 septembre dernier, la Croix de des oreilles, comme les empreintes

Courbe peu prononcée

lobe long et étroit

LE FAUX

Hanfstaengl has ideas about culture.

Hitler's "Putzy" Is Here

DR. ERNST "PUTZY") HANFSTAENGL, intimate friend of Leader Hitler and Harvard-educated head of the Nazi Foreign Press Department, is in London.
He is staying at Claridge's Hotel.

Above left: A camp caricature of Hitler by Thomas Theodor Heine, printed in the left-wing journal *Tage-Buch* in 1930. (*Author's collection*)

Above right: This suggestive report from the *Daily Express* in September 1934 prompted a libel writ from Hitler's 'Putzy', Dr Ernst Hanfstaengl.

Right: A mischievous German take on the death of General Sikorski from the magazine *Das Reich* in 1943. The original caption reads: 'I'll put my cards on the table, General. I am from the British Secret Service. You don't fit with Britain's plans any more – Will you take tea, or do you prefer an aeroplane?' (*Author's collection*)

Floating Mystery Ball Is New Nazi Air Weapon

SUPREME HEADQUARTERS, Allied Expeditionary Force, Dec. 13—A new German weapon has made its appearance on the western air front, it was disclosed today.

Airmen of the American Air Force report that they are encountering silver colored spheres in the air over German territory. The spheres are encountered either singly or in clusters. Sometimes they are semi-translucent.

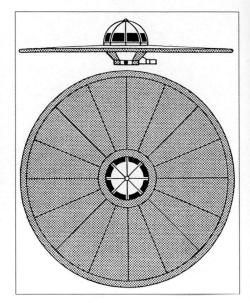

The original Foo Fighter headline, 13 December 1944.

A speculative illustration (published in 1959) of a supposed German 'flying disc'. (*Author's collection*)

A remarkable photograph of searchlights and anti-aircraft fire during the phantom air raid on Los Angeles in February 1942. (*Author's collection*)

A facsimile death certificate for Heinrich Poncke, one of several dozen German soldiers washed ashore on the south coast of Britain in the autumn of 1940. (*Courtesy of the County Registrar of Sussex*)

A sea flame barrage in action at Studland Bay, Dorset. (*Author's collection*)

In 1954 the German film biography *Canaris* suggested that Operation Sealion was cancelled after the *Abwehr* chief revealed the existence of British flame weapons to the German High Command. (*Author's collection*)

In 1939 Polish cavalry fought as dismounted troops, rather than charging tanks. (*Author's collection*)

A selection of headlines detailing the Invasion That Never Was.

Rouged German Airmen

BY A SPECIAL
CORRESPONDENT

OFFICERS of the German
air force in a prisoners-
of-war camp in England
spend part of their pay on
face creams.

Two shot down had waved
hair, rouged cheeks, painted
lips and enamelled fingernails
and toenails.

The medical profession has a
word for men of this type. It
classifies them as moral deviates, a class with curious ten
dencies, including outbursts of
emotional violence admirably
suited to the ruthless tactics of
the Luftwaffe.

The silliest myth of the war? From the *Daily Mirror*, April 1941.

By the most famous and the most feared spy of all time!

HITLER's SPY RING

by "E.7"

Author of "Women Spies I Have Known"

Determined to penetrate into the secrets of this network of Nazi espionage, the author discovered an organization so vast that, as he says: "No one living in the British Isles could have any idea of what it really means, nor of the myriads employed in it." A true story—but a story far more enthralling than any novel. 10/6.

HURST & BLACKETT

Two titles from 1940 which fuelled the fifth column myth. (*Author's collection*)

several senior RAF officers who arrived in an Avro Anson. Their story possibly tallies with an article published in the *American Mercury* in May 1943, which stated that 'two Hurricanes took off to trail the mystery plane with orders to force it down but under no conditions to shoot at it'. However, there is no record of Srom having flown that day in the Operations Record Book for 245 Squadron, while the convoy patrol undertaken by Bauman between 9.35 and 10.40 pm would not have taken him anywhere near Hess. In all likelihood the various other RAF pilots who claimed to have been scrambled to intercept Hess on 10 May were simply mistaken.

Several sources have claimed that Hess was the target of an assassination attempt while at Mytchett Place. According to a former army intelligence officer named John McCowen, the three would-be killers were German and arrived by parachute near Luton Hoo on the night of 28 May 1941. After being captured and interrogated, the trio revealed that they had expected to find Hess at the London Cage at Cockfosters, and to obtain help from *Abwehr* agents already in Britain. They were later executed without trial at the Tower of London. Predictably there is no record of any such agents being captured in 1941, or executed, and the facts seem highly unlikely. In June 1942 Hess was moved from Mytchett to Maindiff Court near Abergavenny, apparently because it was feared that a group of Poles were planning to break into the camp, kidnap Hess, and beat or kill him by way of revenge for Nazi atrocities in Poland. Indeed in an MI5 file released by the PRO in 1999 there is an odd reference to a reported gun battle between Polish soldiers and guards at Mytchett, although no precise details are given. However, as with so many aspects of the Hess affair, the whole truth is never likely to emerge.

More imaginative even than the occult explanation of the Hess mission is the theory that the real Rudolf Hess was replaced with a double, and that the man who died at Spandau in 1987 was not the Deputy Führer at all. The most celebrated proponent of the so-called doppelgänger theory is Dr Hugh Thomas, a former army surgeon who examined Hess in September 1973 while attached to the British Military Hospital in Berlin. The publication of his book *The Murder of Rudolf Hess* in 1979 prompted questions in the House of Commons and the Bundestag, and generated further controversy in 1988 when it appeared in revised form under the title *Hess: A Tale of Two Murders*. Thomas relied on his own medical expertise. During the First World War Hess was known to have been wounded twice: once by shrapnel in June 1916, followed by a more serious chest wound caused by a rifle bullet on the Romanian front in July 1917. According to Thomas, the 'major scars on his chest and back' caused by both wounds should have been highly visible even after 60 years, yet were not recorded by any one of the 58 doctors who examined Hess after 1941. Thomas was unable to locate any detailed contemporary medical notes, but made a number of assumptions which hypothesised extensive tissue damage and a large exit wound on the back. Thomas also accepted muddled assertions that Hess had been treated by the renowned chest surgeon Ferdinand Sauerbruch, whose technique for treating gunshot wounds usually entailed the partial removal of a rib. The fact that Hess refused to see his wife and son until 1969 was also cited as further evidence.

After concluding that the man he had examined in Spandau in 1973 was not the real Hess, Thomas suggested a plot far stranger than fiction. By this version, Hess took off from Augsburg in a Bf 110 intending to fly to Sweden, but was shot down on the orders of rival Nazi leaders who opposed the peace plan. A second Bf 110 coded NJ+OQ with an imposter at the controls was then dispatched from Aalborg in Denmark, although quite what the substitution was meant to achieve remains obscure. A no less convoluted version was offered by Professor Peter Waddell in 1999, in which Hess was kidnapped from Sweden by SOE agents. In order to prevent reprisals against British prisoners of war, an SOE agent impersonating Hess was made to bale out of an aircraft over Scotland. The real Hess was later executed in Scotland in 1942 on the direct orders of Churchill.

All of which is quite simply fantastic. It is abundantly clear from contemporary photographs, as well as from the wreckage on public display at the Imperial War Museum, that Hess's aircraft was coded VJ+OQ, and that the Bf 110 in which he flew from Augsburg to Scotland had the necessary range. The most damaging evidence against the *doppelgänger* theory was unearthed in 1989, when a BBC journalist named Roy McHardy located a copy of the original Hess medical file in the Bavarian State Archives. The file included several reports on the bullet wound sustained in 1917, including the following description from December of the same year:

> Three fingers above the left armpit, a pea-sized, bluish-coloured, non-reactive scar from an entry wound. On the back, at the height of the fourth dorsal [thoracic] vertebra, two fingers from the spine, a non-reactive exit gunshot wound the size of a cherry stone.

No operation had been necessary. The wound had been a clean through-shot from a small-calibre rifle which left minor scarring, in a different location to that suggested by Thomas. No amount of minor quibbling about ancillary details can hide the fact that Thomas had based his entire hypothesis on incorrect information. Furthermore his claim that he possesses a copy of a letter from Lord Willingdon to William Mackenzie, the Canadian Prime Minister, discussing Hess and 'the problem we have with the double' cannot be verified since Thomas claims that the Official Secrets Act precludes him from publishing it. It should be clear to anyone that the two photographs of Hess which appear in this book are of the same individual. His wife Ilse described the double allegation as 'ridiculous', while fellow prisoner Albert Speer dismissed it as 'utter nonsense.' And why on earth would Hess's double accept an uncomfortable term of life imprisonment without disclosing his true identity? The notion is simply preposterous.

Yet another fanciful story emerged from Germany in 1987. According to the German historian Werner Maser, Hess was temporarily released from his cell on the night of 17/18 March 1952, during a Russian tour of duty at Spandau. Without the knowledge of the western powers, Hess was taken to a secret location where he met senior officials from the German Democratic Republic. On the instructions of Stalin he was offered his freedom and a leading position in East Germany, on condition he declared himself to be a socialist. Hess, however, is said to have remained loyal to Hitler and turned down the proposal. The Russians in turn warned Hess to reveal nothing of his outing, and that he would remain in Spandau until his death. The story seems somewhat far-fetched.

In the second version of his book, *Hess: A Tale of Two Murders*, Dr Hugh Thomas put forward the proposition that the double who died in Spandau on the afternoon of 17 August 1987 was murdered. The official version holds that Hess hanged himself in a garden shed in the grounds of the prison, by looping the electrical cord of a reading lamp around his neck and suspending this from a window latch. After attempts were made to revive him in situ he was rushed to the British Military Hospital, where, after further unsuccessful attempts at resuscitation, he was pronounced dead at 4.10 pm. A suicide note addressed to his family was found in his jacket pocket, and the initial autopsy performed on 19 August found that death had resulted from asphyxia, caused by compression of the neck due to suspension. It is worth recording here that Hess had attempted to take his own life on several previous occasions. In June 1941 he threw himself over a balcony at Mytchett Place near Aldershot, breaking his left leg, and stabbed his own chest with a breadknife in February 1945. Even as late as 1977, at the age of eighty-three, Hess tried to cut his wrists with a table knife.

Thomas argues that the neck injuries were consistent with throttling, that the suicide note was forged, and that the Hess double was murdered by SAS personnel on the orders of the British government, to whom Hess and/or his double had been an embarrassment since 1941. His son Wolf Hess also believes that his father was murdered, but dismisses the *doppelgänger* theory. Quite why the authorities waited until 1987 to murder Hess is not explained, while some of the additional evidence cited by Thomas is flawed. He notes that neither of the autopsies carried out in August 1987 noted the 'massive' gunshot wounds dating from 1917, although as we have already seen this theory would be comprehensively demolished in 1989 when his complete medical file was unearthed in Munich. Thomas also found it suspicious that the corpse measured a height of 5 feet 9 inches (1.75 metres), whereas Hess was said to have been a tall man who stood about 6 feet 1 inch (1.85 metres). Again, his original medical file reveals the truth, which is that Hess was 5 feet 10 inches tall (1.77 metres), and that a reduction of 2 cm in height as a result of stooping in old age is quite normal.

In 1989 the murder theory gained some support from the testimony of a Tunisian medical orderly, Abdallah Melaouhi, who had acted as Hess's nurse since 1982. Melaouhi claimed that on the day in question he was delayed by guards, and that when he finally arrived at the garden summerhouse (in fact an elderly Portakabin) there were two unfamiliar men present dressed in

American uniforms. He also stated that furniture had been thrown about, as if during a struggle, and that there was no cord around Hess's neck, the electrical flex still being attached to the lamp and plugged in. Melaouhi was also of the opinion that Hess was so debilitated and arthritic that he was unable even to tie his own shoelaces, let alone knot a cord around his neck. He even ? that at the British Military Hospital the British, French and American directors later toasted the passing of Hess with champagne.

This evidence was largely contradicted by Lieutenant-Colonel Tony Le Tissier, the British Governor at Spandau. In his book *Farewell to Spandau*, Le Tissier pointed out that the only delay in Melaouhi's arrival was caused by difficulty in locating him, eventually in the mess, and that even then the log at the main gate showed there was little delay before he arrived at the summerhouse. There were four reading lamps in the Portakabin, and therefore more than one cord. The two men in American uniform were medics who had been called to assist with the resuscitation, and in fact continued in these attempts with the help of Melaouhi. The furniture had been pushed aside in the course of their previous efforts to revive Hess. As for his medical condition, Hess wore a truss and probably found bending to tie his shoelaces problematic, but he could write legibly and thus tie a knot.

Probably the last great Hess conspiracy theory emerged in 2001, again in *Double Standards* by Picknett, Prince and Prior. As well as postulating that the reception committee at Dungavel included the Duke of Kent, brother of King George VI, the authors also surmise that the Duke's death in a flying accident in August 1942 was an assassination, in which the real Rudolf Hess also perished. For reasons of space it is not possible to explore this theory fully here, but in summary it runs as follows. The Duke of Kent remained in favour of a negotiated peace, and with others continued to work toward this end after Hess arrived in May 1941. Although Hess was officially held first at Mytchett Place, and then Maindiff Court in Wales, he was also confined at several locations in Scotland, including Braemore Lodge near Loch More. Beyond doubt is the fact that on 25 August 1942 the Duke took off from Invergordon in a Short Sunderland flying boat. Officially he was on a morale-boosting visit to RAF personnel stationed in Iceland, although the memorial erected by his widow indicated that the Duke was engaged in an unspecified 'special mission'. About 60 miles after take-off the Sunderland crashed into a remote hilltop near Caithness, some ten miles off course, killing everyone on board bar the rear gunner. Various explanations have been offered through the years, including pilot error, drunkenness, magnetic rocks, faked German radio messages, and a cover-up to hide the fact that the Duke himself was at the controls.

The authors of *Double Standards* present a convincing case that there were sixteen men on board the Sunderland, rather than the fifteen listed in official reports. However, the rest of their hypothesis is harder to credit. This suggests that the extra man was Hess, picked up by the Duke's flying boat from Loch More, and en route to Sweden. Rather than meeting with an accident, the aircraft was sabotaged in the same fashion as the B24 Liberator in which the

Polish leader General Sikorski would perish in July 1943. Beyond the fact that the evidence presented in support of this theory is circumstantial in the extreme, there are at least two major flaws in the assassination plot. First, it scarcely seems credible that Hess could have been collected or snatched by the Duke without the aid of a small private army. Second, if Hess was indeed on board the doomed aircraft, then it raises the spectre of the fantastical *doppelgänger* theory, and the almost total suspension of disbelief which that entails. Instead, the likely explanation is that the crash was simply a tragic accident caused by poor or impaired navigation, whoever may have been at the controls.

Today few would disagree that Rudolf Hess was kept far too long in captivity, a hapless pawn in a prolonged game of chess between former Allies turned Cold War adversaries. However, it is important to remember that the underlying purpose of the Hess peace mission, the last serious attempt to reach an Anglo–German *détente*, was in no way humanitarian. Hess was a staunch Nazi, and like Hitler desired a peace which would allow Germany to continue the war in the east, leaving the Reich free to initiate the Holocaust unhindered. Against this background it matters little that the original point of the war, the liberation of Poland from foreign occupation, was never achieved. Therefore it would be quite wrong to conclude that Hess should be admired for his efforts, or that Churchill should be criticised for rejecting his proposals out of hand, rather than putting them before his Cabinet or the Commons.

CHAPTER NINE

The Man Who Never Was

On 26 January 1943 a 34-year-old Welsh labourer named Glyndwr Michael swallowed a quantity of phosphorous rat poison, intending to take his own life. Discovered in a London warehouse, Michael was taken to St Pancras Hospital where he died two days later. The deceased, who had been suffering from mental illness, left no will, and an inquest held on 4 February went unreported by local papers. The mortuary register recorded simply: 'Michael, Glyndwr; 34; phosphorous poisoning; suicide; lunatic; cost of proceedings £1.'

Following the publication of *The Man Who Never Was* by Ewen Montagu in 1953, the story of how Glyndwr Michael came to be buried in a grave in a hilltop cemetery above the Spanish town of Huelva, beneath the headstone of one Major William Martin, has become one of the most celebrated legends of the Second World War. As the centrepiece of a deception codenamed Operation Mincemeat, Michael's body was released from a submarine into the sea north-west of Gibraltar, chained to a briefcase in which forged letters suggested that Allied intentions in southern Europe hinged on the invasion of Greece and Sardinia. As predicted by the planners in British intelligence, Charles Cholmondeley and Ewen Montagu, the papers were seen by the *Abwehr* and accepted as genuine, with the result that the Allies landed in Sicily on 10 July almost unopposed. Brilliant though this scheme was, the refusal of the authorities to reveal the true identity of the erstwhile Man Who Never Was until 1995 only served to ensure that the story assumed a wholly unwarranted mystique. For in truth the mechanics of Operation Mincemeat were hardly novel, and its true military value overstated. Moreover, the questionable postwar manoeuvrings of its supposed architect, Ewen Montagu, would result in an unnecessary posthumous manhunt second only to the quest to name Jack the Ripper.

Mincemeat would certainly have remained a closely guarded secret but for the literary aspirations of Alfred Duff Cooper, a capable Conservative politician who served as Churchill's Minister of Information between 1940 and 1942, and subsequently as British Ambassador to France. In November 1950 Cooper published a novel, *Operation Heartbreak*, which was clearly based on detailed inside information about Mincemeat. Within its pages an ageing officer named 'Willie Maryngton' dies of despair and pneumonia, after observing his fiancée Felicity leaving what he takes to be a brothel. Felicity happens to be a secretary in military intelligence, and her employers decide to utilise Maryngton's corpse for 'a military operation of immense magnitude' in which 'success must depend largely upon the enemy's ignorance of when and where it will be launched'. The body is dropped from a submarine off the coast of an unspecified Axis-friendly neutral country, clutching a package containing false documents from the Chief of the Imperial General Staff, as well as letters from his fiancée, which are duly photographed by the enemy. This macabre but ingenious deception is appraised as having 'powerfully contributed to the success of one of the greatest surprises ever achieved in military history'.

Cooper's somewhat dull novel was not submitted for security clearance prior to publication, and provoked outrage in Whitehall. Both MI5 and the Chiefs of Staff considered the book a highly damaging breach of the 1911 Official Secrets Act, in that it disclosed the workings of an operation which the intelligence services might wish to repeat, and quite rightly demanded that its author should be prosecuted. However Cooper was still living in Paris, and threatened to reveal that he had the story direct from Churchill, who 'in his cups' had not warned that national security might still be involved. Fearing an embarrassing political scandal involving a senior diplomat, the Attlee government had to content itself with a letter warning Cooper that if he dared to return to the United Kingdom as a civilian he would be charged, although in time the storm blew over, and in 1952 Cooper was made Viscount Norwich.

Duff Cooper died in 1954, but in the meantime several press reporters smelled a story and began to dig deeper. Interest was further spurred by a brief mention of 'a clever enemy ruse' involving 'the body of a British courier washed ashore in Spain' in the memoir of a former *Wehrmacht* general named Westphal. At the head of the press pack was Ian Colvin, then the foreign editor of the *Sunday Express* and later deputy editor of the *Daily Telegraph*. Before the outbreak of war Colvin had been a press correspondent in Berlin, who had 'plunged very deeply into German politics' and kept Churchill in touch with developments there. After a hint dropped over dinner by an unnamed Cabinet Minister, Colvin concluded that the 'mischievous reality' of the deception scheme spelt out in 'Operation Heartbreak' must have some basis in fact, and late in 1952 set out on an arduous investigative trail which led him to the grave of Major William Martin, Royal Marines, in the Roman Catholic section of the cemetery outside the town of Huelva. The date of death on the slab was 24 April 1943, which tied with the invasion of Sicily, and in the light of further local enquiries Colvin knew he had his man.

Publication of the revelation was another matter, for Colvin had served as an officer in the Royal Marines and was therefore subject to the Official Secrets Act. The story is taken up by the celebrated scientist R.V. Jones in his memoir *Most Secret War*. In 1952 Jones had been recalled to the Ministry of Defence as

Director of Scientific Intelligence, and thus took a seat on the Joint Intelligence Committee:

> At my first meeting I heard a discussion about what should be done because Ian Colvin had worked out the facts of the operation, and had written a book which he had submitted for security clearance The JIC decided, very unsportingly, I thought, to hold back Colvin's account while they invited Ewen Montagu, who had been in Naval Intelligence and was involved in the deception, to write an officially approved account which came out as *The Man Who Never Was* in 1953 . . . I had much sympathy for Colvin over his shabby treatment.

A barrister by profession, Ewen Montagu had taken silk six months before war was declared, and after a short spell with Humber Command as an acting Lieutenant-Commander, joined the Naval Intelligence Division. There he served as a liaison officer on the Twenty Committee, the body which ran German double agents, through which he met Charles Cholmondeley, a junior officer in B Division of MI5. Montagu's own account of his wartime role in the operation is examined in detail below, but it is sufficient to state here that he returned to the Bar in 1945, and then sat as a judge on the Western Circuit. The call from the Joint Intelligence Committee in 1953 gave Montagu just three days to complete a sanitised account of Operation Mincemeat, which was to be serialised in the *Sunday Express* between 1 and 22 February. Montagu later recorded that his professional experience in preparing complex legal briefs at short notice equipped him well for the task, which was completed over a weekend at his cottage on the Solent. Following newspaper serialisation it was published in book form by Evans Brothers in July, and became an immediate best-seller.

Read in isolation, this hastily prepared official version appeared comprehensive. It explained that the 'wild idea' was first suggested by an officer identified only as 'George' (i.e. Charles Cholmondeley), and that after Mincemeat was approved at high level the pair set about procuring a suitable body. Sir Bernard Spilsbury, the eminent Home Office pathologist, advised that a victim who had succumbed to pneumonia would be most appropriate, as the fluid in the lungs would suggest death by drowning. The coroner for the St Pancras district, William Bentley Purchase, was asked to locate a suitable unclaimed body, which was then put on ice while a plausible identity – 'Major Martin RM' – was manufactured, and the necessary documents forged. On 17 April 1943 the body of Major Martin was dressed in battledress in an unnamed London mortuary and driven by van 400 miles to Greenock in Scotland, where it was loaded onto HMS *Seraph*, the submarine that would drop the body off the Spanish coast en route to Gibraltar. Montagu gave details of the launching of the corpse, and also the text of the false documents carried. Operation Mincemeat was, he concluded, an unequivocal success, resulting in the strong but needless reinforcement of Axis forces in Greece, Sardinia and Corsica.

With the benefit of hindsight, *The Man Who Never Was* is no less interesting for what Montagu was obliged (or chose) to omit. Writing as he did in 1953, Montagu was unable to make any mention at all of Ultra decrypts, and the fact that intercepted enemy signals revealed that the *Abwehr* had accepted the false documents as genuine within three days of 'Major Martin' being released into the sea. And because Charles Cholmondeley was still a serving MI5 officer, he was referred to only as the pseudonymous George, and thus unfairly (but inevitably) relegated to a supporting role.

More surprising is the fact that Montagu failed to mention that the concept of Operation Mincemeat was far from new. During the First World War a 'haversack ruse' had been successfully employed by Generally Allenby's forces in Palestine in October 1917, by which false documents were planted on the Turks, having been dropped between the lines by a mounted officer named Meinertzhagen who feigned a wound. This deception was described in detail in the Official History, although the War Office was more sensitive about plans on the Western Front to plant a forged diary on a German corpse, revealed by General John Charteris in 1925 and quickly suppressed. In August 1942 the haversack ruse was replicated in the Middle East when a false map was planted on the enemy shortly before the battle of Alam Halfa, supposedly with the aid of a corpse. The body was left in a wrecked scout car of the 11th Hussars on ground facing Afrika Korps forces south of Qaret el Abd, and primed with a map revealing 'good going' across a sector of desert where in fact the ground was bad. Accepting this false intelligence as genuine, a number of Rommel's tanks were routed into an area of soft sand and bogged down. Add to this the possibility that managed corpses played a part in the myth of a failed German landing on the south coast of England in 1940, and one could be forgiven for concluding that by 1943 corpse deceptions were already an established military tactic. Indeed the same Mincemeat tactic would be repeated by Peter Fleming in Burma in 1944, albeit without success.

On 25 September 1942 an RAF Catalina flying boat carrying a naval courier named Lieutenant James Turner crashed off Cadiz during an electrical storm, after which his body was recovered by Spanish police from the beach at Tarifa. In Turner's inner pocket was a letter from General Mark Clark to the Governor of Gibraltar, which named certain Free French agents in North Africa and gave the proposed date of the Allied landings codenamed Torch as 4 November, although in the event these were delayed until the 8th. For the Allies, this should have marked an intelligence disaster of epic proportions. However Turner's body was returned by the Admiral of Cadiz with the letter still inside his jacket, and apparently unopened. A team of technicians was flown out from Britain in an effort to determine whether the papers had been examined, and concluded they had not, although doubts remained. Turner was buried on Gibraltar, but for reasons which remain obscure still featured in the Navy List for the rest of the war.

This earlier incident had become confused with Operation Mincemeat by the time Colvin interviewed several Spanish and German participants a decade later, which explains some of the more garbled aspects of his account, *The Unknown Courier*, published in 1953. Whatever the truth, it is inconceivable that the Cadiz incident was unknown to the planners of Mincemeat seven months later, or that they were ignorant of the earlier haversack ruse. Despite this, Montagu maintained to the end that the idea of floating a corpse ashore had been conceived by Cholmondeley independently. Not only is the supposed coincidence too great, but if in 1942 British intelligence were unsure whether the documents carried by Turner had been seen by the enemy, Operation Mincemeat could not realistically have been expected to work the following year, unless sympathetic *Abwehr* contacts were primed in advance.

Unsurprisingly, in his published account Montagu failed to disclose the true identity of the corpse who served as Major William Martin. The body was said to be that of 'a young man in his early thirties' who had died of 'pneumonia after exposure' late in 1942 and was then kept on ice for six months. According to Montagu, relatives of the dead man agreed to release his body on condition that he was given a decent Christian burial, and that his name remain secret, on the ground that he had died insane. To preserve this supposedly sworn anonymity, Montagu went to considerable lengths to ensure that The Man Who Never Was would never be identified. The London mortuary in which Major Martin was dressed before his journey north was described as being south of the River Thames. Montagu also described how the driver of the van, a racing car driver named Jock Horsfall, almost rammed a 'tram-standard' after the driver caught sight of a queue outside a cinema 'opposite' the mortuary, at which a 'spy film' was being shown, and began laughing. In fact in 1986 the morgue was identified as Hackney, on the north side of the river and never adjacent to a tram route or cinema. In 1953, however, the convincing fiction of the near-accident lent the book added veritas.

Indeed, the appearance of *The Man Who Never Was* gave some the impression that Montagu had taken a brave decision to publish and be damned, as John Masterman later would in 1972. In his definitive history of the use and abuse of the 1911 Official Secrets Act, David Hooper describes Montagu's book as having 'slipped through the net' while serving to 'raise some Security Service eyebrows'. Nothing could be further from the truth, although it is interesting to note that, while sitting as a judge at Hampshire Quarter Sessions in 1951, Montagu heard an appeal by two junior employees from the Royal Aircraft Establishment at Farnborough, convicted of minor offences under Section 2 of the Act. In reducing their fines from £50 to £20, Montagu handed down a ruling which still stands as the sole occasion on which a sentence under Section 2 has been reduced on appeal. Whether the government's failure to prosecute Duff Cooper the previous year had any bearing on this enlightened decision must remain a matter of conjecture. However some have suggested that Cooper may have first learned the facts of Operation Mincemeat from Montagu himself, a fellow student at Trinity College, and not from Churchill. It remains an intriguing possibility.

The Man Who Never Was boasted a classic title, the credit for which went to the editor of the *Sunday Express*, Howard Keeble. Colvin was awarded the inadequate sop of a written introduction to the newspaper serialisation, sight of two heavily weeded War Office files containing nothing not included in Montagu's book, and permission to publish his own account of the operation, by then rendered largely redundant. Montagu's book proved an immediate best-seller. A striking jacket design featuring a faceless Royal Marine stared out from posters and advertisements everywhere, and the book has remained in print ever since. Two years later a film version appeared, in which an American actor named Clifton Webb played Montagu, who in turn took a brief cameo role as a critical Air Vice-Marshal at a Chiefs of Staff conference. Charles Cholmondeley had to remain content with an uncredited role as technical advisor. Whether at any time he shared in any of the financial rewards enjoyed by Montagu is unknown.

Yet Cholmondeley must have been irritated. A fragment of Cholmondeley's original proposal for Operation Mincemeat finally appeared in the Official History of wartime deception operations in 1990, revealing a detailed proposal by which he even anticipated purchasing a corpse from a London hospital for the 'normal peacetime price' of £10. Although Montagu gave 'George' credit for originating the scheme in *The Man Who Never Was*, the fact that Montagu alone wrote the book meant that his role as the public face of Operation Mincemeat left the impression that he was the sole architect. That impression was further expressed in the short introduction by Hastings Ismay, who wrote that Montagu had 'originated' the plan. The film version two years later served only to reinforce this myth, with 'George Acres' appearing as Montagu's junior, working for and taking orders from him. Two years after publishing *The Man Who Never Was*, Evans Brothers published *The Big Lie* by John Baker White, which described Montagu alone as 'the architect of the deception' who 'had the idea of creating a fictitious courier' and was merely 'aided' by others unnamed. Little can be read in Montagu's Hitchcock-like cameo in the 1955 film, yet the closing scene in which his character places his own MBE on the grave of Major Martin surely stretches dramatic licence too far. In fact Montagu never once visited Huelva before his death in 1985.

No further details about Operation Mincemeat emerged until 1972, when John Masterman published *The Double Cross System*, his bombshell account of the work of the Twenty Committee. The text was written as an official report in 1945, and published in America 27 years later to avoid the necessity of Defence Notice Committee approval. Masterman revealed little not already disclosed by Montagu two decades earlier, but did reproduce an extract from Twenty Committee minutes for 4 February 1943 (also the date of the coroner's inquest into the death of Glyndwr Michael), which named Montagu and Cholmondeley as the members responsible for 'putting forward' the plan. Tellingly, Masterman also confirmed that the earlier Cadiz incident played a part in the planning of Mincemeat:

Shortly before the invasion of North Africa an aeroplane had crashed, a body had been washed ashore in Spain, and some fortunately unimportant papers had been shown to the Germans. It therefore appeared that a similar incident might be faked and turned to good account before some suitable major operation.

Quite why Montagu continued to give a contrary account after *The Double Cross System* appeared in 1972 can only be guessed at. Two years later, Frederick Winterbotham's unofficial but equally seismic book *The Ultra Secret* for the first time made public the breaking of the German Enigma codes, and the work of Bletchley Park. The dam had been broken, and having retired from the bench in 1973, Montagu wrote a more complete account of wartime activities, *Beyond Top Secret U*. In a short chapter devoted to Mincemeat, Montagu filled in some of the background to the deception, albeit still ignoring Cadiz, and finally credited Charles Cholmondeley by name, 'George' having by then retired from the Security Service to deal in horticultural machinery in Wells.

Cholmondeley at least now received due credit, albeit too little too late. Yet it was the identity of the original man who never was, Major William Martin, which continued to exercise the minds of several dedicated investigators, among them Roger Morgan, a civil servant, and Winston Ramsey, editor of *After the Battle* magazine. Both had approached Montagu independently, and both ran up against the former judge's dubious assertions of universal legal copyright. In reply to a letter from Ramsey, Montagu stated in 1976 that there was 'no other source other than my book from which the story can be obtained with any degree of accuracy' while reserving the right to 'pass' anything written on the subject. There is no copyright in historical fact, and the official précis written by Masterman in 1945 can hardly be dismissed so lightly. Nevertheless, in 1974 Montagu had threatened to sue the publishers of a book by Janusz Piekalkiewicz, which included photographs purporting to show the body of 'Major Martin' in a London morgue, and on the deck of a Spanish launch after being retrieved from the sea. Although no writ was uttered, damages were paid, and in this irregular manner Montagu was able to stifle the publication of further research until his death in July 1985.

Undeterred, in August 1986 Morgan finally succeeded in identifying the mortuary where 'Major Martin' was defrosted and dressed before his long journey north, in Hackney. In 1943 there had been no cinema within a reasonable distance showing a likely spy film, nor had enemy action since moved the mortuary north of the Thames, which underscored the lengths to which those in the know had gone to obscure the truth. Morgan also offered up a tentative candidate for the man who never was, one Reginald Harrison, a homeless man who had died of tubercular pneumonia in Archway Hospital in December 1942. Shortly afterwards, historian Martin Gilbert edged closer to the truth in suggesting that the dead man had been a Welsh gardener who had killed himself with weed killer, on the basis of a disclosure made by Colonel John Bevan some years before. In 1988 Colin Gibbon and James Rusbridger suggested that the body was that of a Welsh barman named Emlyn Howells, whose relatives, none the wiser, had attended the burial of an empty coffin in a cemetery at Treorchy, twenty miles from Cardiff. Rusbridger, who repeated the guess in his book *The Intelligence Game* the following year, died in 1994, but Gibbon eventually obtained an exhumation order from the Home Office, with the object of submitting Howells's remains to an examination which might prove the validity of his candidate. However, this macabre exercise was called off following a surprise discovery by Roger Morgan in a file declassified by the Public Record Office in November 1995, indexed as ADM 223/794.

Thanks to the Open Government Initiative of 1994, an Admiralty file by Ewen Montagu on 'Naval Deception' had been declassified without fanfare, and contained not only the definitive account of Operation Mincemeat, but also the long-coveted name – Glyndwr Michael. His true identity was subsequently confirmed to Morgan by the Ministry of Defence, and further research revealed Michael to have been the illegitimate son of illiterate South Wales mining stock, born in Aberbargoed on 4 January 1909 to Thomas Michael and Sarah Ann Chadwick. Against this background, the gravestone at Huelva is seen to offer substantial clues, interpolating Glyndwyr, An(tonia) and the Welsh connection. Sadly that link had been severed by 1995, and Morgan was unable to trace any surviving members of the Michael family.

The naming of Glyndwr Michael also served to shed light on why Montagu and others were so keen to keep his identity secret. In *The Man Who Never Was*, Montagu recalled that the task of procuring a suitable corpse had thrown up unforeseen difficulties:

> At one time we feared we might have to do a body-snatch – 'do a Burke and Hare' as one of us put it; but we did not like that idea, if we could possibly avoid it. We managed to make some very guarded inquiries from a few Service Medical officers whom we could trust; but when we heard of a possibility, either the relatives were unlikely to agree or we could not trust those whose permission we would need not to mention to other close relatives what had happened.

By 1977, in *Beyond Top Secret U*, Montagu felt able to state that his team had 'searched and searched' for a suitable body. Furthermore:

> I gave a solemn promise never to reveal whose body it was and, as there is no-one alive from whom I can get a release, I can say no more than that it was the body of a young man who had died of pneumonia. As I am not identifying him, I can perhaps add the ironic fact that he was a bit of a ne'er-do-well, and that the only worthwhile thing he ever did he did after his death.

The truth is probably that no such inquiries were made, no consent sought or obtained from Glyndwr Michael's relatives in Wales, and no promise of anonymity made. Instead it is far more likely that the very 'body-snatch' Montagu professed to dislike was not avoided at all, and that a body was simply hijacked. Even in wartime such 'Burke and Hare' activity was technically illegal, and ran contrary to a raft of legislation and procedures, including the rules relating to coroners and registrars, and the Removal of Bodies from England Regulations 1927. No relevant registry records survive from this period, but in any event may never have been made in the case of Glyndwr Michael. A failure to contact and gain consent from living relatives is probably chief among the unspecified 'various reasons' offered by Montagu for not obtaining a genuine photograph of Michael for his faked ID card.

There is in fact more than a hint of professional unease in the following passage from the biography of coroner Bentley Purchase, written by Robert Jackson shortly after his subject died after falling from the roof of his home near Ipswich in September 1961:

> Purchase insisted that his name should not be mentioned. His action in providing the body had the sanction not only of the government but the man's own relatives, but he was still worried about the effect on public opinion of the unorthodox disposal of a body which had been in his keeping.

As a serving judge, and a Queen's Counsel to boot, Montagu too would undoubtedly have been sensitive over any past conduct tainted by illegality, even though it is hard to conceive that anyone in their right mind would condemn any wartime aspect of Mincemeat. For it is beyond dispute that Charles Cholmondeley's 'wild idea' ranks as one of the most successful deception operations of the entire war.

Yet even with the identification of Glyndwr Michael, questions over Operation Mincemeat remain. Curiously, it was never integrated into the main strategic deception plan for the invasion of Sicily, code-named Barclay. Although Barclay was approved by the Chief of Staffs' Committee on 10 April 1943, and is available for inspection at the PRO, in discussing various methods for feeding disinformation to the enemy, no mention whatsoever is made of Mincemeat. Nor was it mentioned in the definitive chronicle of the Allied planning for Husky by Richard Leighton, published in the *US Naval Institute Proceedings*. According to Masterman, the Controller of Deception 'sponsored' the scheme only at a late stage, and in May 'took responsibility for the developments' after the body had been washed ashore in Spain. All of which only serves to underline the fact that Mincemeat stood outside the central planning both for Barclay and Husky, and was simply part of a larger whole which paved the way for the successful conquest of Sicily in little more than a week.

Montagu's account gave rise to yet another myth, namely that Mincemeat alone made the landings successful. When *The Man Who Never Was* appeared in book form in 1953, the introduction penned by Ian Colvin for the *Sunday Express* serialisation was abandoned in favour of a short foreword by General Hastings Ismay, the Chief of Staff between 1940 and 1946, who wrote that:

> The operation succeeded beyond our wildest dreams. To have spread-eagled the German defensive effort right across Europe, even to the extent of sending German vessels away from Sicily itself, was a remarkable achievement. Those who landed in Sicily, as well as their families, have cause to be especially grateful.

Montagu repeated these words in *Beyond Top Secret U*, but Ismay's bold claim had little foundation in reality. True, from early May 1943 the enemy were deceived into rating the defence of Greece, Sardinia and Corsica on an equal footing with Sicily. In June the reconditioned 1st Panzer Division, with 83 tanks and 18,000 men, were moved from Brittany to Greece, while another 22 tanks were diverted to Corsica. On Sicily itself, there were just 30,000 German troops by July, and 42 tanks, together with a larger but much less effective Italian force. Mussolini alone was convinced that the blow would fall on Sicily, but by this stage in the war was little heeded in Berlin. Defences were concentrated in the west and north of the island, rather than the south, and motor torpedo boats were transferred to the Aegean. Indeed even two weeks after the main Allied assault on Sicily on 10 July, Hitler still felt sure that a heavier attack would fall on Greece, and on the 25th sent Rommel to command his forces there.

Yet Mincemeat cannot claim sole credit for this. The plan hatched by Cholmondeley and Montagu did not exist in a vacuum, and formed part of an ongoing and methodical policy of strategic deception. In the Mediterranean, Operation Barclay sought to tie down Axis forces in the south of France and the Balkans peninsula, and to secure the greatest possible degree of surprise for the assault on Sicily. By late 1942 British deception agencies had already succeeded in convincing the *Abwehr* that the British army was 50 per cent larger than it actually was, and capable of attacking in several directions, when in fact there were insufficient landing craft for more than one operation. As part of Barclay bogus radio transmissions continued to talk up British military strength, and Mediterranean convoys were routed so as to aid the general deception, while on the day – 10 July – surprise was also achieved on Sicily by landing in rough weather. Against this background Mincemeat may be seen as simply a dividend which undoubtedly distracted attention from the island, but was not responsible for all German troop movements in southern Europe during the summer of 1943. Indeed the documents conveyed by Major Martin told the enemy little or nothing they did not already expect.

In closing, it is perhaps relevant to Operation Mincemeat that the Americans were always nervous about the assault on Sicily. Forceful objections to the attack had been raised at the Casablanca Conference in January 1943, partly informed by the sheer obviousness of Sicily as a target, while Eisenhower later tried to impose a condition that the landing was to be cancelled if there was reason to believe that more than two German divisions were defending the island. It can hardly have helped that early in May the US Naval Secretary, Colonel Frank Knox, declared publicly that Sicily was next in line for occupation. Clearly, much turned on the success of the various deception operations, which was reflected in the fact that it was deemed expedient to enlist the services of Section B1A of MI5, which ran turned German agents in Britain. Charles Cholmondeley seems to have envisaged just such a critical mission in his original written proposal, quoted in the Official History:

> While this courier cannot be guaranteed to get through, if he does succeed, information in the form of the documents can be of a far more secret nature than it would be possible to introduce through any other normal B1A channel.

It remains a matter of conjecture just how far these channels ran in relation to Major Martin. The Official History states that the corpse was released into the sea off Huelva because the German vice-consul there was known to be 'highly competent', while Montagu referred to a 'very active German agent' at Huelva who boasted 'excellent contacts with certain Spaniards'. After being retrieved from the sea on 30 April the body was handed over to the Spanish naval headquarters at Huelva, but the briefcase dispatched straight to Madrid, from where the *Abwehr* appear to have been keen to endorse the false documents as genuine, and to emphasise the importance of the find. By 11 May Foreign Armies West (FHW), the traditionally sceptical army intelligence department, had described the Martin material as 'absolutely convincing', while an appraisal delivered to Admiral Dönitz on the 14th offered that 'the genuineness of the captured documents is above suspicion' and assessing as 'slight' any suggestion that 'they have intentionally fallen into our hands'.

Quite what transpired between Huelva, Madrid and Berlin between 30 April and 9 May, when the first appreciation reached the German High Command, is impossible to say. However, the suspicion remains that unspecified intelligence channels on both sides left less to chance than is apparent from the information so far disclosed by official papers, and that some in the *Abwehr* welcomed – and even expected – the arrival of Glyndwr Michael, alias Major William Martin, RM.

CHAPTER TEN

Canaris and the Abwehr

In late 1934 Wilhelm Canaris was marking time as the commandant of Swinemunde Fort on the Baltic, patiently awaiting retirement with the rank of Rear-Admiral. The following January, very much to his surprise, he was appointed as chief of the German military intelligence service by Admiral Raeder, whose reputed dislike of Canaris was overridden by a desire to prevent the *Abwehr* falling under the control of the army. In February 1944 the labyrinthine and allegedly inefficient *Abwehr* was finally absorbed by the SS, and in July Canaris was arrested on suspicion of treason. On the evening of 8 April 1945 he was tried before an SS *Standgericht* (summary court) at Flossenburg and sentenced to death. The following morning he was hanged – twice, according to some accounts – and burned on a common funeral pyre.

Although at least three major biographies of Canaris have been published since 1949, as well as countless studies of the *Abwehr*, there is little or no consensus on whether the Admiral acted as a British agent, or was simply a courageous German patriot who opposed the Nazi creed. Whatever the truth, the myths, legends and fictions surrounding Canaris are legion. He is said to have conducted an affair with Mata Hari while in Madrid in 1916, and then betrayed her to the British secret service once she had outlived her usefulness. Some allege that in the same year Stewart Menzies, later head of MI6, was sent to Spain to kill or capture Canaris, evidently without success. Some accounts portray him as a powerful and omnipotent Nazi leader, able to command all German forces on land, sea and air, as well as the SS and Gestapo. Others link him to an attempt to frustrate the sinking of the *Royal Oak* at Scapa Flow in October 1939 and the assassination of Reinhard Heydrich in May 1942, while a film biography made in 1954 suggested that he secured the cancellation of Operation Sealion by showing the German High Command film of British flame defences. It hardly helped that Canaris himself revelled in intrigue, and fostered the belief that he was descended from the Greek freedom fighter Konstantin Kanaris, when in fact his family hailed from Lombardy. Had he survived the war, he might well have been flattered by the fact that he has appeared as a character in a string of novels and thrillers, including *The Eagle Has Landed* (1975), *Sea Wrack* (1980), *The Canaris Fragments* (1982) and *Shingle Street* (2002). Some even suggested that rumours of his demise were much exaggerated. In his highly unreliable account *Secrets of the British Secret Service*, published in 1948 under the name E.M. Cookridge, Edward Spiro reported that the previous year the French Intelligence Service had discovered Canaris 'in Argentina, living under an assumed name'.

Few, if any, of these theories have any basis in reality. However, in 1983 the intelligence historian Nigel West was able to establish as a fact that Canaris passed information to the Allies through his Polish mistress, Halina Szymanska. This much was afterwards confirmed by Andrew King, a former MI6 passport control officer in Zurich and a member of the same Z network. Szymanska was the wife of the former Polish military attaché in Berlin, who Canaris helped to escape to Switzerland in September 1939, where she was installed as a typist at the Polish legation in Berne. MI6 gave her the designation Z-5/1, and equipped her with a false French identity in the name of Marie Clenat. In February 1940 Canaris sent an *Abwehr* officer named Hans Bernd Gisevius to Switzerland under vice-consular cover to provide support for Szymanska. Canaris himself seems to have met with Szymanska on relatively few occasions, in Italy and France as well as Switzerland. As we shall see, the popular consensus is that the information passed by Canaris to London via this conduit was in the nature of political rather than military intelligence, although this is impossible to verify. Nevertheless, Gisevius too was in contact with MI6, and in this way information was passed from the *Abwehr* to British intelligence. Misinformation no doubt flowed the other way, and although no details are available there can be little doubt that in this way Allied counter-espionage and deception operations great and small were actively assisted by elements within the *Abwehr*.

Surprisingly, the core of the astonishing revelation about agent Z-5/1 had been made public as early as 1951, although at the time the significance of Halina Szymanska's story seems not to have been appreciated. For this we have to thank Ian Colvin, the veteran journalist whose role in the tortuous story of The Man Who Never Was was examined in Chapter Nine. Unfortunately, there is rather less to admire in his contribution to the Canaris debate. In 1951 Colvin published *Chief of Intelligence*, a speculative assessment of the Admiral's career later reprinted as *Hitler's Secret Enemy*. The book invited readers to make up their own minds on whether Canaris had acted as a British agent, and, as with The Man Who Never Was, Colvin claimed his curiosity had first been aroused by chance remark over dinner with a senior establishment figure. His source this time was Sir Christopher Warner, an under secretary at the Foreign Office, who hinted that

British intelligence was not badly equipped. As you know, we had Admiral Canaris, and that was a considerable thing.

In about 1950, a Polish diplomat introduced Colvin to one 'Madame J', then living in Surrey. Madame J was in fact Halina Szymanska, although Colvin obscured her true identity, and during her lifetime it was never expressly acknowledged that Szymanska had been a mistress to Canaris. To Colvin, Madame J acknowledged that she had known the Admiral, but denied ever having been a spy. By her account (albeit edited by Colvin), during his visits Canaris had never asked Szymanska for information concerning the Allies, but did volunteer information about Hitler's plans:

> The Admiral never asked me to find out anything for him about the Allies, although he must have known that I was in touch with my own countrymen in Berne, and, through them, with the British. Not long after I had arrived in Switzerland he made a visit to Berne. That was in the winter of 1939 . . . During his first visit I could not be sure that Switzerland was not going to be invaded next, so I asked him whether I should go on to France. 'No, not France, that is an uncertain place.'
>
> I don't suppose you could call Admiral Canaris an indiscreet man or he would not have held that high position in Germany for so long. But he could be very outspoken. He told me that winter of 1940 that Germany would certainly make war on her treaty partner Russia sooner or later . . . During the first stages of the Russian campaign he visited me again – that would have been in October 1941 – and said that the German front had run fast and bogged down in Russia and that it would never reach its objectives. But he was most interesting when he was talking about the tension within Germany and the conspiracy that was gathering against Hitler.

When Colvin asked Szymanska if Canaris had known that she had the ear of British intelligence, she replied that his 'calculated indiscretions' were exclusively 'in the sphere of high politics', but that she could 'sense from them what was imminent'. Furthermore:

> He would not have told me of purely military matters – small treason such as agents deal in . . . At times the tension in him affected me deeply when he spoke of their aims against Hitler. I asked the British sometimes, 'Shall I tell him to go ahead?' The British were very correct in such matters and said nothing. But the British Secret Service could keep secrets, and throughout the war this link was undiscovered.

Colvin met Madame J again some months later, when she instructed him to 'make it plain that he did not give away ordinary military secrets, otherwise the Germans will say that he was a British spy'.

In his book Colvin covered his meetings with Madame J in isolation, and perhaps doubted the truth of her story. Certainly all details of the Admiral's anonymous Polish ladyfriend were ignored by all subsequent biographers, including André Brissaud (1973) and Heinz Hohne (1979). It was not until

1983 that the truth of Halina Szymanska's story was confirmed by Nigel West, at a stroke rendering much of what had previously been written about Canaris redundant. Had Colvin stopped there, his part in the development of the Canaris story (and mythology) would mirror his role in the story of The Man Who Never Was: that of a determined investigative journalist who touched on the truth, but by virtue of being first on the case in a climate of close official secrecy, was unable to unravel the full story. However, in his introduction to a biography of Canaris by André Brissaud, published in Britain in 1973, Colvin made a claim which was as unlikely as it was startling:

> I am able to add here a detail, unrevealed in my own book twenty years ago, as it was still too sensitive then for publication. Major-General Sir Stuart Menzies, the wartime Head of British Intelligence, to whom in his Westminster office in October 1942 I explained my theory that his opposite number in Germany was in reality working against Hitler with the object of shortening the war, interrupted the conversation, saying with a smile: 'I think I know what is going on in his mind. Would you like to meet Canaris?'

As we saw at the beginning of this chapter, an earlier myth runs that Menzies had been sent to Spain to eliminate Canaris during the First World War. Astonishingly, Colvin then went on to relate that in 1942 Menzies (whose Christian name he spelt incorrectly) considered sending him abroad in order to establish contact with the head of the *Abwehr*. Perhaps Colvin considered that the glowing testimonial later provided by Churchill in *The Gathering Storm* was proof enough of his credentials for the job:

> He [Colvin] plunged very deeply into German politics, and established contacts of a most secret character with some of the important German generals, and also with independent men of character and quality in Germany who saw in the Hitler movement the approaching ruin of their native land.

Even bearing in mind this lavish praise, quite why the head of MI6 would have chosen a journalist working in the German section of the Foreign Office to undertake such a sensitive assignment is not explained by Colvin. In the event, however, the mooted rendezvous was overtaken by events:

> The matter was left that Sir Stuart required a week or two to obtain official approval for myself and one of his staff to meet Canaris . . . When I next saw Sir Stuart, however, he appeared disturbed and embarrassed by some awkward press reference that had been made in the interim to Admiral Canaris by the British propaganda services. It had been reported in a London newspaper that the Admiral was a disaffected anti-Nazi. 'Every time we build something up,' said Sir Stuart sadly, 'something like this happens and destroys what we have built.'

He then went on to say that he could no longer proceed with the plan for a meeting with Canaris. 'It has also been pointed out to me,' he explained, 'that you are a friend of Winston Churchill. We have to protect the old man and we have to be very careful not to offend the Russians.'

Colvin then went on to pin the press leak on Kim Philby, the MI6 section head and communist mole who defected to Moscow in 1963. In this way Colvin helped fuel the legend that during the war Philby did all he could to sabotage contact between British intelligence and the *Abwehr* for fear that collaboration might lead to peace in the West, leaving Germany free to fight the Soviet Union on a single front. Colvin's supposed sources, Warner and Menzies, died in 1957 and 1969 respectively, and thus were conveniently unable to contradict his version of events. The idea that Colvin would have been sent to meet Canaris is most unlikely, and the whole intrigue almost certainly invented. Since by 1942 British intelligence had already been in touch with Canaris for at least two years, via Halina Szymanska, it must be assumed that Colvin's memoir is fiction.

Just as falsehoods about Canaris have multiplied down the years, a rich seam of myth and legend has arisen around the vexed question of whether the *Abwehr* as a whole were engaged in a secret war against the Nazi regime. Certainly some *Abwehr* personnel served the Allies as double-agents, and some were involved in the July 1944 bomb plot which came close to killing Hitler. Moreover several senior officers testified for the prosecution at Nuremberg, including Erwin von Lahousen and Hans Bernd Gisevius. In recent years it has been noted with increasing regularity that certain operations against Britain were conducted in such a thoroughly incompetent manner that the very intent behind them may be called into question. David Mure, who served under Brigadier Dudley Clarke in the deception unit known as A Force, questioned whether the *Abwehr* were 'suckers or saints', observing that

I had not been the chairman of a deception committee controlling several agents for more than a couple of months before I began to suspect, from my own transmissions and from the study of previous traffic, that the complacency and inefficiency displayed by my opposite numbers might well be deliberate . . . Let me give three examples which strain the credibility to suggest otherwise than that the *Abwehr* was doing all in its power to help.

The examples cited by Mure include the cases of Tricycle, the Yugoslavian double-agent Dusko Popov, who the *Abwehr* continued to trust long after others would have smelt an entire midden of rats, and of a notional White Russian operative code-named Lambert, who proved useful to the Allied cause in the North African and Mediterranean theatres:

It never appeared odd to the *Abwehr* that over a period of three years their star 'agent' Lambert, whilst right in detail, was invariably wrong in effect. Also that he was so apparently devoted to the *Abwehr* cause that having arrived in 1940 with £1500 he had survived without replenishment for three years.

Other examples discussed elsewhere in this book include the remarkable speed at which Operation Sealion's planners were made aware of notional British flame defences in July and August 1940, conducting their own trials six days before the first British flame barrage was tested successfully. There is also the enthusiastic manner in which The Man Who Never Was and his forged papers were accepted as genuine by the *Abwehr* in April 1943.

Another possible example of deliberate *Abwehr* incompetence is provided by the four spies landed by sea near Hythe and Dungeness on 3 September 1940, all of whom were swept up in a matter of hours. One, Charles Kieboom, was a conspicuous Dutch Eurasian, discovered with binoculars and a spare pair of shoes draped around his neck, while another was arrested after attempting to order champagne cider in a public house at 9.30 in the morning. Because their capture had been public, and because one, Jose Waldberg, managed to remain at large for a day, and send back three valueless signals by wireless, they could not be turned by MI5, and were committed for trial at the Old Bailey. One, Sjoerd Pons, was acquitted, but the others received mandatory death sentences under the 1940 Treachery Act.

In 1952 Colonel Oreste Pinto gave an account of the capture of this ill-starred quartet which merits mention, if only as a reminder that even memoirs by former serving officers must sometimes be treated with caution. Pinto served as head of the Dutch section at the Royal Victorian Patriotic School, the interrogation centre at which refugees were screened after arriving in Britain. In his popular book *Spycatcher*, Pinto claimed to have played a key role in the capture and interrogation of all four spies, at a location very far from Dungeness, and offered a wholly fictitious account of the action. By this account, at dawn on 8 September Pinto received a decoded message from an agent in France that four spies would be landed on the south coast by U-boat, at map reference 432925. Accompanied by a dozen Field Security men, dressed in plain clothes, Pinto drove west from London for five hours to reach a 'small, secluded cove' where his group lay in wait for the *Abwehr* visitors. After a brief struggle three were detained, but the fourth spy could not be found. At daybreak the FS men fanned out to search 'every inch' of the cove thoroughly, but still to no avail. Pinto:

> I clenched my fists in my exasperation and watched the approaching line of searchers. It was light enough to see the white blur of each face but not to recognise the owner. I looked along the line from right to left and then back again. Suddenly the solution hit me and I laughed aloud . . . The captain and I strolled along the line of searchers, long enough to recognise each one. Eight, nine, ten. We were nearing the end of the line. Eleven, twelve and – we halted and I put a hand on the last man's shoulder. 'Good morning, Van der Kieboom,' I said. He was the thirteenth man.

In reality Kieboom had been arrested on the coast road near Hythe by a sentry from the Somerset Light Infantry, replete with shoes and binoculars, having demonstrated no guile whatsoever. Map reference 432925 is a fictional location, and it is said that Pinto's account was so at variance with the facts of the case, and the others examined, that both his books were passed for publication by the War Office without amendment. His other study, *The Boys' Book of Secret Agents* (1955), is unlikely to have troubled the Whitehall censor. While Defence Notice approval might excuse a certain degree of factual manipulation, it is clear that Pinto's motives in publishing *Spycatcher* and *Friend or Foe?* were self-aggrandisement and financial gain. *Spycatcher* was later televised by the BBC, and the book issued with a cover quotation attributed to Eisenhower that Pinto was 'the greatest living expert on security'. It is highly unlikely that the former Allied Supreme Commander ever expressed such a view, even as an act of charity.

Even reliable accounts may on occasion give rise to misconceptions. One myth surrounding the *Abwehr* espionage network in Britain arose after 1972, in the wake of the publication of *The Double Cross System* by Sir John Masterman. Masterman had completed his official report into the workings of the Twenty Committee in September 1945 while still a serving MI5 officer. The text was published by Yale University Press in 1972, thus avoiding the need for Defence Notice clearance in Britain, where permission to publish had been denied to Masterman since the early 1950s. The report detailed how every enemy agent sent to Britain (bar one) had been expected by MI5, since the *Abwehr* had unwisely given prior notice of their arrival to the Welsh double agent SNOW (Arthur Owens), and also explained how most were turned into double agents after capture, to send back false information to their *Abwehr* controllers. Few doubted Masterman's startling claim that 'by means of the double agent system we actively ran and controlled the German espionage system in this country,' while the implication that MI5 had exercised complete control over the notional enemy network was reinforced by the following passage:

> Innumerable precautions had to be taken with every agent and indeed with every message on the assumption (which later turned out to be false) that the Germans had several and perhaps many independent agents of whom we had no knowledge, and that these agents' reports could be used to check the reports of our own controlled agents.

Over the years several dubious accounts have emerged of alleged German agents who double-crossed the double-cross system, notably *The Druid* by Leonard Mosley in 1981, which claimed an SD agent had operated undetected by MI5 from May 1941 onwards. This account was exposed as false by Nigel West in his myth-busting study *Counterfeit Spies*, although West himself uncovered circumstantial evidence that an independent spy may have been at liberty on the south coast as early as September 1940, whose reports on defence dispositions near Rye and Beachy Head appear in German files. West suggests that at this time the Soviet military intelligence service, the GRU, ran several active networks in Britain, and that some intelligence gathered for Moscow may also have reached Berlin. One member of the Communist Party of Great Britain, a merchant seaman named George Armstrong, was tried at the Old Bailey in May 1941, having offered to supply details of Atlantic convoys to the German consul in Boston. His appeal against the death penalty was dismissed on 23 June, the day after the German invasion of the Soviet Union reversed CPGB policy overnight. Against this background, Masterman's account may not stand as the last word on German intelligence operations in wartime Britain after all, at least as far as the period between September 1930 and June 1941 is concerned.

In fact Masterman contradicted his own assessment in respect of one German agent, a hapless male in his late twenties whose body was discovered in a Cambridge air raid shelter on 1 April 1941, and who carried forged papers in the name of Jan Willem Ter Braak. Given the implications of an active enemy agent remaining at large for some six months, the published version of Masterman's account covers Ter Braak with surprising brevity:

> It is more than probable that he was a parachute agent (perhaps the only agent) who succeeded in eluding capture, but who was unable to make contact with the Germans . . . It is not altogether fanciful to speculate how much more happy and useful his career might have been if he could have fallen into the hands of the Security Service and become a double agent.

Although some accounts claim that Ter Braak was tailed and investigated while still alive, the truth is that MI5 only learned of his existence after his death. It was established that Ter Braak first surfaced in the city early in November 1940, claiming to be a Dutch refugee. As well as lodgings he also rented an office in Rose Crescent. In addition to a wireless transmitter, his possessions were found to include a number of bus tickets, which suggested that he had been touring airfields around the country. His true identity was never established, and the MI5 report concluded that he had probably taken his own life after running out of ration books and funds. It was impossible to guess at the nature or value of any intelligence he may have managed to pass back to Germany, although later anecdotal evidence connected him with air raids on marshalling yards used by the military.

Today he remains buried in an unmarked grave in the cemetery at Great Shelford, the only German spy known to have succeeded in double-crossing the double-cross system.

CHAPTER ELEVEN

Myths in the Field

The following chapter is necessarily something of a mixed bag, being a collection of assorted wartime myths whose common denominator is that they all concern armies and land operations.

Of all the myths to emerge from the Polish campaign, the most persistent is that Polish cavalry units charged German armoured columns, broke their sabres and lances on tanks, and were massacred in droves. A further elaboration offered that the Poles had mistakenly believed that the enemy 'tanks' were no more than cars dummied-up with wood and canvas, of the type used by Germany in pre-war exercises. Although the tale is rarely mentioned in official histories, the following brief paragraph from the *Eastern Daily Press* is typical:

> An instance of the useless sacrifice of brave men was an order to 2000 or 3000 cavalry to charge tanks in the Katowice area in the first days of the war. Only 100 cavalry returned from the desperate encounter.

In fact this never happened. Although the Polish army of 1939 boasted eight cavalry brigades, and considered its mounted troops an elite force, they fought chiefly as dismounted infantry. On 1 September the 18th Lancer Regiment of the Pomorska Cavalry Brigade charged an unprepared German infantry unit at Krojanty, and caused considerable panic until several armoured cars appeared and turned the Polish riders under a barrage of withering automatic fire. This single incident was reported in exaggerated form first by Italian journalists, and quickly exploited by German propagandists. In truth, in a month of fighting the Polish army gave a far better account of itself than did the French, Belgian and British forces in May 1940, and managed to account for 674 German tanks lost or damaged. Polish anti-tank gunners were particularly effective, and obliged the Panzer arm to abandon the large white *Balkankreuz* as its standard marking on armoured vehicles. Nor is it true that the Polish air force was destroyed on the ground during the first few days of the campaign.

The Poles had sensibly withdrawn most of their modern aircraft to secluded airfields days before the invasion, leaving only obsolete machines on the targeted bases. In this way most of Poland's first line aircraft survived to fight another day, even if they were themselves outnumbered and outclassed by the *Luftwaffe*.

Myths about spies and parachutists were rife in Poland, as they were in the West as Hitler strove to complete the conquest of Europe in 1940. Although Britain was not invaded, rumours of landings by German troops were commonplace, particularly in the wake of the celebrated Cromwell alert issued on Saturday 7 September. The many stories of bodies on beaches have already been examined in Chapter Six, while bemused accounts of nocturnal panics and false alarms are legion. Countless sticks of German paratroops were said to have met a sticky end, such as that reported by a Mass Observer near Newport on 10 September, to the effect that 500 Germans had landed nearby, 499 of whom were shot in three seconds. The last was said to have escaped. A similar story was recorded by Anthony Armstrong, a Home Guard in the Sussex village of East Downing, in his book *Village at War* (1941):

> We never found out the real truth of that alarm. Rumours varied from a sentry's mistake in identifying baled-out British airman to mines being layed [*sic*] by parachute off Dover harbour. One good blood-thirsty story, circumstantial of course in every detail as these stories are, had it that 14 German parachutists had been dropped to capture a big aerodrome behind Dover and 'every man jack of them was riddled before he reached the ground.' Why, within a week, one of our people had met a chap whose brother had a cousin who had himself got three of them; and later I met another man whose friend had written him to say he's accounted for two himself. At that rate it began to look as if half a battalion had been shot on the wing.

One post-Cromwell rumour which spread in Dover held that Folkestone had already been taken, and that German aircraft were operating from Hawkinge airfield. In his 1971 book *How We Lived Then*, Norman Longmate wrote that 'in East Anglia some enthusiastic engineers blew up bridges and laid mines, which killed several Guards officers', although this much-quoted yarn has never been confirmed. Several stories told of a landing at Sandwich Bay. Meanwhile:

> Station Officer Thomas Goodman, a London fireman on relief at Dover, heard of an attempted landing at Sandwich Bay, 14 miles north: the inshore waters, it was said, were black with German dead. Taking a staff car, Goodman set off – to find only baking sands and blue sea, not a soul in sight.

In *The Big Lie*, John Baker White also records rumours of 'a great pillar of smoke rising from Sandwich Bay and the secret burial in the sand dunes of hideously charred bodies'. A more detailed account of a legendary German landing at Sandwich was given by David Collyer in *Deal and District At War*.

According to John Wilson, then a Home Guard messenger boy, on the night of 15 August 1942:

It was about midnight when there was a terrific knocking at our door, and when we opened it there was an army dispatch rider. He informed my father that the invasion alert had gone off and that there was a general call-out on. Dad rushed over to the Home Guard HQ, while I got dressed and set out on my bicycle to knock up the rest of the platoon. Looking across the north-east, towards the Stour Estuary, all hell had been let loose. I could see machine-gun fire, flares, and star shells all going up, and even the anti-aircraft guns at Manston aerodrome seemed to be firing almost horizontally across Pegwell Bay.

One clue as to what was going on that night emerged later. At the Reed Barn school in Ash village was a detachment of the Dorset Regiment. They were on duty in the pillboxes down at Sandwich Bay for three days a week, and then came back for a three-day rest, then went back on duty again. One of the local girls had become friendly with one of the young Dorset lads, but as her parents did not approve, she used to bring him up to our home.

She had arranged to meet him the evening after all that rumpus down at Sandwich Bay, but he did not turn up, and neither did he appear on the following evening, so she started to get worried. We asked some of the Dorset lads what had happened to him, but we couldn't get anything out of them. Father had dealings with the Dorset detachment about rifle and ammunition supply for the Home Guard, so he tackled their sergeant about it after a few days, but all he could get out of him was: 'Well, it was their own fault – they were all asleep!'

Nothing more happened until six or seven months later, when the young lady concerned arrived at our house in tears, having just received a Red Cross postcard from her young man – from Germany!

A similar 'lost patrol' myth has been attached to Hollesley Bay, Suffolk. According to local historian Derek Johnson, in December 1939 a patrol from the Essex Regiment vanished while patrolling the beach between Shingle Street and Bawdsey:

George Wright told of a strange 'do' on a bleak winter night soon after his arrival. George was a corporal wireless operator. One of his jobs was to take hourly wireless reports from the various patrols scattered along the coast. One night late in December 1939, he lost contact with the Shingle Street squad. By 8 am the following morning, all the other patrols were back – but still no sign of the men from Shingle Street. By now there was great concern for the safety of the missing men and a search party was dispatched . . . All that was found was a rifle and a steel helmet near the water's edge.

No trace was ever found of the men, and the affair was hushed up. The general feeling was that the men had been taken by a patrolling submarine or E-boat, in the hope that they could give valuable information on some of the secret radar installations and defences along the coastline.

Sadly the tale is full of holes. No relevant unit histories or war diaries confirm such a loss, while the idea that Home Defence patrols were routinely equipped with portable wireless sets in 1939 or 1940 is a nonsense. Reports of snatched sentries were common in Britain throughout the war, and elderly Home Guards were even reported in German prison camps. Typical is the following story given to the author by George Hearse, concerning his father, also named George:

Being a 1914–18 war veteran my father took part in Home Guard duties in London. Sometime late in 1943 there was an appeal for Home Guard personnel to volunteer for weekend guard duty at a sensitive location on the coast. One man said goodbye to his wife on the station platform in London, expecting to be home in a few days' time. His wife heard nothing more about him until several weeks later, when she was informed he was a prisoner of war in Germany. My father told me this story some time before his death in 1945, and I have no reason to doubt its authenticity.

The snatched sentry legend is in many respects similar to the flurry of press reports which appeared between August and December 1914, when it was reported that a number of sentries (usually Territorials) had been shot dead by unknown assassins. Few if any were actually killed in this way, and the reports were more likely to have been a ruse to keep the population on their toes. The same is undoubtedly true of the deadly motorcyclist, another First World War bogeyman, sometimes reported to be touring the country disguised as a scoutmaster, and offering poisoned sweets to sentries. Remarkably, he too rose like Lazarus two decades later, as former police officer George Ffoulkes recalled:

Between 1940 and 1944 I was a Superintendent of Police in the Balasore district of India, where there was an ordnance proving station. In about 1940–41 two Royal Artillery officers came out from England and, in conversation one night, told me how when they had been posted to a coastal battery in East Anglia, a party of Germans had come ashore, ridden round the countryside on motor bikes, and thrown grenades into some of the coastal batteries.

The incident is more likely to have been an unannounced training exercise by a Home Guard Auxiliary Unit, but like the legend of the snatched sentries, the truth of the matter is impossible to gauge with any certainty.

Another invasion myth which first surfaced in 1954 concerned psychic defence and witchcraft. During the summer of 1940 a gathering of witches was said to have been held in the New Forest with the object of erecting the so-called Great Circle. According to Gerald Gardner, the self-proclaimed King of the Witches, the ancient magical ritual of the Great Circle was invoked only in times of acute national crisis, and in the past had been staged to repulse the Spanish Armada and Napoleon. The ritual itself involved raising 'a great cone of power', which was then directed across the Channel towards 'Hitler's brain'. However the rite proved a serious drain on the life force of the assembled covens, and was repeated only four times before fatalities among the older witches forced the plan to be abandoned. In *Witchcraft Today* (1954) Gardner wrote:

I am not saying that they stopped Hitler. All I say is that I saw a very interesting ceremony performed with the intention of putting a certain idea into his mind, and this was repeated several times afterwards; and though all the invasion barges were ready, the fact was that Hitler never even tried to come.

Another version holds that the rite was staged by a determined Hampshire coven, and involved the deliberate sacrifice of the oldest and frailest member, who volunteered to perform the open-air ritual 'skyclad' (i.e. naked) without the usual protective covering of bear-fat. Unfortunately the gathering took place on the coldest May night in years, and over the next fortnight two other members of the coven also contracted pneumonia and died. Quite how bear-fat might have been obtained in ration-hit Britain is not explained, however. No less far-fetched was the following elaboration proposed by Richard Deacon (as Donald McCormick) in his book *Murder by Witchcraft*:

Fire and wind were the traditional weapons of witches against ships at sea, and it is interesting to recall that in the late summer of 1940 much propaganda was made of the story that German invasion barges were destroyed in mid-Channel by burning oil on the waters . . .

Atrocity propaganda was far less common in the Second World War than in the First World War. Nevertheless, a myth widespread at the time, yet forgotten today, concerned a particularly barbaric punishment inflicted on Allied prisoners by their Axis captors. Two versions from 1942 are recorded by Marie Bonaparte in *Myths of War*:

A 'Cape-coloured' taken prisoner at Tobruk wrote to his wife, in South Africa, that the Italians were treating him well, but added that since she was collecting stamps she should peel the stamp off the envelope, as it was rare. She does so and finds written below: 'It's dreadful, they've cut out my tongue.'

A major captured at Singapore, writes to his wife that the Japanese are treating him well and advises her to remove the stamp from the envelope. Below is written: 'They have cut out my tongue.'

An American version is recorded by Paul Fussell in *Wartime*, which told of a mother who received a letter from her soldier son held in a Japanese PoW cage.

He tells her that he is well and that she is not to worry, and adds that she might like to soak off the stamp on the envelope to give to a collector friend. When she does so, she discovers the usual message that his tongue has been removed. In truth the tongue story is nothing more than an echo of the lurid stories of castration and eye-gouging common to ancient wars. Somewhat less easy to fathom were rumours that Polish officers and men were liable to bite off the nipples of women rash enough to consort with them. This bizarre story was current in 1939 in the vicinity of Coetquidan in Brittany, where the Polish Legion was stationed, and emerged again in Africa in 1942.

The fact that Italian soldiers were rumoured to confiscate tongues from their prisoners seems surprising today, for there remains a strong perception that Mussolini's troops were a cowardly rabble, reluctant to fight, yet all too keen to surrender en masse, often while carrying neatly packed suitcases. The other stereotype was of 'a lot of opera singers' (according to Roosevelt), and vainglorious dandies 'pomaded and scented, accompanied by framed pictures, birdcages and similar domestic amenities, their elegant spare uniforms neatly folded in extra suitcases and trunks'. In North Africa the Italian army retreated so often that their trucks were said to be fitted with five reverse gears, while in London a popular dance-step called The Tuscana was 'supposedly based on the Italian's way of fighting ie one step forward, two steps back'. Later, on the steppes of Russia, it was rumoured that the Duce's frozen soldiers were issued with cardboard boots. Although there is a great deal of truth in these many anecdotes about Italian military ineffectiveness, the charge of inherent cowardice is a myth, for the Italian soldier was more often the victim of inadequate training, poor equipment and incompetent leadership.

The myth and reality of the Italian soldier in combat between June 1940 and September 1943 is the subject of a searching essay by Brian Sullivan published in 1997. Although Mussolini was clearly a supreme military incompetent, he had made it clear to Hitler before the outbreak of war that the Italian army would not be prepared for a war with the West until at least 1943. Following an opportunist attack on France in June 1940, but finding the war unwon, his army was obliged to fight on for over three years with arms and equipment that was almost always inferior to those of their opponents. Training was poor, consisting largely of close order drill and marching, while most soldiers went into combat in 1940–41 having never seen a tank, let alone trained with one. During the same period Italian troops were issued with a motley assortment of rifles of no fewer than four different calibres, ranging from 6.5 mm to 10.35 mm, and creating obvious problems of ammunition supply, while no fewer than seven different calibres of machine-gun were adopted. In June 1940 the great majority of Italy's 10,000 artillery pieces were of pre-First World War design, many of them captured from Austro-Hungarian forces in 1918, and again of a bewildering variety of types and calibres. Of 1,600 so-called tanks, all but 300 were small, turretless L3/35 machine-gun carriers, while trucks and transport were in constantly short supply. The Italian invasion of Egypt from Libya in September 1940 was never likely to succeed, as Brian Sullivan explains:

The problem was that Libya was a country with very scanty water resources. There's no river in the entire country. What water there is is in artesian wells, but to make matters worse there had been a drought previously, so there was even less water than usual. The Italian army had very few motor vehicles. The majority of its forces were infantry in the full sense of the word: they were foot soldiers. Marshal Graziani had some tanks and artillery, but basically if his army was going to reach the Nile Delta it would have to march on foot. And, of course, June, July, August and September is a period of blazing heat. In order for him to cross the Western Desert he had to supply his men with water, and he had a lot of men: well over 10,000.

The result was inevitable, and between December 1940 and February 1941 British and Commonwealth forces captured 150,000 prisoners and 400 tanks. Cowardice played little part. Instead, large masses of immobile Italian infantry were time and again cut off by Allied armour, and had no choice but to surrender, or die of hunger and thirst. The Italian invasion of Greece in October 1940 fared little better, coming just three weeks after Mussolini had demobilised fully one-third of his army for economic and political reasons. As a result the gaps in the ranks were hastily filled with raw recruits, who received little or no training before being thrust into the front line. It is therefore little wonder that the Italians failed to break through, and that Greece eventually had to be subdued by German forces.

After these crushing defeats in North Africa and the Balkans, the Italian army managed a partial recovery. During the spring and summer of 1941 its battle performance improved immeasurably in North Africa, culminating in the defeat of the British 22nd Armoured Brigade at Bir el Gobi in late November. The following year Italian paratroop units fought with skill and courage at Alam el Halfa, and at El Alamein to virtual extinction. Although the three divisions Mussolini unwisely sent to assist Germany in Russia were handicapped by a lack of transport, they fought well enough along the Donetz-Donbas canal from December 1941 and March 1942, although in the final tally lost as many men to frostbite as to bullets. Today the hapless Italian army is remembered only for its poor early showing in the Western Desert, but 75,000 died in Russia and the Ukraine. Field casualties in North Africa totalled just 38,000 dead, although another 17,000 were lost at sea as a result of attacks on transports by the Royal Navy and RAF. In the final analysis, according to Sullivan:

Throughout the war, whether under Mussolini or Badoglio, the Italian soldier had done his best, fighting for what he was told were his country's interests and honour. 350,000 died in battle, succumbed to wounds or perished in prison camps. The incompetent leaders at the summit of the fascist regime and its military-monarchist successor failed to match such selflessness and dedication. The Italian soldier deserved better, even considering the purpose of his war. That he fought for an evil cause in 1940–43 is incontestable. That he fought heroically is undeniable.

In Britain, at least, notable military disasters were often followed by allegations of betrayal and treachery from within. The loss of the *Royal Oak* in 1939, and the disastrous performance of the British army in Norway, Belgium and France in 1940, were all blamed at the time on the mythical fifth column. In much the same way, later costly or ill-fated operations at St Nazaire, Dieppe and Arnhem all led to conjecture that they were compromised by enemy spies.

The facts of the disastrous Dieppe raid are well known. On 19 August 1942 an Allied force of 6,000 men carried out a daylight 'reconnaissance in force' against the French coast at Dieppe, codenamed Operation Jubilee. Intended as an operational trial for an eventual Second Front, and to relieve pressure on the Russians by forcing the German High Command to retain divisions in France in a defensive role, the plan involved a bold frontal assault on the port by two infantry brigades and 27 new Churchill tanks. Once the coastal artillery on the adjoining headlands had been silenced, and the town cleared, a five-mile perimeter was to be established, within which various intelligence gathering missions would to be completed prior to an orderly withdrawal. To ensure complete surprise, the landing was made without the benefit of a preliminary naval bombardment or air attack, and the result was an unmitigated disaster. The Canadian contingent, which comprised three-fifths of the main assault force, was decimated on the beaches. Of the 4,963 Canadian troops who took part in the raid, only 2,210 returned to England, of whom 586 were wounded; 907 were killed, and 1,874 taken prisoner. Indeed the Canadian army lost more prisoners at Dieppe than in the whole eleven months of the later campaign in north-west Europe, or in their twenty months in Italy. A destroyer and 33 other vessels were lost, as well as every last one of the tanks. In the skies above the port, the RAF flew 2,617 sorties and lost 106 aircraft, including 88 Spitfires, with 113 pilots killed or missing. The whole débâcle lasted just nine hours.

Astonishingly, Lord Louis Mountbatten, then the head of Combined Operations, felt able to report to the War Cabinet that the raid had gone off 'very satisfactorily', and that of the men who had returned 'all I have seen are in great form'. In fact rumours of traps and betrayals began to circulate among the survivors almost immediately. A survey by the postal censor in the weeks following Operation Jubilee revealed that 5 per cent of Canadian survivors writing home blamed their horrifying casualty rate (68 per cent) on a betrayal, while returning prisoners later claimed their German captors had boasted of being forewarned. Lord Beaverbrook is said to have been convinced of the truth of the rumour, while one version even held that the tip-off had been deliberate, in order to prove to Stalin that a Second Front was an impossibility. According to historian Eric Maguire, writing in 1963:

> One fact emerged, however: every survivor of the holocaust on those beaches was convinced that the enemy was forewarned. That they should have thought so is not altogether surprising. They point out that after weeks spent at practice embarkations and landings, always under cover of darkness or smoke, they were embarked in broad daylight on the 18th, with no smoke cover and with rumours circulating of German aircraft in some areas. The very fact of Dieppe being the target again was disquieting, and as their briefing had given them no idea at all of the fire-power they were to encounter on the beaches, it is little wonder that they formed the conclusion that their arrival was expected.

Before long, like rumours were being noted by civilian diarists, including Vere Hodgson, who wrote early in October that:

> It is said that the advert for Sylvan Soap Flakes showing a Dieppe Beach Coat was a cryptogram advising the Germans. I remember seeing the advert and wondering why – Dieppe. Scotland Yard is said to be investigating it. No wonder we lost half our forces.

The legend of betrayal gained new impetus in 1963 with the publication of the book *Of Spies and Stratagems*, a war memoir by Stanley Lovell, formerly a senior officer in the OSS, the American military intelligence service which later became the CIA. Then, as now, the book carried some weight, since fully nine years before the publication of *The Double Cross System* it revealed that British intelligence agencies had run a string of double agents in order to pass back false information to their German counterparts. Indeed this might explain why the book did not find a British publisher.

According to Lovell, SIS tipped off the enemy about the Dieppe raid by accident. The raid should have taken place on 18 August, a Tuesday, but was unexpectedly postponed for 24 hours. News of the delay was not passed on to SIS, who therefore proceeded with their plan to bolster the credentials of a particular agent, who had been used in a similar manner during the commando raid on St Nazaire three months earlier. The spy was supposed to have sent 'accurate but retarded information' after the commandos had already achieved their objective, and was to repeat the exercise at Dieppe:

> The message was to be sent late Monday evening and this would be another accurate but 'just too late' bit of intelligence. . . After an agreed upon waiting period, the German radio operator was given a message to flash to Berlin. 'A great Commando raid is laid on, destination Dieppe. Biggest operation since Dunkirk evacuation. Scheduled for Dieppe' . . . Late Monday

evening the message went over the air to Berlin. . . The dangerous game of maintaining a supposed London spy ring information service to the Germans had by chance and a delay at a rendezvous caused the death of perhaps 2,000 brave Commandos.

A broadly similar idea was advanced by Anthony Cave Brown in *Bodyguard of Lies*, published some years later. In 1972, when *The Double-Cross System* was finally published, Sir John Masterman confirmed that the Dieppe raid had been launched without the benefit of any cover plan or deception. Nevertheless, in 1977 a German writer named Gunter Peis repeated Lovell's contrary claim in his own book, *The Mirror of Deception*:

> A great question mark hangs over the dead of Dieppe. Was their heroic sacrifice merely staged in order to test German preparedness on the Channel coast? I found the double agents, intermediaries, radio operators and officers at the German end of the secret 'London sources' who were still able to confirm the fatal advance warning of the attack on Dieppe. The same picture came from several different sources.

By way of evidence, Peis quoted several former *Abwehr* officers, including Herbert Wichmann of the Hamburg Stelle, who said that advance warning of the raid had been received from 'a very reliable, proven agent' in the south of England. These claims possibly inspired the British historian Leonard Mosley, who in 1981 published his controversial work *The Druid*, which claimed to reconstruct the extraordinary career of 'the spy who double-crossed the double-cross system'. The entire book, published by Eyre Methuen as non-fiction, has been comprehensively rubbished by Nigel West in his valuable books *Unreliable Witness* (1984) and *Counterfeit Spies* (1988), and has no credibility as a factual account. Nevertheless, according to Mosley the massacre at Dieppe was the phantom Druid's first success:

> It was quite obvious from the start that the *Wehrmacht* knew they were coming, and had made all the necessary preparations . . . Dieppe was one of the costliest disasters of the war, and the Druid helped make it so.

The major problem with this particular betrayal myth is that it is not substantiated by German records captured during the battle, and at the end of the war. As early as July Hitler had already guessed that a landing would probably take place in 'the area between Dieppe and Le Havre', and defence units stationed on the Channel coast were warned accordingly. The *War Diary* of 302 Division records that the general alert was cancelled on the evening of 18 July, a day before the Allies landed, while a guardbook seized by commandos on the day logged an order issued on 10 August by the commander of the 571st Infantry Regiment garrisoned at Dieppe. This revealed that:

The information in our hands makes it clear that the Anglo-Americans will be forced, in spite of themselves, by the wretched predicament of the Russians to undertake some operation in the West in the near future.

It is therefore clear that although the defenders were expecting some unspecified form of attack 'in the near future', no specific warning had identified Dieppe as the actual target. Haase had also ordered that off-duty gun crews should sleep fully clothed, so as to be ready for immediate action, yet the commandos found many had ignored the instruction. A detailed analysis of *Wehrmacht* records by Professor John Campbell of McMaster University in Ontario also established that no detailed advance warning had been passed on to Field Marshal von Rundstedt's headquarters. The Dieppe attack had already been cancelled, reinstated and postponed over a seven-week period before the men finally stormed the beaches on 19 August, and it is likely that British signal traffic alerted the Germans to a likely operation on the Channel coast, as the order from Haase indicated. Despite this, the legend that the defenders knew the time and place of the attack lives on.

Another Dieppe myth holds that although the raid was a failure, it provided a rich harvest of lessons which were put to good use in Normandy two years later. This falsehood was first offered in several censor-approved books published in 1943, including *Rehearsal for Invasion* by Wallace Reyburn, *Dress Rehearsal* by Quentin Reynolds and *We Landed at Dawn* by A.B. Austin, which described 'a testing and rehearsing of all our combined military, naval and Air Force staff work, a detailed working out of plans on which once completed, weeks could be saved another time'. According to Major-General Sir Leslie Hollis, the lessons learned at Dieppe were merely that 'a frontal attack on a strongly defended position was of little use' and that 'army units destined for amphibious operations must be trained'. The naval commander at Dieppe, Captain John Hughes-Hallett, offered the equally specious assertion that 'we proved once and for all that a frontal assault on a strongly defended port was not on'. The Jubilee planners might have done well to remember that it is not necessary to visit the North Pole to verify that it is cold. True, in July 1944 Eisenhower credited Dieppe as having provided valuable lessons, while Churchill later wrote that in tactical terms the raid was 'a mine of experience', yet this smacks of hindsight. In his book *Unauthorized Action* historian Brian Villa mounts a convincing argument that these later rationalisations were simply part of a smokescreen to obscure the true extent of Mountbatten's culpability for the disaster. Perhaps the best that may be said of Dieppe is that it convinced the German High Command that the Allies would try to take a large port during the early stages of an invasion, and disposed their forces accordingly, when in fact the Allies took their own ports to Normandy. Reynolds's book *Dress Rehearsal* even dared to imply that the Canadians themselves had insisted on undertaking the raid, even though Mountbatten preferred to use more experienced troops, and themselves switched the plan from a flanking to frontal assault. Neither suggestion was true.

Like Dieppe, the facts of Operation Market Garden in September 1944 are well known. On 17 September almost 10,000 men of the British 1st Airborne Division, together with 20,000 American airborne troops, were dropped over Holland at Arnhem, Grave and Nijmegen, in what was the largest airborne operation in the history of warfare. Their task was to secure bridgeheads over the Waal and the Rhine, while an armoured spearhead from 30 Corps plunged down the narrow road to Arnhem, more than 60 miles from the start line. Given that airborne troops are lightly equipped and entirely reliant upon supply from the air, the element of surprise was of paramount importance if the operation was to succeed. Certainly many of the participants were taken unawares, for the planning of Operation Market Garden was completed in little more than a week. Field Marshal Bernard Montgomery was hopeful that it might end the war by Christmas, but in the event the operation was a disaster. Faced with an impossible schedule, 30 Corps failed to relieve the 1st Airborne at Arnhem, who found themselves fighting two crack Panzer divisions, and lost some 6,630 men killed, wounded or captured. Montgomery later described Market Garden as 90 per cent successful, although the result was little more than a sixty-mile corridor leading nowhere, and the King of Holland came closer to the truth in voicing the hope that his people would be spared another of Montgomery's victories.

Allegations that the operation was betrayed to the Germans in advance first surfaced in the book *Spycatcher* (1952) by Oreste Pinto, whose loose attitude towards historical fact was touched on in Chapter Ten. In a chapter titled 'The Traitor of Arnhem', Pinto gave a highly questionable account of 'perhaps the most important spy case in the whole history of espionage', which centred on the activities of the Dutch resistance leader Christiaan Lindemans. Nicknamed 'King Kong' because of his enormous size, Lindemans was arrested on 28 October 1944 after allegations that, far from being a Dutch patriot, he was in fact a German spy. After an intensive two-week interrogation by MI5 he was returned to Dutch custody, where he suffered a nervous breakdown and subsequently committed suicide in a prison hospital in July 1946. Lindemans was never charged or convicted of any crime, but nonetheless he became the peg on which any number of espionage legends were hung, so much so that it is unlikely that the whole truth will ever be established.

What is known is that in September 1944 Lindemans was cleared for operational intelligence duties by the 21st Army Group, and on 13 September crossed the German lines into occupied Holland with the intention of locating a group of Allied evaders near Eindhoven. The mission had been sanctioned by Colonel J.M. Langley of MI9, despite the fact that Oreste Pinto had already warned Langley privately that Lindemans was untrustworthy. Pinto was unequivocal in his appraisal of King Kong's role in the Arnhem disaster:

One man – and one man only – made the Arnhem landings a doomed venture from the start. He was a Dutchman named Christiaan Lindemans. Whether or not we can blame him for the final six months' prolongation of the European war with all its attendant sacrifices and tragedies, we can certainly charge him with the 7,000 casualties suffered by the gallant Airborne Forces during the ten days in which the trap they had dropped into slowly closed its jaws on them. Few spies turned traitors could claim responsibility for dealing such damage at one blow to their country's cause and the cause of their country's allies.

In October 1944 Lindemans was arrested in Eindhoven on information provided by an *Abwehr* informant, Cornelius Verloop, who claimed that King Kong had betrayed Market Garden to a Major Wiesekotter on 15 September, at the *Abwehr* station in Driebergen. According to Pinto, Lindemans made a 'full and detailed' statement in which he confessed that he had met Wiesekotter and told him 'all the secret facts' two days before the Allied airborne carpet arrived on Dutch soil. Pinto went on to assert:

It is true that Lindemans did not mention the word 'Arnhem.' A certain section of the Dutch press subsequently tried to make much of this and claimed that Lindemans could not have betrayed Arnhem because he did not know the exact area of the landings. This argument is puerile nonsense. Lindemans may not have mentioned the actual name but he did tell Wiesekotter that the landings were to take place north of Eindhoven. He said as much in his signed confession . . . One glance at the map would suffice to tell the German military experts what points these airborne troops would be concentrated . . . The obvious targets were the bridges at Grave, Nijmegen and Arnhem.

However the following year Pinto was contradicted by Hermann Giskes, the former *Abwehr* counter-espionage chief in the Low Countries and northern France, whose account of their operations in Holland was published as *London Calling North Pole*. Giskes revealed that although Lindemans had indeed made contact with the *Abwehr*, and warned that Allied troops were standing by for a large-scale airborne landing, his information had been vague:

He knew that English and American parachute and airborne divisions were standing by in England for a big airborne operation . . . In any case there was no mention of Arnhem – King Kong had not mentioned it probably because he simply did not know in what area the airborne attack was going to be made . . . To the IC of the General Staff in Holland he was simply a suspicious foreigner who could well have been sent across for deception purposes.

Giskes took the view that if anything had betrayed Operation Market Garden, it was signals intelligence:

The traffic heard on 15th September was a conclusive indication of the imminence of a large-scale enemy air operation. Apart from this, on the afternoon of the 15th two English aircraft made a reconnaissance of some hours' duration over Nijmegen and Arnhem [and] were given a very large fighter escort . . . I heard that the German Command in Holland attributed this to the fact that a personal reconnaissance was being flown by the commanders of the attacking divisions being held in readiness in England.

At best, therefore, the warning given by Lindemans was simply one of several factors which alerted the Germans in Holland to the coming assault from the sky. As Nigel West points out in *Unreliable Witness*, Lindemans may still have thought that such warning as he did give was sufficient, and this, coupled with the disastrous outcome of the operation, persuaded him to sign the confession described by Pinto. Yet even this is doubtful, for according to Pinto when a trial was mooted the Lindemans dossier quickly went missing:

> When I went to get the vital file it was not in its proper place. I searched carefully on neighbouring shelves and in nearby filing cabinets in case it had been accidently filed away in the wrong place. There was no sign of it . . . There was no entry to show that there had ever been a file on the Lindemans case. In fact the very name 'Lindemans' had been carefully and completely expunged!

The legend of Lindemans as the butcher of Arnhem should have died with the publication of *London Calling North Pole*, but was revived by John Bulloch in *Akin to Treason* in 1966, and exhumed again in 1969 by the Dutch writer Anne Laurens. In her somewhat convoluted account, *The Lindemans Affair*, Laurens concluded that King Kong had been a double agent, and had acted in furtherance of a complicated Allied deception plan:

> The *Abwehr* had poisoned so many networks that they [the Allies] no longer knew where they were. It was imperative that they retaliate by infiltrating an agent into Colonel Giske's organisation. A double agent who would arrive telling such a plausible story that the Germans would swallow it completely.

Laurens also believed that Lindemans had been sacrificed by his Allied controllers:

> Finally, the last most diabolical stroke, a double [agent] was needed who could be sacrificed if need be, if the operation went wrong or if his services became useless, a double therefore who could not pride himself on having many influential relationships.

Although Laurens was unable to identify those responsible for the scheme on the Allied side, she felt certain that:

> They had only forgotten one thing, these Machiavellian leaders, and that was to warn Christiaan that if ever someone from his side accused him of

treason, nobody would lift a finger to help him. Indeed, if necessary, they would plunge him in deeper, if it served their purposes.

None of this makes any sense at all, or explains why Lindemans chose to take his own life. Nonetheless, Laurens went further still, and claimed that the clash between Pinto and Lindemans had its root in the fairer sex. In *Spycatcher* Pinto made several references to King Kong's 'countless amours and intrigues' and 'gross appetites', and wrote that the traitor was both a 'superb muscular athlete with a reputation for turning girls' heads' and 'famed for his sexual prowess'. According to Laurens, this was simply jealousy on the part of Pinto, and represented:

> A curious moral judgment by a man whose private life was, to say the least, stormy. He himself had been accused by his superiors of having had intimate relations with women 'with whom he dropped his guard', even though they were, beyond doubt, enemy agents.

Oddly, Laurens accepted Pinto's claims about a 24-page confession at face value, and was obliged to concoct a fantastical explanation in which Lindemans betrayed Arnhem to the *Abwehr* on the orders of his British spymasters. The notion is quite absurd, and is directly contradicted by a number of other German officers besides Giske. General Kurt Student, chief of Germany's own airborne forces, later stated that nothing was known about the attack until it happened, and described the story that Lindemans had been questioned at his HQ at Vught as 'a big fat lie'. Moreover the two SS Panzer divisions refitting in the area were already in position before 10 September, when Montgomery and Eisenhower met and agreed to execute Market Garden. Furthermore many crucial details of the Allied plan, such as placement of drop zones, were not settled until after Lindemans had crossed the German lines.

The only accurate account of the affair was given by Colonel J.M. Langley himself, who had authorised Lindemans's supposed mission in 1944 and published *Fight Another Day* 22 years later. Of King Kong he recalled:

> He asked to be sent through the lines near Eindhoven to collect evaders he was sure would be hiding with his resistance friends in that area. The relevant Army Group intelligence section had already checked King Kong's credentials and had reported 'nothing known against.' The Dutch army commander agreed to the mission but the head of their counter-espionage section, Colonel Oreste Pinto, sent me a private warning that he believed it possible that King Kong was a German agent, though as yet he had no proof. For King Kong's subsequent action I must accept responsibility.

As we have seen, however, those actions are unlikely to have included an effective betrayal of the Arnhem débâcle. An official enquiry exonerated Langley of any blame on the basis of the security clearance issued by 21st

Army Group, although it also found that he should have taken Pinto's warning more seriously. As to how Lindemans had learned anything of Market Garden:

> Exhaustive enquiries were made into the activities of King Kong during the time he was behind Allied lines, and the indications were that he had been in contact with individuals who knew of plans to use the British and American airborne divisions but that he could not possibly have discovered the actual dropping zones.

Langley also records an intelligence windfall which tends to confirm the account given by Giskes in 1966:

> Months later I was informed that the relevant German intelligence documents had been captured together with one of the officers who had 'worked' King Kong. The latter had reported plans for airborne landings but said that the targets were first Eindhoven and later possibly the bridges across the river Maas at Venlo and Roermond. The German officer stated that King Kong was a very minor agent whose task was to identify Allied units in the immediate battle area and they had not believed his report, putting it down to his boastful imagination.

Imagination is certainly an apposite word when considering the various theories advanced about betrayal at Dieppe and Arnhem.

CHAPTER TWELVE

Crash Myths and Foo Fighters

The most enduring crash legend of the Second World War hinges on the mysterious death of the legendary big band leader Glenn Miller, who disappeared en route to Paris in December 1944. Because his loss was unexpected, and the facts so sparse, several colourful theories developed around Miller's fate, and the case still features in omnibus collections of unsolved aviation mysteries. Like the deaths of Joseph Kennedy Jnr, Leslie Howard and General Wladyslaw Sikorski, also examined in this chapter, speculation and conjecture continue to flourish, providing a field day for fibbers and fantasists alike.

The events leading up to the disappearance of Major Glenn Miller are a matter of historical record. On the evening of Tuesday 12 December Miller and his band gave their last live performance at the Queensbury All Services Club in London's Soho, before preparing to leave for a six-week tour of American bases and field hospitals in France. The weather conditions were terrible, with much of England covered by a heavy fog which grounded most flights across the Channel, including the so-called 'SHAEF Shuttle' between Paris and Bovingdon airfield in Hertfordshire. Miller managed to obtain a favour from a friend, Lieutenant-Colonel Norman Baessell, who arranged a private flight to Villacoublay in a small Noorduyn Norseman from an airstrip at Twinwood Farm, three miles north of Bedford. The pilot, a Flight Officer John Morgan, omitted to register a flight plan, and took off into freezing fog at 1.55 pm on Friday 15 December 1944, on a journey which should have lasted approximately three hours. However the aircraft never reached its destination, and Miller was not missed for three days, until his band arrived at Orly on the 18th.

After taking off, Morgan probably flew west, then south to pass west of Greater London, which at the time was a no-fly zone. The likely flight path would have then crossed the Thames and overflown Sussex, before leaving England above Newhaven or Beachy Head and heading out over the Channel towards France. After Miller was reported missing, both SHAEF and the US Air Force checked with every airfield across the United Kingdom and liberated

Europe in the week before Christmas, yet no trace of the missing Norseman was found, save for one report of an unidentified light aircraft flying out over the Sussex coast on 15 December. The USAAF concluded that the Norseman iced up in harsh weather and crashed into the sea, although at an Eighth Air Force inquiry held on 20 January 1945 it was noted that had this occurred, the wings should have detached and remained afloat for up to 18 hours. However, even if the occupants had survived the ditching, they would hardly have lasted long in the freezing water. Indeed on 15 December 1945, precisely one year after they had disappeared, Miller, Morgan and Baessell were officially declared dead.

Long before, wild rumours began to circulate among American personnel that there had been no crash at all, and that Miller had instead been stabbed to death in a bar fight in a Paris brothel, or shot by an American MP during a similar sordid fracas. Other stories put about in the late 1940s included suggestions that Miller was a German spy, or a black marketeer, or a physical or psychological wreck confined to an ex-servicemen's home, unable to face the world. Later still it was reported that he had been murdered, or disfigured in a fire, or captured by the Germans and executed by the SS. Most of these lurid Miller myths were substantially debunked by his former executive officer, Don Haynes, in a detailed article printed in the special tribute issue of *Down Beat* magazine in 1951, although some are still resurrected in the press from time to time. An earlier attempt to correct various falsehoods had been made in 1946 by Paul Dudley, formerly programme director for the AEF Band:

> The following facts are listed to belie the fictions of the many rumour-happy gossipers who have erroneously reported the details surrounding Major Miller's departure. For those whose carelessly flapping tongues have reported that they witnessed Glenn taking off in a twin-engine Douglas C-47, it was actually a single-engine Norseman C-64, an all-metal plane equipped with a one-way radio, fixed landing gear and a reputation for treachery in bad weather. For those badly informed 'experts' who claim that Miller was flying without orders, he was proceeding under official order issued by SHAEF (Rear) to travel via Military Aircraft to the Continent on or about December 15th. For the hundreds of others whose adventuresome imaginations have claimed that 'they were supposed to have been on the same plane', it was a seven-passenger ship. It was flown by a pilot who had completed a lengthy tour of combat missions, Flight Officer Johnny Morgan.

In truth the latter 'fact' was itself erroneous, for Morgan was simply a ferry pilot and is said to have been inexperienced at instrument flying. Other Miller myths that have emerged over the years include the claim that the Norseman lacked sufficient range to fly to Paris non-stop (easily refuted by its 1,150-mile range at normal cruising speed), and that the lack of wreckage in the Channel indicates the aircraft crashed in England, either in the Chiltern Hills or South Downs. On several occasions wreckage recovered from the sea bed has been heralded as belonging to Miller's Norseman, including artefacts discovered by a diver off Calais in 1973, and engine parts trawled up by fishing boat off Newhaven four years later.

A sensationalist article printed in the German tabloid *Bild* in 1997 claimed that a British diver named Clive Ward had located the remains of the Norseman off Calais in 1985, that there were no signs of human remains, and that the aircraft was undamaged. The same article claimed that a German journalist named Udo Ulfkotte had uncovered evidence that Miller did arrive in Paris on 14 December, but died of a stroke the following day while visiting a brothel. None of these revelations were backed by documentation, but *Bild* nevertheless managed to construct an elaborate (if highly unlikely) conspiracy theory involving fake crashes and missing bodies, all for the sake of maintaining American morale. Stranger – and sadder – were a series of bizarre claims made by the bandleader's younger brother Herb Miller, who stated in 1983 that the Norseman had indeed taken off from Twinwood Farm, but had been forced to land after thirty minutes because his brother was too ill to continue the flight. By this version Glenn Miller died of lung cancer in a military hospital the following day, after which Herb himself fabricated the story of the Channel crash because his brother had wanted to die a hero, rather than bedridden. The US military authorities politely declined to substantiate the tale, and quite why Herb Miller chose to publicise it remains obscure.

While it is entirely plausible that Miller's Norseman iced up above the Channel and dropped like a stone, it is equally possible that it was inadvertently brought down by Allied bombers in the bomb jettison zone north-west of Dieppe. The theory was first put forward in 1984 by a former RAF navigator named Fred Shaw who, in December 1944, was on Lancasters with 149 Squadron. According to Shaw, on the afternoon of 15 December his crew were returning as part of a large force from an aborted raid on the German town of Siegen. In accordance with standard practice, the force was obliged to drop their bombs inside the southern jettison zone before returning to base, and did so just after 1.40 pm. During this operation Shaw saw a small aircraft flying far below them, which was tipped over by blast waves from the bombs and plunged into the sea. Although the type was relatively uncommon in Europe, Shaw recognised the aircraft as a Norseman since he had become familiar with the type while training at Manitoba in Canada.

Shaw's claim has been the subject of heated debate ever since, but seems to hold up under scrutiny. While Shaw failed to report the incident on returning to base, it is clear that it was discussed amongst 149 Squadron aircrew at the time, and the Norseman would have needed to deviate from its probable course by only eight degrees to enter the eastern edge of the bomb jettison zone. Given that Morgan was an inexperienced instrument flyer, navigating by magnetic compass alone over featureless water, such an error would have been all too easy to make. For many years the story was dismissed on the ground that the returning bomber force reached the zone at 1.40 pm, when Miller was still on the ground at Twinwood Farm. However, this anomaly was explained by aviation historian Roy Nesbit, who pointed out that in 1944 the Americans used local time when writing up records, whereas the RAF used Greenwich Mean Time – precisely one hour different. Shaw passed away in 1992, although in 1999 his logbook was auctioned by Sotheby's for a staggering £22,000. The true fate of Miller and his aircraft is never likely to be established with absolute certainly. Ice or bombs, however, there remains little real mystery.

The death of Lieutenant Joseph P. Kennedy Jnr in August 1944 has also given rise to a latter-day conspiracy theory. Although little known in his own right, Kennedy was the eldest son of the former American Ambassador to Britain, also named Joseph, and brother to Teddy, Bobby and Jack Kennedy, the latter becoming the 35th President of the United States before his assassination in Dallas in 1963. In 1944 Joe Kennedy was an experienced combat pilot in the US Naval Reserve, and had volunteered for a hazardous operation known as Project Anvil, in which stripped down B17 and B24 bombers were refitted as radio-controlled flying bombs for use against German submarine and V-weapon bases. On 12 August Kennedy and another pilot took off from Fersfield in Suffolk in a B24 Liberator call-signed Zootsuit Black, laden with twelve tons of Torpex explosive, intended for launch against a V3 target at Mimoyecques near Calais. Once airborne, the two men took their B24 flying bomb up to 2,000 feet, and once over the Blyth estuary near Southwold, prepared to head south towards a point near RAF Manston in Kent, where they would bale out. However at 6.20 pm, when the radio controller in the escorting Ventura aircraft transmitted a test signal to Zootsuit Black, the aircraft was destroyed by two almighty blasts, and the wreckage spread over a mile-wide area.

Joseph Kennedy and his co-pilot Wilford Willy were killed instantly, and today his death is often cited as the first in a long line of tragedies to befall the hapless Kennedy family. Nevertheless, in 1986 a former *Luftwaffe* artillery officer named Karl-Heinz Wehn claimed to have captured Joe Kennedy in France on 14 July, a full month before the drone explosion above Suffolk. According to Wehn, who was then serving with a flak battery near Grimbosq, south-west of Caen, his battery hit an American four-engined bomber which then crashed into the sea near Bayeux. Two crew members baled out of the stricken aircraft and landed close to his gun position, where they were captured by men of the 12th Panzer Division. The two men were then questioned by Wehn:

The first prisoner said his name was Joe Kennedy, First Lieutenant, US Air Force. 'I didn't understand at first,' Wehn recalled, 'and asked him to repeat this. He did, adding that he was from Hyannisport, near Boston, Massachusetts, USA. When I asked him what he did before the war, he said he helped his father. When I asked him what his father did, he said he was the American Ambassador in London before the war, then owned a shipping company in Boston.'

Wehn also claimed that the man's flight overalls carried an identity tag which confirmed his name, rank and number. Later that day, the two Americans were handed over to a detachment of SS troops, and were shot dead while trying to escape across a river. The bodies were supposedly buried on 15 July just outside the churchyard at St-André-sur-Orne. Assuming Wehn was telling the truth, the simplest explanation would be that he encountered another flier named Joe Kennedy, who thought that by claiming to be the son of a prominent American he might make his period in captivity more comfortable. However, no other pilots called Joe Kennedy appear in American military records, let alone in the US Naval Reserve. If Joe Kennedy Jnr really did die in combat in France in July 1944, it is hard to imagine why his death would have been transposed to Project Anvil, and in the final analysis it is hard to conclude otherwise than that Wehn was mistaken. In closing, many American sources cite Kennedy as having died on a combat mission over the English Channel, but this shorthand description is plainly misleading. And although 147 properties in the Blythburgh area sustained some form of damage, postwar American claims that three complete Suffolk villages were obliterated are somewhat exaggerated.

A B24 Liberator aircraft also features in the mysterious death of General Wladyslaw Sikorski, leader of the Free Polish forces and the Polish government in exile. On the night of 4 July 1943 a heavily laden RAF Liberator took off from the short airstrip on Gibraltar bound for Britain, only to plunge into the sea half a mile offshore, killing Sikorski and everyone else on board except the Czech pilot, Edward Prchal. Despite several official inquiries and reports the cause of the accident was never established, which in turn gave rise to much speculation and rumour. The common thread running through this conjecture was that Sikorski had been assassinated, although whether the plot was British, Russian or German in origin remained the subject of heated debate, particularly in the late 1960s.

The least likely candidates are the Germans. On 13 April 1943 Berlin radio had announced the discovery of the bodies of some 10,000 Polish officers in a mass grave in the Katyn Forest near Smolensk, and blamed the Russians for the massacre. Moscow countered that the Germans were responsible for the atrocity, but few were convinced. As early as December 1941 Sikorski had pressed Stalin on the fate of 14,000 missing Polish officers, only to be told they had fled to Manchuria. On 26 April 1943 Moscow broke off diplomatic relations with the Free Polish government, and accused Sikorski of colluding with the Nazis over Katyn. Given that a rift of this kind between Allies was a godsend to Berlin, and that Sikorski was a staunch anti-communist, it seems safe to assume Sikorski was more use to the Germans alive than dead.

Indeed, when Sikorski was killed in July Goebbels's propaganda machine wasted no time in broadcasting the news across Europe, and claimed the crash had been engineered by the 'British Secret Service' because the Free Polish leader had undermined Allied relations with Stalin. German radio also described Sikorski as 'the last victim of Katyn' and wondered whether the pilot, Edward Prchal, would feature in a future Honours List. In their book *They Spied on England*, published in 1958, Charles Wighton and Gunter Peis offered that General Erwin Lahousen, the head of *Abwehr* II, confirmed that *Abwehr* agents caused the crash by putting sugar in the Liberator's fuel tanks. However, Lahousen's contemporary diaries make no mention of such an operation, and this supposed claim of sabotage seems highly unlikely.

While pointing no fingers, the idea that Sikorski's aircraft was sabotaged was also advanced by the controversial historian David Irving in his book *Accident: The Death of General Sikorski*, published in 1967. This minutely researched volume remains the definitive account of the events surrounding the crash, and revealed that there had been two previous attempts to kill the Polish leader. In March 1942 a bomb was found in the aircraft carrying Sikorski from Prestwick to Canada, en route for a meeting with President Roosevelt, while in November a Lockheed Hudson carrying him from Montreal to Washington suffered sudden engine failure shortly after take-off, resulting in a crash landing. Irving also established that De Gaulle had also been involved in a suspicious near-accident involving a Wellington bomber in April 1943. Even in wartime these circumstances seem highly suspicious. Indeed, Stalin was apparently fond of repeating the German canard that Sikorski was murdered by British intelligence, yet this seems unlikely, if only because two MI6 men named Pinder and Lock were among the victims on board the general's Liberator.

In writing his book Irving 'failed to obtain the close cooperation' of the pilot Edward Prchal, who was still alive and well and living in the United States. That Prchal declined to cooperate is hardly surprising. The following year a play by Rolf Hochhuth called *Soldaten* (translated as *Soldiers*) was staged in London, which implied that Churchill had arranged the death of Sikorski for political motives. Hochhuth claimed he had based his information on the evidence of an anonymous 'English colonel who had been in charge of the sabotage team', now living in Switzerland, who had lodged documentary proof of the operation in a Swiss bank vault. The playwright also let it be known that Prchal had been 'paid a large amount of money to do the job', in the mistaken belief that he had been fatally stabbed in a bar brawl in Chicago some years earlier. Unsurprisingly, the undead Edward Prchal sued for libel and was awarded substantial damages.

The official RAF Court of Inquiry into the incident opened in Gibraltar on 7 July 1943. Prchal, an experienced flyer, was unable to explain the crash beyond stating that the controls had seized. He was said to have indicated that his co-pilot, Squadron Leader W.S. Herring, was unfamiliar with the Liberator, and in trying to raise the undercarriage may have operated a lever which locked the controls, although later Prchal denied suggesting this. Prchal also denied that the aircraft had been overloaded, or that he had smuggled a large quantity of furs and oranges on board. The fact that Sikorski himself selected Prchal as his pilot shortly before the flight tends to suggest that the Czech was innocent of deliberately causing the crash, although the Governor of Gibraltar, General Sir Noel Mason-Macfarlane, seems to have harboured suspicions:

There was one very extraordinary fact. The pilot, like nearly all pilots, had his idiosyncrasies, and he never under any circumstances wore his Mae West

. . . He stoutly maintained in evidence that he had not departed from his usual practice, and that when he started his take off run he was not wearing his Mae West. The fact remains that when he was picked up out of the water he was found to be not only wearing his Mae West, but every tape and fastening had been properly put on and done up.

After three weeks the inquiry ruled out sabotage as the cause of the accident, but failed to identify any precise cause. A second inquiry, ordered by Churchill a fortnight later, was similarly unable to pinpoint the fault, but cleared Prchal of any blame. The rumours were slow to fade, however, and a number of mysterious deaths and murders have since been linked with the Sikorski case. These include the diver Lionel 'Buster' Crabb, who vanished in Portsmouth harbour in 1956, and two Polish women, Christina Granville and Countess Teresa Lubienska, stabbed to death in 1952 and 1957 respectively. The Polish officer who discovered the bomb on the earlier flight in March 1942 is often reported to have been killed after being hit by a tram or lorry, although in reality he succumbed to pneumonia after a period of mental illness.

Another air death to which myth and legend attach is that of actor Leslie Howard, who was killed when a civilian BOAC airliner was shot down over the Bay of Biscay in June 1943. Howard was returning to Britain from Lisbon with his business manager, Alfred Chenhalls, and although such flights were always hazardous in wartime, the Douglas DC3 should have been safe from attack by virtue of its pale blue colour scheme, wing stripes and civilian identification code. Instead of shadowing the DC3, however, a squadron of Ju 88 fighter-bombers from KG 40 shot the airliner down. There were no survivors, and the tragedy quickly attained the status of an unsolved mystery. Questions were raised in the House of Commons over whether the aircrew had baled out, leaving the thirteen passengers to their fate. One rumour held that Churchill had planted his own double on the flight in order to cover his return journey from North Africa, with tragic results, although this was later denied by Churchill himself:

The regular commercial aircraft was about to start from the Lisbon airfield when a thickset man smoking a cigar walked up and was thought to be a passenger upon it. The German agents therefore signalled that I was on board . . . The brutality of the Germans was only matched by the stupidity of their agents. It is difficult to understand how anyone could imagine that with all the resources of Great Britain at my disposal, I should have booked a passage in an unarmed and unescorted plane from Lisbon and flown home in broad daylight.

The 'thickset man' was apparently Alfred Chenhalls. Others felt that Howard himself was the target, on the basis that he was a British agent, or because films such as *49th Parallel*, *Pimpernel Smith* and *The First of the Few* were of 'inestimable value' as Allied propaganda. Another theory holds that Wilfrid

Israel, the founder of the Jewish Refugee Mission in London, was the real target, and was suspected by Germany of recruiting Jewish scientists to the Allied cause. Yet another theory held that important documents were on board the aircraft. The true reason for the destruction of the DC3 will never be known, for the relevant *Luftwaffe* operational records were destroyed at the end of the war, and surviving aircrew from KG 40 were understandably reluctant to discuss the incident.

Myths and legends attach to many aircraft types, and most lie beyond the scope of this study. That said, the timing and impact of the propaganda surrounding the Boulton Paul Defiant must stand as an exception. Designed to destroy unescorted bomber formations, the Defiant carried no forward armament but packed a formidable punch from four Browning machine-guns mounted in a turret behind the pilot. Because the 'Diffie' bore a superficial resemblance to the Hurricane, at the time of the Dunkirk evacuation it was said that German fighter pilots were fooled into bouncing the type from behind, and were shot down in droves. Indeed on 29 May 1940 the only operational Defiant unit, 264 Squadron, claimed to have shot down 37 enemy aircraft during two sorties over the Channel, without loss to themselves. The achievement 'remained unequalled throughout the war' and Squadron Leader Phillip Hunter was later awarded the Distinguished Service Order. On this day of days 264 Squadron received a signal from 11 Group:

> The Air Officer Commanding sends sincere congratulations to 264 Squadron on their excellent performance in shooting down over 30 enemy aircraft without losing a single pilot, one of whom brought back his aeroplane minus both elevators and an aileron.

The Defiants' miraculous performance was gleefully reported in daily newspapers, and even by several diarists of the day. Shortly afterwards Lord Beaverbrook wrote to Boulton Paul in his capacity as Minister of Aircraft Production:

> Thirty-five Junkers bombers, 13 Heinkel bombers and 30 Messerschmitt fighters fell to the guns of the Defiants. That was the bag! That was the fruit of your labours, of the skill and devotion which has made the Defiant so formidable a defender of our homes and our liberty. It is a magnificent achievement. The pilots in the RAF rejoice in the splendid weapon which you have given them. I send my warmest congratulations to you all.

The senior figures perpetuated the myth of the deadly Defiants, but the truth was very different. Having entered service in October 1939, teething problems saw all aircraft of the type grounded in January 1940, with the result that Defiants only became operational in March, and first saw combat on 12 May. The very next day five out of six were shot down during an encounter with the *Luftwaffe* over Holland, while over four days in July 264 Squadron lost eleven aircraft and fourteen aircrew. A second Defiant squadron, 141, lost six out of seven aircraft on 19 July on a coastal patrol, and both units were hurriedly moved out of the firing line.

As for the glorious turkey-shoot above Dunkirk on 29 May, it never took place. Although the Defiants claimed a total of 37 enemy aircraft destroyed, including 15 Bf 109 fighters, on the day in question total German air losses in all areas amounted to just 14 machines. How many fell to the Diffies is impossible to say, although the total was almost certainly less than ten, and only two of these Bf 109s. Meanwhile Defiants were being shot out of the sky like so many pheasants, and the various puffs and congratulations sent to 264 Squadron and Boulton Paul supportive gestures to beleaguered servants, at a time when the BEF were being evacuated from France and the war appeared lost. The Defiant was quickly reassigned as a night fighter, and later relegated to air sea rescue and target-tug duties. Remarkably, despite its essential failure as a combat type no fewer than 1,062 examples of the Defiant had been built by the end of the war.

A rather less desperate RAF myth held that night fighter pilots ate prodigious quantities of carrots to improve their night vision. The story was first attached to Group Captain John Cunningham of 604 Squadron, who emerged from the war as the leading night fighter ace with 20 confirmed kills. On 23 December 1940 Cunningham was the first RAF pilot to bring down an enemy bomber with the aid of radar, but since the new air interception (AI) equipment was still a closely guarded secret, the press were informed that Cunningham possessed miraculous night vision. The nickname 'Cat's Eyes' Cunningham inevitably followed, as did reports that he ate vast quantities of carrots, whose Vitamin A content helped to maintain his extraordinary powers. The falsehood is said to have served two purposes, in that it deceived the enemy in relation to new developments in airborne interception radar, while at the same time promoting the value of carrots in rationed, blacked-out Britain. However, it seems unlikely that the Germans ever gave the story much credence. Cunningham, incidentally, detested the nickname that was forced upon him.

During and after the Second World War it was often rumoured that several Allied pilots had deserted to neutral Sweden, either through cowardice or dubious political allegiance. In the flippant language of Coastal Command aircrew, a spell of comfortable internment in Sweden was apparently referred to as 'Going to Brighton'. However, thorough research by Rolph Wegmann and Bo Widfelt has established that the story is groundless in relation both to RAF and USAAF personnel. An associated rumour concerning American aircrew of German extraction was also commonplace up and down the country, a typical example being given by Derek Johnson in *East Anglia at War*:

The story concerned a group of fliers based at Rougham. Being of German extraction, these men refused point blank to strike at German targets because they might be dropping bombs on relatives. The men were grounded until replacement crews arrived from the States, but a number of planes were sabotaged. When the bombers finally set off on a mission, several were supposed to have blown up over the Channel. A secret investigation was carried out, several arrests were made, and after a drum-head court martial, a number of men were executed on the spot.

Another dubious legend involving the USAAF centres on the cursed airfield at Boreham, near Chelmsford in Essex, which enjoyed one of the briefest service lives of any Field of Little America. In May 1943 the 861st Engineer Aviation Battalion began work on building a new airfield at Boreham, work which involved moving a large stone in Dukes Wood. According to local lore:

A certain stone, thought by some to be of significance, it was possibly marking the grave of a witch, was found and removed. A disease amongst the cattle nearby was attributed to the witch's revenge for desecrating her grave.

Others held that the stone was an ancient pagan altar, or marked the spot where a gamekeeper called William Hales had been murdered in 1856. It is said that local workers refused to disturb the stone, and that a bulldozer was badly damaged in what should have been a simple task. In October, before the airfield construction work was complete, a Thunderbolt from the 56th Fighter Group attempted a wheels-down emergency landing, and struck a bulldozer with its landing gear, killing the driver, while the station commander later died of a heart attack. Given that the infamous stone has for many years been displayed in the car park of the St Anne's Castle public house in Boreham, it would seem that its powers have waned with the passage of time. And if superstition of this stripe seems far-fetched in wartime, it is worth noting that the last recorded prosecution for assault on a supposed witch was recorded in East Dereham, Norfolk, in January 1941, when magistrates heard that a Mr Sutton had punched a Mrs Spinks after she had tortured him by 'witchcraft of the Dark Ages' for five years. Mrs Spinks in turn claimed that Sutton had behaved in a manner that would shame even Hitler.

The verdant mythology of UFOs, flying discs and so-called 'Foo Fighters' would require a book of its own to cover in detail, while much postwar commentary is so outlandish as to fall into the realm of pure fantasy. This is particularly true of the growing body of literature dealing with Nazi flying saucers and secret bases in Antarctica, which space precludes us from exploring here. Nevertheless, the several reports filed before the alleged saucer crash at Roswell in New Mexico in July 1947, which marks the dawn of modern UFO mythology, make for fascinating reading, none more so than the phantom Los Angeles air raid early in 1942. On 25 February, less than three months after the Japanese attack on Pearl Harbor, unidentified aircraft appeared in the night sky above Los Angeles, triggering widespread alarm and a blackout lasting five hours. At least a million residents of southern California were woken at 2.25 am by the wail of sirens, which also summoned 12,000 air raid wardens to their posts, all of whom assumed the alert to be a drill. At 3.16 am, as searchlights probed the pre-dawn sky, anti-aircraft batteries began firing the first of 1,430 shells, which in turn caused scattered properly damage and several fatalities on the ground. Despite this impressive barrage, however, none of the mysterious enemy raiders were brought down.

Quoting one Beverly Hills resident, who described the action as unfolding like a vast movie premiere, the *New York Times* reported the following day:

> Residents from Santa Monica southward to Long Beach, covering a 39 mile arc, watched from rooftops, hills and beaches as tracer bullets, with golden yellowish tints, and shells like skyrockets offered the first real show of the Second World War, on the United States mainland.

It was no coincidence that the man put in mind of a premiere was one Tom Clark, described as the enemy alien control coordinator for the Far West. For the phantom bombers laid bare a phantom fifth column, as the same paper reveals:

> During the blackout police telephones were busy with reports that airplanes had fallen here and there, that 'Japanese' were flashing signals from hilltops and that 'a Japanese' had been seen with a short wave radio apparatus on a rooftop, probably communicating with the approaching aircraft. Another report, discounted by officials along with some of the others, was that gunfire had destroyed a big long floating bag resembling a balloon high in the air.

The general enthusiasm for reporting and arresting fifth column suspects matched that seen in Poland, Holland and France two years earlier:

> Most of the [30] arrests were made on complaints of air raid wardens, who said the prisoners were attempting to signal or actually signalling with flashlights or lights in their homes. Some prisoners were turned over to the Federal Bureau of Investigation, several were fined and others were held for court hearings. FBI spokesmen said that they had been requested by Army officers not to discuss the arrests.

Well-worn fifth column myths had been floated in the wake of the attack on Pearl Harbor, when it was said that Japanese working on Oahu had cut large arrows in fields to guide the attacking planes towards their target. Another story told of a dog barking in Morse on a beach for the benefit of a Japanese submarine skulking offshore.

At the time, the closest the press came to linking the Los Angeles flap with a UFO was in describing the target as a 'big long floating bag' at high altitude. Some eyewitnesses claimed to have seen as many as 27 aircraft, yet others saw none at all, while a syndicated photograph appeared to show searchlights converging on a single large target, surrounded by exploding anti-aircraft shells. Others still experienced what might now be recognised as a classic UFO sighting, including Paul Collins, an employee of the Douglas aircraft company at Long Beach. While returning home Collins was stopped by a warden in Pasadena, then saw bright red spots of light low on the horizon to the south, moving in an unnatural manner:

> They seemed to be 'functioning' or navigating mostly on a level plane at that moment – that is, not rising up from the ground in an arc, or trajectory, or in a straight line and then falling back to earth, but appearing from nowhere and then zigzagging from side to side. Some disappeared, not diminishing in brilliance at all, but just vanishing into the night. Others remained pretty much on the same level and we could only guess their elevation to be about 10,000 feet.

Soon afterwards, Collins observed the red lights being fired upon by anti-aircraft guns:

> Taking into account our distance from Long Beach, the extensive pattern of firing from widely separated anti-aircraft batteries, and the movement of the unidentified red objects among and around the bursting shells in wide orbits, we estimated their top speed conservatively to be five miles per second . . . We did not see the enormous UFO seen by thousands of observers closer to the coast. Very likely it was below our horizon and a few miles further up the coast at that time.

Other witnesses are said to have seen a large machine which appeared impervious to AA salvos, and remained stationary before proceeding at a leisurely pace over the coastal areas between Santa Monica and Long Beach. In an official report sent to President Roosevelt, his Chief of Staff, General George C. Marshall, was able to offer nothing more than guesswork over far-fetched fifth column activity:

> As many as 15 airplanes may have been involved, flying at various speeds from what is officially reported as being 'very slow' to as much as 200 mph and at elevations from 9,000 to 18,000 feet . . . Investigation continuing. It seems reasonable to conclude that if unidentified airplanes were involved they may have been from commercial sources, operated by enemy agents for purposes of spreading alarm, disclosing locations of anti-aircraft positions, and slowing production through blackout. Such conclusion is supported by varying speed of operation and the fact no bombs were dropped.

This memorandum, written on 26 February, remained classified until 1974, and in the aftermath of the 'raid' itself local papers such as the *Long Beach*

Independent complained of a 'mysterious reticence' about the whole affair and that 'some form of censorship is trying to halt discussion of the matter'. Admiral Knox, the US Naval Secretary, later announced that the phantom raid had been nothing more than a false alarm triggered by jittery war nerves, but many remained unconvinced. Indeed some were adamant that the raid was a propaganda exercise staged with the object of relocating vital industries further inland. Whether official reticence owed anything to the mass panic caused by Orson Welles's celebrated radio broadcast of *War of the Worlds* in 1938 is impossible to say.

By 1944 sightings of unidentified – and unidentifiable – aircraft types had become commonplace for Allied pilots and aircrew, who dubbed them 'Krautballs' and Foo Fighters. The latter name was derived from a then-popular cartoon character named Smoky Stover, who was fond of observing 'Where there's foo, there's fire'. Foo Fighters were sighted both in Europe and the Pacific theatre, and were thought to be secret weapons of German or Japanese origin designed to interfere with the ignition systems of bombers. Few if any official reports reached the public, yet many were lodged by aircrew, and on 13 December 1944 Eisenhower's Supreme Headquarters Allied Expeditionary Force (SHAEF) in Paris issued a remarkable press release, variously headlined 'Floating Ball is New Nazi Air Weapon' (*New York Times*) and 'Like Toys on a Christmas Tree' (*South Wales Argus*). The *NYT* version ran thus:

> A new German weapon has made its appearance on the western air front, it was disclosed today. Airmen of the American Air Force report that they are encountering silver coloured spheres in the air over German territory. The spheres are encountered either singly or in clusters. Sometimes they are semi-translucent . . . The new device, apparently an air defence weapon, resembles the huge glass balls that adorn Christmas trees. There was no information available as to what holds them up like stars in the sky, what is in them, or what their purpose is supposed to be.

According to Reuters, the dispatch from one Major Marshall Yarrow was 'heavily censored' at SHAEF, and no more particulars emerged for a fortnight, when a substantive Foo Fighter story appeared in the New York *Herald Tribune* of 2 January 1945. This quoted a Lieutenant Donald Meiers, who testified that:

> There are three kinds of these lights we call Foo Fighters. One is a red ball which appears off our wing tips and flies along with us. No. 2 is a vertical row of three balls of fire, flying in front of us. No. 3 is a group of about 15 lights which appear in the distance, like a Christmas tree up in the air, and flicker on and off . . .
>
> On another occasion, when a Foo Fighter picked us up, I dived at 360 miles an hour. It kept right off our wing tips for a while, and then zoomed up into the sky. When I first saw the things off my wing tips I had the horrible thought that a German, on the ground, was ready to press a

button, and explode them. But they don't explode, or attack us. They just seem to follow us, like wills-o'-the-wisp.

In Britain, the *Daily Telegraph* ran a brief but broadly similar report a day earlier:

Phoo Fighters are the big topic among our intruder pilots. These are strange orange lights which follow their planes, sometimes flying in formation with them and eventually peeling off and climbing. Some have come within a few yards and have been shot out. Another type of phoo fighter appears under the wings, making a series of dull flashes.

Official sources attributed these sightings to combat fatigue, hallucinations, ball lightning and St Elmo's Fire, but already a myth had been born. Since 1945 the Foo Fighter legend has been endlessly churned and exaggerated, initially by Harold Wilkins in his 1954 book *Flying Saucers on the Moon*. In his second chapter, titled 'The Coming of the Foo Fighters', Wilkins wrote that:

It was in the war year, 1944, when both British and American pilots had singular experiences; but not a word of it has ever appeared in any British newspaper. In that year, censorship was stringent, but though other mysteries have been revealed since, this one has never had the veil of silence removed from it, so far as Britain is concerned . . .
   I happen to know that two British war pilots reported to intelligence officers, after a flight, that strange balls of fire had suddenly appeared while their own planes were on high-altitude flights. These mysterious balls had seemed to indulge in a sort of aerial ballet dance and had, so to speak, pirouetted on the wing tips of the planes. When the planes went into a power dive, these balls followed them down and outdistanced them, despite the fact that the planes were biting into the air with a strident scream at the vertiginous speed they were making. Other pilots reported that they had seen strange balls of blazing light flying in precise formation. The crew of one British bomber reported that 15 or 20 of these balls had followed their bomber at a distance.

Wilkins (whose other books include *Captain Kidd* and *Skeleton Island*) went on to relate the experiences of several American pilots over the Rhine area, the first of which had taken place in November. It was even said that on one occasion a luminous ball had entered a USAAF bomber through a hatch and flown up and down the fuselage, although Wilkins cited no official reports beyond the *Herald Tribune* news story from January 1945. Although the Foo Fighter legend has since been substantially debased, the elusive reality behind the candid SHAEF dispatch of 13 December 1944 remains both baffling and fantastical.
   Even before Wilkins published *Flying Saucers on the Moon*, a connected mythology concerning Nazi flying discs was already in circulation. In 1952 an

engineer and test pilot named Rudolph Schriever told the West German press that he had designed a 'flying top' for the *Luftwaffe* in 1941, which was flown the following year. His remarkable claims were enlarged in the book *German Secret Weapons of the Second World War*, written by Rudolf Lusar in 1957 and published in an English translation two years later. In this otherwise sensible book, which deals with technical developments across all weapon types between 1939 and 1945, Lusar included a brief and wholly unverifiable section on 'flying saucers' which ran as follows:

> During the war German research workers and scientists . . . built and tested such near-miraculous contraptions. Experts and collaborators confirm that the first projects, called flying discs, were undertaken in 1941. The designs . . . were drawn up by the German experts Schriever, Habermohl and Miethe, and the Italian Bellonzo. Habermohl and Schriever chose a wide-surface ring which rotated round a fixed, cupola-shaped cockpit . . . [They] worked in Prague, and took off with the first 'flying disc' on February 14 1945. Within three minutes they climbed to an altitude of 12,400 metres, and reached a speed of 2,000 km/h in horizontal flight. It was intended ultimately to achieve speeds of 4,000 km/h.

Lusar also conjured an illustration of the miraculous machine, suggesting that Klaus Habermohl had been captured by the Russians, while Walter Miethe joined Werner von Braun in the USA, thus fuelling a Cold War flying disc race.

Beyond their essentially fantastic nature, the principal objection to these claims is that neither Schriever or Lusar provided any corroborative evidence of any kind. The same is true of a claim first made in 1967 that the War Office had set up an investigation into foreign aerial objects in 1943, headed by a Lieutenant-General Massey, which was discontinued the following year after Massey reported that the phenomenal craft were not German, and that the *Luftwaffe* themselves were just as concerned by the phenomenon. On the evidence of *Who's Who*, this particular British officer never existed, and Project Massey must be dismissed as a fiction.

Ultimately the Foo Fighter legend remains suspended in a problematic X-Filed limbo, yet it perhaps bears comparison with the more orthodox myth of 'Scarecrows'. These were thought to be special shells fired by flak batteries into Allied bomber streams above Germany, the powerful detonation of which was said to resemble an exploding bomber, with the intention of demoralising aircrew. In fact the Germans had devised no such shells, and what the crews saw were indeed exploding aircraft. To this day, however, many Bomber Command veterans refuse to accept that the ingenious 'Scarecrows' were nothing of the sort.

The Fifth Column in France

In spite of these alarums and excursions in Louvain, I found time to attend an examination of suspected spies in Everburgh that afternoon. A special section had been created in each division to deal with spies and their twentieth-century cousins, the fifth columnists. It was called the Field Security Police. After four days of war in a country already overrun by Hitler's civilian army the divisional FSP were getting a bit rattled; they had been working night and day interviewing spies pretty continuously since they had arrived; and as they consisted of only one officer and ten NCOs, and had anything up to 500 spies and bogus spies to interview each day, they were extremely glad to get helpers. I knew their officer and, with a view to helping him later, I attended one of his examinations and watched him in action in the courtyard of the local school. He sat at a little table in the middle with a revolver in front of him.

Opposite herded into a corner by the NCOs were about 100 dejected-looking people, the suspects. I had never seen such a motley collection before in my life; the only thing common to them all was dirt, they were uniformly filthy, having just spent the night in the courtyard. Every walk of life seemed to be represented; there were priests, beggars, nuns, soldiers, shopkeepers; and every nationality; Belgians, Poles, Germans, Austrians, Czechs – even Indians.

I reflected how many CID officers would normally be employed in peace-time to interrogate such a number of alien criminals. Yet here today, in circumstances far more grave, was one officer with a handful of helpers, doing a day's work, only equalled I supposed, by the sum of all the work done by all the officers in Scotland Yard in a month.

The first suspect, a civilian, was brought up to the table. He was accompanied by a little woman who appeared to be the witness.

The captain consulted his notes.

'You were seen entering a house in Everburgh dressed as a Belgian soldier,' he said. 'You came out dressed as a civilian. You are a deserter. But I am not concerned with that. This lady says that you had a box with you at the time. It contained a portable wireless set.'

'That is a lie,' said the man.

'Do you admit that you had a box with you?'

'Yes.'

'What was in it?'

'Food. I will tell you what happened if you like.' The man now tried to be funny. He appeared quite intelligent. 'Since it seems to interest you so much,' he continued. 'There was a cake my wife baked for me. Let me see – and there were two pieces of bread and butter.' He scratched his head. 'Yes – then there was a sausage.' He looked at the woman who was giving evidence against him, 'but that old sow ate the sausage.'

There was an absolute torrent of abuse from the woman at this. She gabbled her words so indignantly and so fast that I could not make out what she was saying. The captain was evidently quite used to dealing with jokers. After one look at the fellow's identity cards he had decided what to do.

'Take him away. Hand him over to the French police,' he said.

This is a most extreme thing to do because the French police are not lenient with suspected spies; they treat them as guilty until they prove themselves innocent, giving them about a quarter of an hour in which to do it. Most of the other suspects, after an inspection of identity cards, were allowed to depart in peace – or rather in indignant rage; they all went off quietly, no one pelting is with stones and pebbles, as the sergeant told me one Belgian had done on a previous occasion; they were all only too glad to get away.

The Field Security Police are not the only set of detectives and general legal advisors in the division; there is also the Provost Section. In peace-time they provide the 'red caps' and any soldier will tell you what a nuisance they are when they come round on Friday evening, telling you to do up your buttons and trying to catch you out tight.

In war they take on the additional job of providing firing parties for spies, and their power extends over life and death; if the Field Security Police act as CID, the provost officer acts as the High Court judge. His power is prodigious. Our own divisional provost officer came to dinner one night, a Guards officer of the teutonic variety, a man obviously ideally suited to his work.

'Do you really shoot spies?' asked Stimpson, assuming a proper air of awe.

'Of course,' said the provost officer.

'And do you do it entirely on your own? I mean the trial and all that sort of thing.'

'Of course.'

'But I suppose you take very good care that they really are spies, don't you? I mean – it's a sort of absolute power of attorney, isn't it?'

The provost officer nodded his head.

'It's absolute all right,' he said, grinning at the adjutant.

Stimpson told me afterwards that he thought it a very barbarous reply, but he agreed with me that we would both sleep much more easily hereafter.

Extracted from Anthony Rhodes, *Sword of Bone* (1941), pp. 147–9.

APPENDIX TWO

The Rumor Racket

Three sergeants who shared a passion for practical jokes recently founded a little club. They called it Rumors, Inc. The club members devoted their spare time to bootleg lies to the other men in their outfit.

Every day or so the sergeants went into a huddle and polished up a story and released it through proper latrine channels. One morning the chow line buzzed with a new ruling that had just arrived at headquarters: Troops who had been overseas two years were going to be furloughed home on a special program of mass rotation. That one caused tremendous excitement – but nobody ever located the directive.

Another day a man in the know reported that canned beer from the States would be distributed with PX rations. Tongues were hanging out for days – but the PX people knew nothing about the deal. Once the grapevine had it that ten sacks of mail from home had been destroyed when a road mine blew the company jeep into little pieces. Another time there was anxious whispering about the Germans using gas in an adjacent sector and wiping out whole units. Some of the men – particularly the new men – bit every time. Most of the rumors left only a dull hangover of disappointment in the minds of their victims. But the one about poison gas spread terror until the CO called the men together. The sergeants got a big laugh out of their little game. They thought it was good clean fun. It just went to show that Barnum was right – a 'sucker' is born every minute.

Instead of calling their club 'Rumors, Inc.' The sergeants might have called it 'Murder, Inc.' That would have been more accurate.

Rumors can annihilate morale. They can kill men. And lose battles. And sabotage the entire war effort. The Germans are doing it every day.

A man doesn't have to be a mastermind to manufacture a rumor and get it into circulation. Any one can do it. All you need is a good memory or a little imagination – and no conscience.

In wartime especially, the rumor racket thrives. Soldiers have been suddenly thrust into a strange, uncertain environment. They are hungry for news of home, news of military operations. Limited communications and censorship security often bottle up specific details for weeks. The situation leads to worry, to hope, to speculation. Where information ends, guessing begins. Rumors masquerading as cold fact are swallowed whole. The longing to go home – the dream of victory – fear of the unknown – the boredom of waiting – the tension of battle – the discomforts and anxieties and privations of war all blunt a man's judgment and make him over-receptive to hearsay. Good news rumors are welcomed. Even a bad news rumor is better than nothing. At least it's something to gripe about.

Rumors start in a variety of ways. Not all are engineered deliberately by a sergeants' brainstrust. Many a rumor is born innocently enough and passed with the best of intentions from man to man. Unfortunately good intentions don't make a rumor harmless. The evidence is everywhere:

Two battalions, occupying a hill in a forest near G-, had been in contact with the enemy for several days. One afternoon the Germans hit with an infantry attack supported by tanks. A bedlam of firing and yelling echoed through the thick woods. Three men from one of the battalions rushed down the hill to the CP to report the progress of the battle. 'Our casualties are terrible,' a Pfc panted. He described how his outfit had been overrun, cut off and captured. The major lost no time in ordering a light tank platoon into action. Hours later the situation quietened down and the true facts of the attack were discovered. Two enemy tanks had penetrated the front line. They crashed around in the woods but did no heavy damage. One tank was promptly knocked out and the other withdrew. The German infantry had been driven back before it reached our line. In the entire operation, three Yanks had been wounded.

What had been rumored as a disastrous rout turned out to be quite a different matter. The men who had made the false report at the Bn CP thought they were honestly describing the situation. They had lost their heads. They promised it would never happen again – but the harm had been done.

All too often, under the pressure and confusion of attack, soldiers exaggerate the strength of the enemy and the extent of the losses he is inflicting. Their eyes and ears play monstrous tricks. Being prepared for the worst, they recognise the worst even when it has not arrived.

One dark night when the Germans counter-attacked a dug-in company with a flame-throwing tank, two Yanks panicked at the wrong time and rushed to the rear. One of them was slightly singed and the other had an arm wound. On the way back they ran into two supply men who were waiting with ammunition destined for their company. They warned them to scram because the company had been wiped out and the enemy tank was heading towards the improvised dump. The supply men didn't wait for verification of the rumor. They jumped into their jeep and made tracks. It was a tragic mistake. Eventually the company was destroyed – not by the initial attack – they repulsed that one – but because they never got the ammo that the supply men were sent to deliver.

Rumors run rampant under critical battle conditions – when they are hardest to control and when they can sabotage on the greatest scale. Truths and half-truths are quickly distorted beyond recognition. A chance remark at breakfast about a battalion's being in a tough spot has, by noon, grown to the point where that battalion is wiped out. A brief comment that a rifle company is running into stiff resistance will be magnified before sundown until a whole regiment has been forced to retreat ten miles.

A division commander offers this suggestion for controlling the rumor racket at the front line: 'If men would put some stock in the old adage about believing half of what they see and none of what they hear, they'd save lives and get this war over sooner.'

When you're at the front you can't be too careful about reporting what you see. Adding two and two and getting five is bad arithmetic – it leads to dangerous reports.

This incident took place a few weeks ago on the M-bridgehead. When the 88s opened up some shots fell in the Bn CP area which was located in a direct line with the guns and the bridge site. They caused a few casualties. The officer in charge of the CP immediately ordered it moved to the right rear. As the movement began, an ammo carrier from an adjacent company passed by. He sized up the situation (he thought) and hurried back to report to his CO that the Bn CP was withdrawing. On the strength of this news the CO of G Company cleared up the misunderstanding in time to forestall a wholesale evacuation. Just an example of a rumor at work. The ammo carrier believed he was reporting only what he had seen with his own eyes. In the excitement he failed to distinguish between a movement and a withdrawal. There's a big difference.

In other cases, men observing relieved units going back to the rear area have jumped to the conclusion that a retreat is in progress. Instead of getting the facts they start a hot rumor that takes a long time to cool off.

One of the most persistent of all front-line rumors deals with the dropping of German paratroopers. The report is turned in, units are alerted to round up the invaders – and more often than not, neither parachutists nor any evidence of their landing are discovered.

Usually the facts reveal an over-active imagination on the part of the observer. Here is the result of one investigation: 'Reports of 15 parachutes falling during the afternoon were run down and found to be balls of anti-radar window. Rumors were started by AAA men who had seen shining objects falling through their field glasses. This may account for a large percentage of our recent parachute alerts. Our watchfulness should not be relaxed. The dropping of enemy agents is still considered a strong possibility. However, all observers should make efforts to distinguish parachutists from 'window,'* which appear similar at high altitudes on clear, sunny days. Whenever there is

---

* Metallic strips, tissue paper thin, dropped from aircraft to interrupt radar detection.

any doubt, observer should include in his report altitude of drop and any other pertinent information that would aid in evaluation.'

Similarly, a sentinel in another sector reported that a hostile plane had dropped parachutes beyond a wooded area. No one else saw the chutes but the sentry stuck to his story. His report on the location, time and course of the plane checked exactly with the AAA records showing that an enemy plane had flown over at the specified hour. Rumors about German paratroopers in the woods spread quickly – until the official explanation was published: 'Flak bursts following the plane in the moonlight gave the appearance of parachutes.'

Quite a different type of rumor recently flared up in an occupied town near the German border. It was sparked by enlisted drivers of a unit attached to an infantry regiment stationed nearby. They told a lurid tale of two men from another regiment of the same division who had been found murdered. According to their story, which had all the excitement of a yarn out of *True Detective*, the partially disrobed bodies had been discovered in the second-floor bedroom of a home. The drivers hadn't actually seen the bodies but they had talked to a corporal who knew a man who had. Later in the week the total of Yanks murdered by civilians under mysterious circumstances had fattened to seventeen.

The Regimental Civil Affairs Officer began to probe for the facts. He questioned all units and attached units in the area. He made additional inquiries through civilian channels. The only basis for the grisly tale appeared to be that when a large neighbouring city had been taken, three or four French soldiers had been shot by civilian snipers during the clean-up fighting. Who was responsible for planting this rumor? It was probably the work of Nazi agents, plotting to foster bitter feeling between the American troops and French civilians. Nevertheless, the story demonstrates clearly one of the common earmarks of every successful rumor. The drivers who repeated the story originally hadn't actually seen the evidence. They had only talked to someone who knew someone else who claimed to be an eyewitness. Any respectable rumor must have authority to give it credibility.

Usually the authority is two or three times removed – 'someone who knows the buddy of a sergeant at Headquarters.'

Most of the rumors that have wide circulation in combat zones can be filed in three pigeonholes:

First – the deliberate falsehoods invented for the amusement of a small group – like the rumors spread by the first-mentioned sergeants.

Second – the rumors which result from an overheard remark and which are exaggerated and distorted and garbled in the retelling so that the final product bears no resemblance to the original.

Third – the rumors that come from an imperfect or too hasty estimate of the situation.

No matter what their source or how they start, rumors never accomplish any good. The more they are repeated, the more harm they do. Some rumors are bloodless. They simply deflate morale and cause needless disappointment. Some pack dynamite. They confuse and slow military operations, lead directly or indirectly to casualties. The only safe way to deal with front line rumors is to adopt an 'I'm from Missouri' attitude. Close your eyes to hearsay. Don't pass information on to the next foxhole that you can't personally vouch for. The CO will keep your unit posted on the battle picture. He'll let you know when other outfits are withdrawing – when enemy parachutists are landing in your rear. By ignoring chance and spurious remarks you'll save yourself a lot of worry. And by refusing to pass on 'unofficial' reports you can also make life a lot less rocky for the next fellow.

A sergeant in the field artillery recently made this excellent statement: 'One of the best allies the Krauts have is the rumor-spreader. He's the fellow who knows nothing and tells all. To troops fresh in combat, the rumor-spreader can lower efficiency and directly hamper military operations. To experienced troops the rumor-spreader is harmless because they've seen the result of his line. It's to the new men that he does real damage.

Ninety-nine per cent of the rumors are unintentional but they're just as harmful as the one per cent. Casual remarks and conversations overheard are the main sources of rumors. In combat the best thing to do is to ignore all you hear except from official sources. Report only what you see and when in doubt, state your doubt. I'm particularly interested in rumors because on about D plus 5 to D plus 10 they scared me more than anything before or since. They scared me to the point that I couldn't concentrate on my job. Anyone going into combat should keep his mouth shut and his ears shut to everything but official statements – and above all, keep your eyes open. You'll catch onto the game faster and live longer.'

Most experts admit that the world's greatest rumor factories are Nazi-controlled. Right now much of their tremendous output is directed towards one objective: Divide the United Nations – make them suspicious of one another – get them to bickering among themselves. After they've quibbled about little matters they'll split wide open on the major issues. The rift will undermine the efficient prosecution of the war. More important, it will make it impossible for them to enforce an effective peace.

Germany's survival as a power depends in a large measure on the success of its propaganda program. Its rumor mills are operating around the clock. Their production can't be curtailed by Allied bombers over the Reich. The mills operate underground with branches everywhere. Munitions are powerless to cope with Nazi rumors. A 105 can't explode an idea. A tank can't crush a concept. Reasoned action by the individual can kill a rumor, and his only weapon is common sense.

The Germans use various techniques in spreading rumors. Whispering campaigns, phony radio broadcasts, puppet orators, cleverly planted news items are just a few. Vital cog in the mechanism, however, is the fellow in the foxhole, the riveter in the shipyard, the housewife in the crossroads village. These people must co-operate as rumor mongers. They must pass on the sugar-coated lies, the counterfeit facts, the distorted half-truths that the enemy thrusts their way. If they don't fall into line, if they suppress the rumors they hear, the rumors will never achieve wide circulation, never become best-sellers, never gain wide acceptance. The whole Nazi program will bog down.

A story current not long ago had the USSR pulling out of the war as soon as the Red Army had pushed the Germans over the Soviet border. Do you remember? The wise guys had it all figured out. They shook their heads and warned: 'Watch Russia drop the Allies like a hot potato.' Did a German start it? That's typical of the way the Nazi rumor specialists are working to drive a wedge of distrust into the solidarity of the United Nations. The headlines of any paper today show just how groundless the prediction was. The men who had it all doped out have dropped that rumor now. Now they're mongering another lie – details different – objective the same.

Another typical tale spread by German propaganda agencies declared that almost no Britishers were engaged in front-line fighting and that they were pushing Dominion and Colonial soldiers and troops into all the hot spots. Thousands of Americans, Canadian and Australians were duped by the story until the facts were published. The figures on casualties and the actual disposition of British forces punctured the rumor flat.

Every whispering campaign against one of our Allies does serious damage – even though the falsity is eventually established. It seems to be a trait of human nature to believe the worst about the next fellow in the absence of black and white evidence to the contrary. When we hear that one of our Allies is a blackguard, we are, perversely, likely to be believe it on the flimsiest hearsay. When we are asked to believe that our Allies are fair and honest, we are unfortunately likely to insist on documentary proof. That sort of prejudice is particularly dangerous in times like these.

What happened to the rumor so prevalent a short time ago that Hitler was dead and buried? Wishful thinking gave that one wide acceptance. Legal minds assembled a lot of evidence that seemed to substantiate the Dictator's demise. His absence from the German scene could be explained in no other way. It was welcome news. Unfortunately it wasn't true.

Rumors about the sudden death of Churchill are beginning to appear with some consistency. The news is whispered about on a packed underground train or in a crowded pub – started by an unknown who has a friend who is very close to one of the under-secretaries in the War Office. Sometimes the dead man is Eisenhower. Sometimes Roosevelt. There are never any details – just the simple fact of death. Official denials can quickly squelch the lie. But meanwhile much worry and apprehension have been created. The day is coming when peace rumors will begin to flash around the world. Already a few premature reports have popped up in certain front line sectors. Fortunately not many men have been fooled.

The Germans capitalized on this type of demoraliser near the end of World War One. The Belgian radio announcement of victory early in September travelled with a speed no other news had been able to match during the war.

The denial, half an hour later took a couple of days to catch up with the first report. Troops relaxed – and Germans who might have been captured were able to retreat out of reach. Similar below-the-belt tactics can be expected now that World War Two is nearing its climax. Be on your guard. Don't swallow any tale about hostilities being over until you get it officially from your CO.

The Nazis pulled a neat trick out of their grab bag on 8 January of this year. It took many people by surprise and for a time threatened friendly relations between the American and British at a critical moment when the Germans were staging their Ardennes counter-offensive. A broadcast masquerading as the regular BBC news program praised the heroism of British troops in checking the Boche drive and accused the Yanks of falling down badly. Naturally this announcement made the Americans boil.

Although few of them actually heard the broadcast it didn't take long for the story to make the rounds. Many papers in the States picked it up. Some large metropolitan dailies gave the story front page prominence. Anglo-American relations were getting it squarely on the chin.

The true facts of the deception came later. The broadcast was traced to a station known as 'Arnhem Calling' – a powerful station operated by the Nazis in Holland, using the same wavelength as BBC. 'Arnhem Calling' relays genuine BBC broadcasts to the Allied troops and even picks up some AEF programs. But there's a catch. After the familiar chimes of Big Ben are heard, the Germans fade out the real program and substitute their own propaganda news bulletin – delivered in perfect English. Later they fade back to the original program. Subsequent broadcasts over this same bogus station were equally clever – and almost as disruptive. But troops at the front are learning to spot the voice of the announcer. They have nicknamed her 'Mary of Arnhem' and now when Mary begins to throw mud at the British or the Americans or the Russians, they have a good laugh and forget it.

The next rumor you hear may not be immediately recognisable for what it is. It won't be spoken in a sinister tone of voice. You won't be able to detect the chuckle of Goebbels in the background. The rumor may sound extremely reasonable. So have your guard up. All rumors have this in common: they pretend to convey facts – but the factual evidence is invariably flimsy. Usually the rumor is based on nothing more reliable than hearsay.

Many people repeat rumors because they like to be first with a new tidbit of information. It makes them feel important. There's no law against spreading rumors – yet. But it's a hobby that no-one can be very proud of these days. The time may come when rumor-mongers are classified as war criminals.

An organisation in Boston called the Rumor Clinic made a comprehensive collection of current rumors. Each week some of these tales were publicly debunked. Speaking from vast experience, the Rumor Clinic gave this advice. It was intended for civilians, but it's just as sound for GIs: 'The next time you hear some red-hot dope or some inside information, ask the fellow who tells it to put up or shut up. He may be a fifth columnist, he may be just another good fellow who has innocently fallen for the Axis line, but you put him straight. This is a total war; we're all in it together. If you are a good American you will work for the USA, not for Hitler. And if you're working for the USA you won't peddle any Nazi rumors about your fellow Americans or your Allies, and you'll squelch the fellow who does.'

Remember this classic advice about a rumor that runs down somebody else: 'Who's behind it, and how does it help me if I believe it?'

24 February 1945

Extracted from *20 Army Talks*, published by the Information and Education Division of the US Army, dated 1 July 1945. In the same vein, readers may care to peruse pages 266–7 of *The War As I Knew It* by General George S. Patton, first published in 1947.

Notes

INTRODUCTION

'. . . corpse factory' but see Fussell (1989), pp. 42–3
'. . . by the *Luftwaffe*' see Chapter One
'. . . by the USAAF' *Nationaler Zeitung*, 10 April 1944
'. . . home made news' Harrisson & Madge (1940), p. 57
'. . .' Driberg (1949), p. 175
'. . . Donegal coast' West (1998), p. 138–9
'. . . severed limbs' Fussell (1989), p. 272
'. . . resistance movement' see generally Foot (1976); Keegan (1995), ch. 6; West (1998); Moore (2000)
'. . . Pearl Harbor' Keegan (1995), p. 17
'. . . overripe corpse factory' Nicholas (1996), pp. 159–60
'. . . Allied bombing' Rubinstein (1997), ch. 4; Keegan (1995), p. 25
'. . . area bombing' Neillands (2001); Keegan (1995), pp. 26–7
'. . . James Bacque' Bacque (1989). See also *Crimes and Mercies* by the same author (1997)
'. . . has been challenged' Keegan (1995), pp. 10–11

CHAPTER ONE

'In the opening . . .' Hayward (2002), pp. 1–30
'. . . Führer had gone off' *Eastern Daily Press*, 7 September 1939
'. . . friendly enemy' Bonaparte (1947), p. 88
'. . . Prussian Guards' Hayward (2002), p. 22
'. . . brutal Prussian' Turner (1961), p. 269
'. . . Oreste Pinto' Pinto (1953), pp. 99–116
'. . . various towns . . .' *EDP*, 7 September 1939
'. . . each air raid' *EDP*, 7 September 1939
'German paratroops were reported . . .' *EDP*, 6 September 1939
'. . . ethnic *Volksdeutsche*' De Jong (1956), p. 44
'. . . general brutality of' *EDP*, 5 September 1939
'. . . to take prisoners' *EDP*, 14 September 1939
'. . . tobacco leaves' Bonaparte (1947), p. 80
'. . . scrap metal' De Jong (1956), p. 42
'. . . the Polish Ambassador' *EDP*, 4 September 1939
'German bombers have . . .' *EDP*, 4 September 1939
'. . . the Commons' Hansard (Commons), 7 September 1939, p. 567

'. . . mustard gas' De Jong (1956), p. 47
'. . . supplying gas shells' Bonaparte (1947), p. 81
'. . . Lord Halifax reminding' Hansard (Lords), 14 September 1939, p. 1,058
'. . . near Jaslo' *EDP*, 18 September 1939
'. . . claims of atrocities' *New York Times*, 13 September 1939
'Already the truth . . .' *EDP*, 9 September 1939
'. . . General Emilio Mola' De Jong (1956), p. 3
'Miniature wireless' De Jong (1956), pp. 46–7
'Crops and pasture . . .' De Jong (1956), p. 45
'. . . German shoes' Biddle (1976), p. 171. See also Garlinski (1985), p. 15
'. . . town of Thorn' De Jong (1956), p. 46
'Hans Roos . . .' Roos (1966), p. 167. See also De Jong (1956), p. 50
'Many helped clear . . .' De Jong (1956), p. 151
'. . . priests or monks' De Jong (1956), p. 156
'. . . like the Greeks' *The Times*, 11 April 1940
'In Northern Schleswig . . .' De Jong (1956), p. 167
'Members of the . . .' *The Times*, 22 April 1940
'Here it was also . . .' De Jong (1956), p. 61
'. . . British government' Colville (1985), p. 114
'. . . widely-syndicated' Gillman (1980), p. 77
'Norway's capital . . .' *Chicago Daily News*, 28 April 1940
'Every move we . . .' *The Times*, 8 May 1940
'. . . hastily assembled' Glover (1990), p. 23; Colville (1985), pp. 130–1
'. . . six to one' Gillman (1980), p. 71
'. . . Norwegian foreign minister' McInnis (1940), p. 152
'Although Quisling . . .' Glover (1990), pp. 42–3
'An official Norwegian . . .' De Jong (1956), p. 179
'. . . such as Baedeker' De Jong (1956), p. 172
'. . . the main operations' Glover (1990), pp. 28–9
'. . . at a high cost' Pallud (1991), p. 153
'. . . Home Office issued' *EDP*, 11 May 1940, p. 1
'An Air Ministry . . .' Glover (1990), p. 30
'. . . 200 parachutists' *The Times*, 11 May 1940, p. 6
'. . . delivery boys' *Daily Telegraph*, 15 May 1940
'. . . every kind of trick' *Daily Express*, 14 May 1940
'Holland's internal . . .' *EDP*, 13 May 1940
'. . . 2000 uniforms' This report is probably an exaggeration of an incident from November 1939,
    recorded by De Jong (1956), p. 66
'. . . atrocity propaganda' Pater-Downes (1971), p. 62
'Some of the parachutists . . .' *The Times*, 13 May 1940, p. 6
'. . . equipped with dummies' *EDP*, 13 May 1940, p.5. On dummies see also Gray (1942), p. 65
'At Ostend . . .' *Evening Standard*, 17 May 1940
'. . . pulls a lever' *EDP*, 14 May 1940, p. 3
'Outlandish as these . . .' Gillman, p. 108
'. . . wrote to Roosevelt' Glover (1990), p. 35
'Indications of . . .' West (1981), p. 121
'Fifth column reports . . .' Ironside (1962), p. 347
'. . . signalling going on' Ironside (1962), p. 377
'. . . units in London' *Daily Herald*, 17 September 1940
'. . . telegraph poles' West (1981), p. 122
'. . . a scoutmaster' Jones (1978), pp. 162–7
'One cannot name . . .' quoted in De Jong (1956), p. 74
'All the passengers . . .' *EDP*, 14 May 1940, p. 5
'Among the evacuees . . .' Gillman (1980), p. 101

'All boys of 16 . . .' PRO, FO 371/25189
'At once embark . . .' PRO, FO 371/25189
'. . . Department EH' Gillman (1980), pp. 109–10
'. . . the French press' De Jong (1956), p. 88
'A late report . . .' *The Times*, 23 May 1940, p. 5
'The parachute soldier . . .' *War Illustrated*, 7 June 1940, p. 604
'. . . poisoned meat' De Jong (1956), p. 187
'. . . burnt in fields' De Jong (1956), p. 187
'. . . central police station' De Jong (1956), p. 188
'. . . at Gennep' De Jong (1956), p. 185
'. . . local tulip fields' Gillman (1980), p. 107
'. . . the security service' De Jong (1956), p. 79
'. . . ringletted wigs' Gillman (1980), p. 30
'Complicity on . . .' Moen (1941), p. 33. See also Barlone (1942), p. 66
'. . . Maggi soup' Hayward (2002), p. 20
'. . . grown chicory' Horne (1969), p. 270
'A Belgian lady . . .' Hodson (1941), p. 182
'Near Brussels six . . .' Hodson (1941), p. 265
'I heard of a . . .' Hodson (1941), p. 309
'One man much . . .' Hodson (1941), p. 200
'Hereabouts news . . .' Hodson (1941), p. 200
'. . . sinister officer spies' Hayward (2002), pp. 98–9
'Men in British . . .' Hodson (1941), p. 274
'A regiment . . .' Hodson (1941), p. 271, p. 242
'A Scots soldier . . .' Hodson (1941), p. 186
'. . . Douglas Williams' Williams (1940), p. 31, p. 56, p. 68
'. . . Bernard Gray' Gray (1941), p. 83, p. 112
'. . . born in Paris' Horne (1969), p. 528
'. . . J.H. Patterson' Bond (1997), p. 43
'. . . Angel of Mons' Hayward (2002), pp. 46–61
'At one place . . .' Williams (1941), pp. 68–9
'Gunner William Brewer . . .' Collier (1961), pp. 63–4
'. . . killed on the spot' Bonaparte (1947), p. 88
'. . . Jean Cocteau' Bonaparte (1947), p. 89
'On the 24th . . .' Calder (1991), p. 123
'Miss Elsie Seddon . . .' *EDP*, 24 May 1940, p. 4
'We discussed German . . .' Mitchison (1985), p. 62
'A rather absurd . . .' Lehmann (1978), p. 90
'The weekly comic . . .' Allingham (1941), p. 193
'He will say . . .' quoted by Turner (1961), p. 269
'In Heugot's . . .' Barber (1976), pp. 163–4
'. . . from Luxembourg' De Jong (1956), p. 85
'. . . station masters' Bonaparte (1947), p. 89
'. . . poisoned sweets' Horne (1969), p. 528
'Arras was said . . .' Koestler (1941), p. 172
'. . . in Paris' Bonaparte (1947), p. 86
'. . . scare refugees' Bonaparte (1947), p. 86. That the fifth column panic was deliberately
    engineered 'by Goebbels' with this aim in mind is nonsense – ignore Foot (1976), p. 29
'. . . with water' Bonaparte (1947), p. 86
'. . . Paul Reynaud' Glover (1990), p. 44
'. . . French units ordered' Barlone (1942), p. 48
'. . . at Abbeville' De Jong (1956), p. 83
'. . . downed aircrew' see for example *After The Battle* magazine, 54 (1986): 'Show Trial at Luchy'
'The fifth column . . .' Barlone (1942), p. 52, p. 66

'. . . André Morize' Shennan (2000), p. 12
'. . . Robert Richardson' Shennan (2000), p. 12
'. . . 20,000 organised' Ziegler (1995), p. 23
'Great zeal was . . .' Jones (1978), pp. 161–2
'My best friend . . .' Gardiner (n.d.), p. 8
'. . . Saxon-Steer' West (1981), p. 120
'. . . Dorothy O'Grady' West (1981), p. 131
'. . . Marie Ingram' West (1981), p. 130
'. . . peace fanatics' *Sunday Dispatch*, 14 April 1940
'. . . Evening Standard' *Evening Standard*, 16 February 1940
'. . . the 'hysterics'' *The Times*, 23 April 1940
'All liberal-minded . . .' quoted in Gillman (1980), p. 79
'After the withdrawal . . .' Royde Smith (1941), p. 10
'We found that . . .' Lafitte (1940), p. 116
'. . . Ministry of Information' Gillman (1980), p. 110
'. . . William Donovan' *New York Times*, 20–23 August 1940
'. . . a mere 43 per cent' Calder (1991), p. 117
'. . . magistrates dismissed' West (1981), p. 123
'He emphasised that . . .' Colville (1985), p. 225
'. . . and New Zealanders' Bonaparte (1947), p. 85
'. . . attacking Java' Bonaparte (1947), p. 85

CHAPTER TWO

'. . . at Waltham Abbey' West (1981), p. 153; Bulloch (1963), p. 171
'. . . Saboteur of Lyness' Korganoff (1974), p. 201
'. . . German news item' West (1984), pp. 58–9
'Prien is thirty . . .' Shirer (1941), p. 190
'. . . at least eleven' Weaver (1980), pp. 176–7
'. . . Italian photographer' West (1981), p. 153
'. . . removed from his post' Bulloch (1963), p. 171; West (1984), pp. 68–9
'. . . Curt Reiss' West (1984), p. 60
'The spy was . . .' Farago (1971), p. 188
'In 1927, twelve . . .' Singer (1959), p. 73
'Equipped with . . .' Singer (1959), p. 74
'Home Office records . . .' West (1984), p. 70
'. . . confirmed to McKee' McKee (1959), p. 168
'. . . all fifteen living' West (1984), p. 72
'No watchmaker . . .' West (1984), p. 71
'In the midst . . .' Singer (1953), p. 82
'The subsequent history . . .' Singer (1959), p. 79
'In 1927 . . .' Cookridge (1947), p. 63
'Knight of the Iron . . .' Cookridge (1947), p. 65
'In Kiel a great . . .' Cookridge (1947), p. 66
'The omission of . . .' Cookridge (1947), p. 67
'How important . . .' Schellenberg (1956), pp. 62–3
'A notable example . . .' Felix (1963), p. 123
'. . . Lauren Paine' Paine (1984), p. 83
'It was in pursuit . . .' Cousins (1965), p. 147–8
'What is interesting . . .' Deacon (1978), p. 155
'. . . one Robbie Tulloch' Weaver (1980), p. 169
'. . . by scuba divers' Weaver (1980), pp. 167–8
'. . . refused to believe' Korganoff (1974), p. 198; Weaver (1980), p. 15; Snyder (1976), p. 178

'. . . stores stencilled' Snyder (1976), p. 178

'On Sunday, the 15th . . .' McKee (1959), p. 115; p. 170

'As H.J. Weaver . . .' Weaver (1980), p. 165

'. . . Arandora Star' Perry (1972), p. 14; Calder (1991), pp. 113–4

'. . . court-martial for mutiny' Frank (1954), p. 9

'I base my . . .' Frank (1954), p. 193

'During the First World War . . .' Hayward (2002), p. 27

CHAPTER THREE

'. . . on the Mole' Hodson (1941), p. 266

'. . . marking time' Gelb (1990), p. 178

'. . . regulation haircuts' Knightley (1982), p. 216

'. . . the most wonderful' Chatterton (1940), p. 5

'. . . to glory's tune' *The War Illustrated*, 14 June 1940

'. . . come back in glory' Ponting (1990), p. 92

'The English Channel . . .' *Sunday Dispatch*, 2 June 1940

'. . . requisitioned from civilian' Montgomery (1958), p. 50

'. . . gangster weapon' White (1955), p. 40

'The general view . . .' Hodson (1941), p. 254

'Germans using gas . . .' PRO, WO 106/1626. In 1941 it was also falsely reported that the
    Germans were using gas in the Crimea – see Ziegler (1995), p. 211

'. . . vivid description' Gray (1942), pp. 83–4

'. . . group of Hampshires' Collier (1961), p. 64

'. . . Coldstream Guards' Howard and Sparrow (1951), p. 41

'. . . oxygen cylinder' Rhodes (1942), p. 165

'. . . tracer bullets' Harris (1980), p. 23

'. . . yellow billowy cloud' Rhodes (1942), p. 163

'. . . Siegfried Line' Royde Smith (1941), p. 9

'. . . wood and canvas' White (1955), p. 39

'. . . had to prod' Williams (1940), p. 69

'. . . crewed by women' Hodson (1941), p. 309

'. . . other nations' Rhodes (1942), p. 150

'. . . Russians in England' Hayward (2002), pp. 31–45

'In September 1939 . . .' Montgomery (1958), pp. 49–50

'. . . 1st Armoured Division' Fraser (1983), p. 74

'. . . static and slow-moving' Bond (1997), p. 44

'. . . split his headquarters' Ponting (1990), p. 91

'At almost every . . .' Hatherill (1971), pp. 26–8

'. . . sugar beet and rain' Gray (1942), p. 23

'Major D.F. Callander . . .' Bond (1997), p. 42

'Twice the 30th . . .' Atkin (1990), p. 35

'The BEF of 1940 . . .' Hadley (1944), p. 147

'Not one man . . .' Williams (1940), p. 16

'. . . just 500' Ponting (1990), p. 89

'. . . careful study reveals' Bond (1997), p. 41

'Down the street . . .' Hadley (1944), p. 62

'There was nothing . . .' Atkin (1990), pp. 66–7

'At Helchin . . .' Harman (1980), p. 93

'. . . as 'automatons'' Gray (1942), p. 78

'May 22nd was likewise . . .' Howard and Sparrow (1951), p. 35

'. . . at Furnes' Lord (1983), p. 199

'. . . driver named Cole' Collier (1961), p. 178

'At the entrance . . .' quoted in Atkin (1990), p. 71
'A couple of Redcaps . . .' quoted in Atkin (1990), p. 71
'. . . Anthony Rhodes' Rhodes (1942), p. 149
'. . . bogus doctor' Rhodes (1942), p. 162–3
'. . . take no prisoners' Ponting (1990), p. 92
'. . . stray dogs' Atkin (1990), p. 101
'. . . James Hodson' Hodson (1941), pp. 243–4
'. . . Douglas Williams' Williams (1940), p. 56, pp. 68–9
'. . . Bernard Gray' Gray (1940), p. 83, p. 113
'. . . demonisation of the Hun' Hayward (2002), pp. 70–95
'On march passed . . .' Aitken (1977), p. 106
'Waiting on Dunkirk . . .' Chatterton (1940), p. 209
'You never knew . . .' Chatterton (1940), p. 209
'. . . into straightjackets' Collier (1961), p. 153
'. . . poison capsules' Collier (1961), p. 54
'. . . drew prostitutes' Collier (1961), p. 53
'Not many regiments . . .' Hodson (1941), p. 266
'One lad carried . . .' Hodson (1941), p. 277
'One of the minor . . .' Divine (1959), p. 264
'. . . one police inspector' Collier (1961), p. 243
'. . . pay would be docked' Fussell (1989), p. 38
'. . . abandoned on the quays' Glover (1990), p. 33
'. . . Anthony Eden' Atkin (1990), p. 234
'. . . talking freely' Calder (1991), p. 123
'Today I heard . . .' Perry (1972), pp. 11–12
'Several people . . .' King (1970), p. 57
'The Dunkirk episode . . .' King (1970), p. 85
'In the circumstances . . .' Hadley (1944), pp. 143–4
'The fact that . . .' Montgomery (1958), p. 68
'Several books . . .' Calder (1991), p. 96
'. . . just 26,000' Ponting (1990), p. 91
'. . . remain sealed.' Lord (1983), p. 282
'Crews aboard several . . .' see generally Lord (1983), pp. 222–4; 241
'Seven of our consorts . . .' quoted in Atkin (1990), p. 203
'. . . RNLI crews' Vince (1946), pp. 34–6
'Every time a Hurricane . . .' Atkin (1990), p. 206
'A new and more . . .' Chatterton (1940), p. 30; p. 37
'. . . bad poetry' Neave (1972), p. 212
'. . . sake of Allied solidarity' Neave (1972), p. 102
'Defence of Calais . . .' Harman (1980) p. 124
'. . . every hour you' Neave (1972), p. 105
'It was painful thus . . .' Churchill (1949), p. 71
'Calais was the crux . . .' Churchill (1949), p. 73
'As the commander . . .' Guderian (1952), p. 120
'I was vexed . . .' Churchill (1949), pp. 134–5
'. . . deliberately sacrificed' David (1994), p. 239
'At this time . . .' David (1994), p. 240
'. . . Brittany peninsula' Fraser (1983), p. 77
'. . . enthusiastic support' Churchill (1949), p. 169
'There was a tendency . . .' Glover (1985), p. 236
'When this news . . .' Churchill (1949), p. 172
'I then asked . . .' Churchill (1949), p. 42
'. . . in 1949 Gamelin' Divine (1959), p. 35
'The regrettable instances . . .' Alexander (1997), p. 161

'. . . Admiral Darlin' Shennan (2000), p. 11
'. . . not made easier' Atkin (1990), pp. 209–10
'. . . forced out of boats' Wilson (2000), p. 180
'. . . hard and well' Alexander (1997), pp. 161–76
'. . . just 7,000 officers' Kersaudy (1981), p. 80. The figure given by Ponting (1990), p. 184, is
       lower ie 4,000
'Some months later . . .' Muggeridge (1973), pp. 99–100
'. . . French Air Force' see generally Deighton (1979), pp. 354–5
'. . . 7,000 French 75 mm' Horne (1969), p. 667

CHAPTER FOUR

'At Le Paradis . . .' see Jolly (1956)
'. . . at Wormhoudt' see Aitken (1977)
'The distasteful truth . . .' Harman (1980), p. 107
'. . . 'previous murders'' Harman (1980), p. 89n. In the revised edition, published in 1991,
       Harman deleted wording which suggested there had been a 'German allegation' of a massacre.
'What was presented . . .' Atkin (1990), pp. 97–8
'Atkin also referred . . .' ibid, p. 152
'While SS troops . . .' Calder (1991), p. 94
'The excuse . . .' Bond (1997), p. 46
'. . . have been overplayed' Sydnor (1977), p. 96; Pallud (1991), pp. 352–4
'. . . future Desert Fox' Deighton (1979), pp. 332–3
'There followed . . .' Harman (1980), p. 97–8
'C Company, in . . .' Rissik (1953), p. 26
'C Company was . . .' Lewis and English (1949), p. 16
'. . . howitzer crews' Macksey (1965), p. 217
'We came to . . .' Affidavit sworn 13 October 1989
'. . . Harry Miller' quoted by Macksey (1965), p. 213
'My platoon went . . .' Affidavit sworn on 25 September 1989
'. . . vicinity of Beaurains' Affidavit of George Iceton, sworn 27 September 1989
'. . . at Dainville' Blaxland (1973), p. 141
'Suddenly round . . .' Gun Buster (1940), p. 120
'After crossing . . .' Gun Buster (1940), p. 136
'. . . the Official History' Ellis (1953), pp. 94–5
'They were . . .' Butler and Bradford (1950), pp. 109–10
'As they stood . . .' Butler and Bradford (1950), p. 110
'I was asked . . .' Affidavit sworn 11 September 1989
'. . . Maurice Buckmaster' Ruby (1988), pp. 12–13
'Buckmaster records . . .' Affidavit sworn 20 September 1989
'. . . as early as 1966' Stein (1966), p. 69
'. . . never been envisaged' Moore (1996), p. 21
'. . . less than one hundred' Atkin (1990), pp. 11–12, p. 173; Collier (1961), p. 241; Calder
       (1991), p. 107; *The Times* 17, 20 and 23 May 1940; *Daily Telegraph*, 4 June 1940
'. . . overseas to Canada' Moore (1996), p. 21, p. 26
'. . . German paratroopers' Pallud (1991), p. 153
'The German prisoners . . .' Sydnor (1977), p. 102
'We suffered . . .' statement to Laurence Turner, 1981
'An officer of 7 RTR . . .' Harman (1980), pp. 106–7
'I continued into . . .' statement to Laurence Turner, 1981
'. . . quoted in the Official' Ellis (1953), p. 93. Hepple wrote his report on 24 May 1940
'. . . Laurence Turner' *Sunday Express*, 25 October 1981
'. . . George Self' Bond (1997), p. 46

'The three French . . .' IWM Sound Archive, 10413
'. . . some so exhausted' Macksey (1965), pp. 227–8
'Elsewhere in his book . . .' Harman (1980), p. 95; p. 253
'. . . renewed public debate' World War Two Investigator (UK), June 1988

CHAPTER FIVE

'Picture if you can . . .' Glover (1990), p. 21
'The following year . . .' Fitz Gibbon (1957), p. 6
'. . . Anderson Committee' Ziegler (1995), p. 11
'. . . Stanley Baldwin' Harrisson (1976), p. 22
'. . . three years later Churchill' Harrisson (1976), p. 22
'By 1938 . . .' Fitz Gibbon (1957), p. 6; Glover (1990), p. 22
'. . . during the whole' Turner (1961), p. 47
'. . . Committee of Imperial' Ziegler (1995), p. 11
'In January 1938 . . .' Ironside (1962), p. 46
'. . . Blitz of 1940/41' Ziegler (1995), p. 176
'. . . the Mental Health . . .' Fitz Gibbon (1957), p. 7
'. . . J.B.S. Haldane' Haldane (1938), p. 31
'Lord Halsbury . . .' Haldane (1938), p. 21
'. . . of Guernica' Neillands (2001), pp. 31–2
'. . . such as Air Raid' John Langdon-Davies (1938)
'It has long been . . .' Klemmer (1941), p. 23
'. . . open trenches' Ziegler (1995), p. 30, p. 71; Mosley (1971), p. 13
'. . . cardboard coffins' Mosley (1971), p. 13; Ziegler (1995), p. 71; Harrisson (1976), p. 24
'. . . lime pits' Harrisson (1976), p. 24
'. . . the Channel' Fitz Gibbon (1957), p. 7
'The reality . . .' Glover (1990), p. 22
'. . . widespread rumours' Brittain (1941), p. 13
'. . . east coast' EDP, 7 September 1939
'In the absence . . .' Harrisson and Madge (1940), pp. 57–8
'. . . a Zeppelin' Harrisson and Madge (1940), p. 62. p. 154
'. . . from Bradford' Longmate (1971), p. 95
'. . . venereal disease' Longmate (1971), p. 95
'One Division . . .' PRO. This Home Defence document was disclosed by the Army Historical Branch
    in 1992 in relation to the Shingle Street controversy, but carries no PRO reference.
'. . . widespread and persistent' The Times, 7 September 1939, p. 3
'. . . pet holocaust' Longmate (1971), p. 216
'. . . circled above' Fussell (1989), p. 40; Perry (1972), p. 87
'. . . German-Swiss resident' Ziegler (1995), p. 69
'. . . polished toe-nails' Thomson (1947), p. 94
'Several pilots . . .' Klemmer (1941), p. 195
'. . . torn to pieces' Ziegler (1995), p. 174
'A young pilot . . .' Klemmer (1941), p. 196
'There was a . . .' Perry (1972), p. 54
'. . . large eagles' West (1981), p. 132
'. . . another 59' Perry (1972), p. 56; Daily Herald, 15 and 17 August 1940
'. . . other than Joyce' Cole (1964), pp. 132–4
'. . . a certain church' Longmate (1971), p. 97
'Indeed an investigation . . .' Calder (1991), p. 110
'Weeks ago there . . .' Royde Smith (1941), p. 66
'Another dead rumour . . .' Royde Smith (1941), pp. 79–80
'. . . that Göring' Longmate (1971), p. 95

'. . . a Junkers 88' Ramsey (1988)

'Three weeks earlier . . .' Savignon (1968), p. 134

'. . . chance encounter' Hayward (2002), p. 22

'. . . of Leyland' Longmate (1971), p. 95

'. . . brutal Prussian' Turner (1961), p. 269

'. . . tank-carrying aircraft' Klemmer (1941), p. 173

'. . . generating earthquakes' Jones (1978), p. 103

'. . . cross-Channel tunnel' Collier (1979), pp. 233–4

'. . . on the Brocken' Royde Smith (1941), p. 8

'. . . overt German threats' *Daily Herald*, 18 September 1940

'It was freely . . .' Klemmer (1941), pp. 178–9

'. . . rocket gun' Ziegler (1995), p. 268

'. . . Park Lane' Ziegler (1995), p. 282

'. . . 400 ton bomb' Ziegler (1995), p. 268

'Remarkably, warnings . . .' Woon (1941), p. 132

'. . . mysterious white threads' Klemmer (1941), p. 176

'. . . sky-blue wool' Thompson (1966), p. 134

'. . . rice and tapioca' Calder and Sheridan (1984), pp. 81–2

'In W-- . . .' Klemmer (1941), p. 177

'. . . about 'arsine'' Longmate (1971), p. 76

'. . . local pickle factory' Royde Smith (1941), p. 11

'. . . lull the population' Royde Smith (1941), p. 132

'. . . induce vomiting' Ziegler (1995), p. 158

'. . . to burst' Jones (1978), p. 103

'. . . the London Underground' Hayward (2002), p. 19

'The German pilot . . .' Klemmer (1941), pp. 181–2

'I have been told . . .' Klemmer (1941), p. 182

'The corollary . . .' Klemmer (1941), pp. 51–2; Woon (1941), p. 78

'. . . coiled springs' Woon (1941), p. 79

'. . . secret anti-raid weapon' Royde Smith (1941), p. 141

'. . . part of the loot' Royde Smith (1941), p. 156

'. . . death rays' Klemmer (1941), p. 53

'. . . British and German . . .' Fussell (1989), p. 48

'Pre-war motorists . . .' Kinsey (1983), pp. 44–5

'. . . the true nature' Kinsey (1983), p. 68

'. . . the Air Ministry' Jones (1978), p. 42

'Invariably he had . . .' Jones (1978), p. 100

'There is now . . .' Perry (1972), p. 176

'. . . supersonic beam' Ziegler (1995), p. 282

'. . . virtually defenceless' Deighton (1980), p. 180

'. . . 30,000 shells' Ziegler (1995), p. 117

'. . . 45 per cent' Klemmer (1941), p. 33

'. . . was so intense' Mosley (1971), p. 143, p. 297; Ziegler (1995), p. 118, p. 208, pp. 235–6; see
    also Perry (1972), p. 197; Woon (1941), p. 97, p. 98

'. . . following catalogue' Ziegler (1995), p. 235

'. . . an express train' Ramsey (1990), p. 222

'. . . Bethnal Green tube disaster' Ramsey (1990), Vol 3, p. 222

'. . . an oil bomb' Ziegler (1995), p. 238

'. . . balloon barrages' Ramsey (1987), p. 95

'. . . RAF Hampdens' Ramsey (1987), p. 97, p. 98

'. . . 278 V1' Ramsey (1987), p. 95

'. . . of KG 27' Ramsey (1987), p. 89; Calder (1991), p. 135

'. . . Dover Castle pub' Ziegler (1995), p. 236

'. . . turkey shoots' Ramsey (1987), pp. 86–95; Woon (1941), p. 80; King (1970), pp. 72–3

'Over 5,000 . . .' Ponting (1990), p. 145
'three sitting MPs . . .' Ponting (1990), p. 146
'. . . Crime in Wartime' Smithies (1982), p. 161
'. . . forced out of' *Hendon Times and Guardian*, 19 January 1940
'It is not only . . .' Mannheim (1941), p. 133
'Indeed almost half . . .' Ziegler (1995), p. 149
'Some men come . . .' Calder and Sheridan (1984), pp. 99–100
'. . . rescue work' Marwick (1976), p. 71
'. . . anti-looting detectives' Smithies (1982), p. 49; Nixon (1943), pp. 146–7
'. . . in Birmingham' Smithies (1982), p. 49
'. . . troops even stood' Harrisson (1976), p. 185
'. . . Café de Paris' Ziegler (1995), pp. 147–8
'The first thing . . .' Monsarrat (1966), p. 288
'It was a gory . . .' Nixon (1943), p. 101
'Coventry: there . . .' PRO, INF 1/292
'Outside London . . .' Ponting (1990), p. 165
'. . . in Belfast' Calder (1991), p. 66; pp. 168–9
'. . . Clydebank' Harrisson (1976), p. 255
'. . . martial law' Harrisson (1976), p. 245
'The Liverpool . . .' Harrisson (1976), p. 243
'. . . East Enders' Fitz Gibbon (1957), p. 63
'. . . the royal family' Ponting (1990), p. 160
'After the big raid . . .' Harrisson (1976), p. 329
'. . . stirring speeches' Ponting (1990), pp. 157–9
'I said to Lotbiniere . . .' Snagge and Barsley (1972), pp. 16–7
'. . . airmen refused' Deighton (1977), p. 232
'. . . Angus Calder' Calder (1991), pp. 103–4
'Later it was . . .' Ramsey (1980), p. 147
'There were a . . .' Stockman (1986), p. 44
'At about 3 pm . . .' Winterbotham (1974), pp. 82–3
'. . . a new verb' Calder (1991), pp. 36–7
'. . . man had been shot' Harrisson (1976), p. 138
'Should not the . . .' Cave Brown (1976), p. 41
'at least 48 . . .' Cave Brown (1976), p. 40
'The name of . . .' Stevenson (1976), p. 153
'The official history . . .' Hinsley (1993), p. 534
'. . . technical error' Jones (1977), pp. 200–6; Collier (1979), pp. 277–81; West (1984), pp. 21–31
'. . . out in time' West (1984), p. 29
'Whoever had . . .' Jones (1977), p. 206
'. . . V1 flying bombs' for typical rumours attached to the first V1 see Nixon (1980), p. 171; Ziegler
    (1995), p. 296
'It would be a . . .' Masterson (1972), p. 180
'. . . Croydon went on' Ziegler (1995), pp. 285–6
'. . . lost six men' Moynihan (1974), p. 180

CHAPTER SIX

Author's note: this chapter is based largely on material explored in more detail in my book *The
    Bodies on the Beach* (2001).

'. . . phantom parachutists' *Daily Herald*, 15–17 August 1940
'By the middle . . .' Hayward (2001), pp. 37–8
'. . . no less than 80,000' *New York Times*, 15 December 1940. Quoted in Hayward (2001), pp. 60–1

'In the whole . . .' Thomson (1947), p. 73
'After dinner . . .' Colville (1985), p. 277
'On making to intercept . . .' Hayward (2001), pp. 33–4
'. . . not to lack daring' unpublished account by Lieutenant T.H. Waterhouse, navigating officer on HMS *Intrepid*, June 2002.
'For two days . . .' letter to ATV in 1992, quoted in Hayward (2001), p. 33
'. . . Channel battle' Fitz Gibbon (1957), p. 79
'According to the censor . . .' Thomson (1947), p. 70
'. . . in Sandwich Bay' Thompson (1966), pp. 233–4; White (1955), p. 22
'Tales begin to come' Brown (1981), p. 120
'What is the . . .' Brown (1998), p. 61
'I hear from . . .' Perry (1972), p. 134
'On the 15th . . .' Brown (1998), pp. 61–2
'15 Division . . .' Hayward (1994), p. 85
'It has been . . .' Hayward (2001), pp. 45–6
'I suppose you've . . .' Hodson (1941), p. 330
'It began with . . .' Royde Smith (1941), pp. 78–9
'. . . in Southampton' Klemmer (1941), p. 188
'The fact is . . .' quoted in Thomson (1947), p. 70
'. . . ticklish circumstances' Thomson (1947), p. 73
'Although in 1914 . . .' Hayward (2002), pp. 4–5
'Our task . . .' White (1955). p. 12–3
'I cannot say today . . .' White (1955), p. 17–8. White's unsatisfactory account informed the risible telling of the failed invasion myth given by Seth (1969), pp. 93–100
'. . . those in the know' Hayward (2001), pp. 43–45
'. . . Petroleum Warfare Department' Hayward (2001), pp. 16–7
'. . . Lord Maurice Hankey' Hayward (2001), p. 4
'Nazi dead said to . . .' *New York Times*, 29 September 1940
'Nazi losses seen . . .' *New York Times*, 21 September 1940
'Letter to the Editor . . .' *New York Times*, 20 October 1940
'. . . Marie Bonaparte' Bonaparte (1947), pp. 109–117
'The British sent . . .' *Daily Mail*, 21 September 1940
'. . . no ordinary refugee' West (1983), p. 340
'. . . Gunner William Robinson' Hayward (2001), p. 1, p. 39. Robinson recounted his story on a BBC television programme in November 1957.
'He was wearing . . .' *The Times*, 22 October 1940, p. 4
'. . . for burial' Folkestone, Hythe and District Herald, 26 October 1940
'. . . German flak trawlers' Foynes (1994), p. 275; White (1955), p. 19–20
'. . . a London railway station' Klemmer (1941), p. 189
'. . . by Clement Attlee' Hansard Vol 430, written answer on 18 November 1946
'. . . of Royal Engineers' Hayward (2001), pp. 4–5
'. . . Operation Lucid' Hayward (2001), pp. 27–32
'By May of that year . . .' Hayward (2001), pp. 9–18
'. . . trial at Dumpton' (2001), pp. 14–5
'. . . Flame Over Britain' Banks (1946), p. 41
'. . . as August 10th' Schenk (1990), p. 139
'At Wilhelmshaven . . .' Schenk (1990), pp. 139–40
'It was decided . . .' Schenk (1990), p. 140; Ansel (1960), p. 244
'. . . planted on German intelligence' see Delmer (1962), p. 20
'The first variant . . .' Hayward (2001), p. 51
'Short Invasion Phrasebook' Hayward (2001), pp. 52–4
'. . . on the radio' Delmer (1962), p. 20
'. . . New York Sun' *New York Sun*, 7 October 1940
'The carnage . . .' *War Illustrated*, 1 November 1940

'350,000 men . . .' Bonaparte (1947), p. 113
'We were caught . . .' *New York Times*, 15 December 1940
'. . . official denials' Hayward (2001), pp. 50–1
'. . . James Spaight' Spaight (1941), p. 95; pp. 214–5
'I first learned . . .' Moen (1941), pp. 162–3
'I noticed several . . .' Shirer (1941), pp. 505–6
'. . . at Charlottenburg' Shirer (1941), pp. 508–9
'Shirer later concluded . . .' Shirer (1960), pp. 772–3
'. . . thanked by name' West (1998), p. 20
'. . . Gare du Nord' Hayward (2001), p. 66, p. 73
'. . . Charles Barbe' Hayward (2001), pp. 66–7
'. . . duly reported' Thomson (1947), p. 71
'. . . near Bognor' Thomson (1947), pp. 72–3
'. . . fact and fiction' Hayward (2001), pp. 68–9
'Evelyn Waugh . . .' Waugh (1952), p. 232
'Thousands of . . .' *News of the World*, 1 October 1944
'. . . biggest secret' *Daily Express*, 4 June 1945
'. . . several questions raised' Hayward (2001), pp. 69–70
'. . . whose wife Mary' Calder (1991), p. 121
'It always seemed . . .' *Daily Express*, 4 June 1945
'And the Germans . . .' *News-Chronicle*, 4 June 1945
'In November 1946 . . .' Hayward (2001), pp. 75–6
'We took no steps . . .' Churchill (1949), p. 275
'. . . Enemy Coast Ahead' Gibson (1946), p. 108
'. . . Peter Fleming too' Fleming (1957), pp. 104–5, pa. 210
'In November 1957 . . .' Hayward (2001), pp. 81–4
'Produced in 1954 . . .' Hayward (2001), p. 77
'The line about . . .' Delmer (1962), pp. 20
'. . . Shingle Street' Hayward (2001), pp. 85–104
'When we engaged . . .' White (1955), p. 124
'. . . corpse deceptions' see Chapter Nine
'. . . Namier' Namier, Diplomatic Prelude, Macmillan, 1948, p.v

CHAPTER SEVEN

Note: references below to W&P are to Watson and Petrova

'. . . gone off with' *EDP*, 7 September 1939
'. . . death and disappearance' Royde-Smith (1941), p. 9
'. . . among British troops' Scannell (1987), p. 121
'. . . American units' Anonymous (1945), p. 157
'. . . Prien' see Chapter Two
'. . . Bormann' Infield (1980), p. 255
'. . . Canaris' see Chapter Ten
'A poll taken . . .' Byford-Jones (1947), p. 83
'. . . variously seen' O'Donnell (1979), p. 302
'In July 1945 . . .' Watson and Petrova (1995), p. 14
'. . . Karl Dönitz' O'Donnell (1979), p. 297
'. . . Georgi Zhukov' Trevor-Roper (1947), p. xlv
'. . . Eisenhower, who voiced' *The Times*, 16 June 1945
'. . . Potsdam Conference' O'Donnell (1979), p. 301
'. . . Izvestiia carried' O'Donnell (1979), p. 302
'. . . the Iron Curtain' Trevor-Roper (1995), p. xvi + xlvii

'No trace . . .' W&P (1995), p. 44
'. . . continued to multiply' W&P (1995), pp. 16–19
'. . . in Colorado' Hitler of the ?, C5 television programme, 22 May 2003
'. . . Nauecilus' Blundell (1995), pp. 92–3
'Throughout the summer . . .' Trevor-Roper (1947), p. xxviii
'. . . Baumgart' Trevor-Roper (1947), p. xxiii
'If you look . . .' W&P (1995), p. 19
'. . . Canadian paper' W&P (1995), p. 75
'. . . at the last minute' Infield (1980), p. 247
'. . . Brazil in 1966' Infield (1980), pp. 254–5
'. . . in 1955' W&P (1995), p. 47
'. . . strewn to the wind' Bezymenski (1968), p. 66
'. . . further bone fragments' W&P (1995), p. 85
'. . . point-blank range' W&P (1995), p. 87
'. . . Hitler Diaries' Harris (1986), p. 15
'. . . the remains' W&P (1995), pp. 87–9
'. . . Russian archives' W&P (1995), p. 167
'. . . relatively uninformed' Thomas (1995), p. 183
'. . . of the capture' Thomas (2001), pp. 147–59
'. . . medical anomalies' Thomas (2001), p. 215
'. . . was 'perhaps' not' Thomas (2001), p. 249
'. . . obscure angles' Thomas (2001), p. 170
'. . . as an exhibit' Ramsey (1976), p. 35
'. . . Artur Axmann' Trevor-Roper (1947), pp. xxxvii–xxxvii
'. . . Stalin informed Harry' W&P (1995), p. 44
'. . . Lev Bezymenski' Trevor-Roper (1995), p. xi
'. . . Bormann biography' *Martin Bormann* by James McGovern (Arthur Baker, 1968)
'. . . Ladislas Farago' Farago (1974), p. 431; Thomas (1995), pp. 220–30
'. . . Reinhardt Gehlen' Trevor-Roper (1995), pp. xi–xiii
'. . . in December 1972' Ramsey (1998), p. 42
'. . . Hugo Beer' Trevor-Roper (1995), p. xii
'. . . J.O.E.O. Mahrke' Ramsey (1998), p. 42
'. . . Nigel West' West (1998), pp. 146–64
'The 'Bormann skull'. . . ' Ramsey (1998), p. 42
'. . . Colonel Bogey' Waite (1977), p. 150
'Hitler's abnormal sex . . .' Hinchley (1963), p. 155
'The genital member . . .' Bezymenski (1968), p. 46; Redlich (1999), p. 229, pp. 374–9
'. . . deliberately falsified' Redlich (1999), p. 229
'. . . Heinz Linge' Redlich (1998), p.229; Heinz Linge, *Bis zum Untergang* (Munich, 1980), p. 68, pp. 93–4
'Two Nazi doctors . . .' Maser (1973), p. 204; Waite (1977), p. 151; Redlich (1998), p. 229
'. . . some doubt' Waite (1977), pp. 151–2
'. . . *Die Zeit*' *Die Zeit*, 21 December 1971
'. . . was impotent' Maser (1973), p. 204
'. . . Ernst Hanfstaengl' *Daily Express*, 19 September 1934; Hinchley (1963), p. 155
'. . . fizzled out' Machtan (2001), p. 292
'. . . Harold Nicolson' Nicolson (1980), p. 168
'. . . the Listener' *The Listener* 15 February 1940, pp. 311–13
'. . . William Shirer' Shirer (1941), p. 137
'. . . Chips Channon' James (1970), pp. 288–9
'. . . crude propaganda' e.g. Kurt Kruger, *Inside Hitler*, Avalon Press, 1941
'. . . contracted syphilis' Maser (1973), p. 195
'. . . seventeenth birthday' Waite (1977), p. 435
'. . . an epileptic' Fussell (1989), p. 46

'. . . sexual pervert' Waite (1977), p. 237; Hinchley (1963), p. 155
'. . . Kurt Kruger' cited in Waite (1977), pp. 433–4
'. . . a Jewish lover' W&P (1995), p. 165
'. . . trigger himself' Tabori (1949), pp. 18–19; Ravenscroft (1973), p. 174; Hinchley (1963), p. 155
'. . . Dresden in 1942' Tabori (1949), p. 53; Blundell (1995), p. 42
'. . . Josef Greiner' see Waite (1977), pp. 427–32
'. . . in 1949' Tabori (1949), unpaginated preface; Waite (1977), pp. 343–5
'. . . subsequent historians' Robert Payne (1973); John Toland (1976)
'. . . Brigid Dowling-Hitler' Waite (1977), pp. 432–3
'. . . *The Flying Visit*' published by Jonathan Cape in 1940
'. . . Air Ministry' PRO, AIR 16/519
'A large number . . .' PRO, FO 898/6
'The moon and tides . . .' quoted by Richard Cox in Sealion (Thornton, 1974), p. 153
'. . . mislead by bogus' see Chapter 8
'. . . seer Nostradamus' Howe (1982), plate 19
'. . . unavowable black' see generally Howe (1982)
'. . . Louis de Wohl' Howe (1967), pp. 205–16
'. . . Hitler's personal astrologer' Montgomery Hyde (1962), p. 189
'Four months hence . . .' Montgomery Hyde (1962), p. 189
'In the light . . .' Montgomery Hyde (1962), p. 190
'. . . the fire escape' Stevenson (1976), pp. 346–7
'. . . highly unreliable' West (1984), p. 169–83
'. . . a quack' Stevenson (1976), p. 346
'. . . Satanist or Luciferian' Spence (1943), p. 12
'. . . mystical mulatto' Spence (1943), p. 7
'. . . shadowy people' Spence (1943), p. 9
'. . . Michael Bentine' Michael Bentine, *The Door Marked Summer*, Granada, 1981, p. 291
'. . . *Satan and Swastika*' by Francis King (Mayflower, 1976)
'. . . *The Occult Reich*' by J.H. Brennan (Signet, 1974)
'. . . *Hitler and the Occult*' by Ken Anderson (Prometheus, 1995)
'. . . Hitler – Black Magician' by Gerald Suster (Sphere, 1981)
'Books written . . .'. Goodrick-Clarke (1985), pp. 224–5
'. . . Stein himself witnessed' Ravenscroft (1973), p. xxi
'. . . knew more about' Ravenscroft (1973), plate caption between pp. 170–1
'. . . a confidential advisor' Ravenscroft (1973), p. xiii
'. . . mind expansion' Ravenscroft (1973), p. 13
'Very considerable . . .' Ravenscroft (1973), p. xiii
'. . . General Patton' Ravenscroft (1973), p. 349
'. . . Karl Haushofer' Ravenscroft (1973), p. 238
'. . . SS took oaths' Ravenscroft (1973), p. 259
'. . . Planetary Doppelgänger' Ravenscroft (1973), p. 307
'. . . anti-human' Ravenscroft (1973), p. 295
'. . . took no verbatim' Ravenscroft (1973), p. 60
'One day we were . . .' Jones (1992), pp. 118–9
'There was to be . . .' Ravenscroft (1973), p. 325
'Many rumours, later . . .' Ravenscroft (1973), p. 328

CHAPTER EIGHT

Note: references below to PPP are to Pickett, Prince and Prior.
References to Nesbit are to Nesbit and Van Acker.
'. . . victim of hallucinations' statement on German radio, 12 May 1941, preserved in PRO, INF
   1/912

'. . . sufficient fuel' Thomas (1979), pp. 40–5; Jackson (2000), p. 23
'. . . land to refuel' Jackson (2000), p. 23
'. . . shot down' Thomas (1979), p. 49
'. . . 1,560 miles' PPP (2001), p. 171
'. . . 3869' Bateman (1987), p. 4
'. . . 3526' Bateman (1987), p. 4
'. . . NJ+OQ' Thomas (1979), p. 50
'. . . from the Clyde' Nesbit (1999), pp. 96–7
'. . . Schiphol' Nesbit (1999), pp. 126–7
'. . . Aalborg' Jackson (2000), p. 23
'. . . from Calais' Svenska Dagbladet, 23 May 1941.
'. . . Reinhard Heydrich' Padfield (1991), p. 188, pp. 195–6; Nesbit (1999), pp. 128–31
'. . . Adolf Galland' Galland (1955), pp. 108–9
'. . . prior authorisation' Nesbit (1999), pp. 125–6
'. . . American parts' Deacon (1991), p. 304
'. . . Double Standards' PPP (2001), pp. 178–82; Nesbit (1999), p. 57
'. . . at least September 1940' Nesbit (1999), p. 33; PPP (2001), p. 131, p. 153
'. . . abortive attempts' Nesbit (1999), p. 40
'. . . Lord Beaverbrook' Padfield (1991), p. 292
'. . . Operation Sealion' PPP (2001), pp. 121–2, p. 168
'. . . chiefly Mussolini' PPP (2001), p. 168, p. 231
'. . . knew and approved of' PPP (2001), pp. 174–6
'. . . paroxysm of rage' Speer (1971), p. 174
'. . . news calmly' PPP (2001), p. 231
'A letter which . . .' PRO, INF 1/912
'. . . driver, bodyguard' PPP (2001), p. 231
'. . . little punitive action' PPP (2001), pp. 243–4
'. . . comfortable quarters' Nesbit (1999), p. 121
'It is no coincidence . . .' Pravda, 19 October 1942
'. . . Myra Hess' Nesbit (1999), p. 121
'The Russians are . . .' PRO, PREM 3/219/7, memo from Churchill to Sir Archibald Sinclair dated 6 April 1945
'Anthony Cave Brown . . .' Brown (1988), pp. 349–50
'. . . Philip Knightley' Independent on Sunday, 24 August 1997
'. . . to KGB' New York Times, 8 June 1991
'. . . Joseph Goebbels' Goebbels (1982), pp. 361–5
'. . . a brilliant coup' McCormick (1993), p. 94
'Hess, however, presented . . .' McCormick (1993), pp. 86–8
'. . . a dummy dressed' McCormick (1993), p. 90
'. . . questioned by Crowley' Deacon (1991), p. 305
'. . . Maxwell Knight' Masters (1984), pp. 126–9
'. . . Louis de Wohl' McCormick (1993), p. 89
'Cast the horoscope . . .' McCormick (1993), p. 88
'. . . totally bizarre' McCormick (1993), p. 91
'As is well-known' quoted by Howe (1967), p. 192
'. . . ongoing peace negotiations' PPP (2001), p. 165
'. . . losing the war' PPP (2001), p. 187
'. . . Lloyd George' PPP (2001), p. 187
'. . . Lord Halifax' PPP (2001), p. 88
'. . . Lord Beaverbrook' PPP (2001), p. 90
'. . . Sir Samuel Hoare' Newton (1996), p. 108; PPP (2001), pp. 87–8, p. 165
'. . . Stewart Menzies' Newton (1996), pp. 142–3
'. . . Anglo German Fellowship' PPP (2001). p. 145
'. . . ample evidence' PPP (2001), pp. 141–3

'. . . a complicated task' PPP (2001), p. 300
'. . . proposed terms' PPP (2001), p. 173, p. 307
'. . . reduction in strength' PPP (2001), p. 249, p. 334
'When Rudolf Hess . . .' Hansard (Commons) Vol 377, cols 594–5; PPP (2001), p. 311
'. . . published in *The Times*' reproduced in PPP (2001), pp. 143–4; pp. 148–9
'. . . libel writs' Nesbit (1999), p. 119; PPP (2001), pp. 245–7
'. . . reception committee' *American Mercury*, May 1943; PPP (2001), pp. 268–9
'. . . Duke of Kent' PPP (2001), p. 269
'. . . a Polish contingent' PPP (2001), pp. 272–3
'. . . Albrecht Haushofer' PPP (2001), pp. 139–41, p. 147
'. . . his widow' Padfield (1991), p. 354
'Some have claimed . . .' Nesbit (1999), p. 66
'. . . a Bristol Beaufighter' PPP (2001), p. 191, p. 268
'. . . promoted as a crack' PPP (2001), p. 237
'Indeed rumours . . .' PRO, INF 1/912; PPP (2001), p. 288
'. . . van Paassen' van Paassen (1941), p. 522
'. . . ties with America' PPP (2001), pp. 316–22
'. . . last significant' Ziegler (1995), pp. 179–80
'. . . ruthlessly exploited' PPP (2001). pp. 310–13
'Three Spitfires . . .' Nesbit (1999), pp. 62–3
'. . . airborne Defiant' Nesbit (1999), pp. 67–8
'. . . was alerted' MacLean (1999), pp. 137–40
'. . . not scrambled' Nesbit (1999), p. 67
'. . . John Costello' Costello (1991), pp. 5–10
'Both statements are incorrect' Nesbit (1999), p. 133
'. . . two Czech' PPP (2001), pp. 186–7
'. . . American Mercury' PPP (2001), p. 188
'. . . no record of Srom' PPP (2001), p. 187
'. . . anywhere near Hess' Nesbit (1999), p.134
'. . . simply mistaken' Nesbit (1999), pp. 134–6
'. . . John McCowen' Nesbit (1999), pp. 102–4; PPP (2001), pp. 309–10
'. . . group of Poles' PPP (2001), p. 354, p. 371
'. . . an MI5 file' PRO, KV237
'. . . most celebrated proponent' see also PPP (2001), p. 9
'. . . Dr Hugh Thomas' PPP (2001), pp. 357–8
'. . . wounded twice' Nesbit (1999), pp. 6–7
'. . . major scars' Thomas (1979), p.1 96
'. . . Peter Waddell' *East Kilbride News*, 23 June 1999
'Three fingers . . .' *Kriegsarchiv*, Munich. Quoted in PPP (2001), p. 358
'. . . from Lord Willingdon' PPP (2001), p. 366
'His wife Ilse . . .' Bateman (1987), p. 22
'. . . Albert Speer' Bateman (1987), p. 22
'. . . Werner Maser' *Gazet van Antwerpen*, 7 September 1987
'. . . official version' Nesbit (1999), pp. 115–7
'. . . suicide note' PPP (2001), p. 475
'. . . over a balcony' Bateman (1987), pp. 16–7
'. . . with a breadknife' Nesbit (1999), p. 110
'. . . cut his wrists' Nesbit (1999), p. 114
'. . . seriously flawed' Nesbit (1999), p. 140
'. . . Abdallah Melaouhi' Le Tissier (1994), pp. 101–4
'. . . Le Tissier' Le Tissier (1994), pp. 101–4
'. . . pilot error' Smith (1982), pp. 32–3
'. . . drunkenness' *The Scotsman*, 5 September 1985
'. . . magnetic rocks' Smith (1982), p. 32

'. . . radio messages' Smith (1982), p. 32
'. . . the Duke himself' *Sunday Times*, 24 March 1996
'. . . their hypothesis' PPP (2001), pp. 377–435

CHAPTER NINE

'On January 26th . . .' Morgan (1996), p. 31
'. . . immense magnitude' Cooper (1950), p. 149
'. . . powerfully contributed' Cooper (1950), p. 166
'. . . threatened to state' Jones (1978), p. 283
'. . . in his cups' Jones (1989), p. 280
'. . . named Westphal' Westphal (1951), p. 150n; Colvin (1953), p. 29; Montagu (1953), p. 13
'. . . plunged very deeply' Churchill (1948), p. 64
'At my first . . .' Jones (1978), p. 283. The meeting would have been in January 1953.
'I had much sympathy . . .' Jones (1989), p. 280
'A barrister by . . .' Morgan (1986), p. 10
'. . . B Division of MI5' Howard (1990), p. 89
'. . . haversack ruse' Wavell (1940), p. 202; (Official History) pp. 30–1; Aston (1930), pp. 191–8
'. . . John Charteris' Hayward (2002), pp. 121–3
'In August 1942 . . .' Young and Stamp (1989), pp. 61–3
'. . . Fleming in Burma' Young and Stamp (1989), pp. 220–5
'On September 25th . . .' Morgan (1986), p.4
'. . . doubts remained' Hoare (1946), pp. 175–6; Masterman (1972), p. 133; West (1981), p. 292
'. . . Montagu maintained' Morgan (1986), p. 4; p. 23.
'. . . tram-standard' Montagu (1953), p. 86
'. . . opposite' *Sunday Express*, February 1953
'. . . slipped through the net' Hooper (1987), p. 247
'. . . Security Service eyebrows' Hooper (1987), p. 98
'. . . Hampshire Quarter' Hooper (1987), p. 98
'. . . Trinity College' Rusbridger (1989), p. 176
'. . . a film version' Morgan (1986), pp. 2–3
'A fragment . . . ' Howard (1990), p. 89
'. . . The Big Lie' White (1955), pp. 124–5
'Shortly before . . .' Masterman (1972), p. 133
'. . . in Wells' Morgan (1986), p. 3
'. . . in Hackney' Morgan (1986), p. 24
'. . . Martin Gilbert' Gilbert (1986), p. 405
'In 1988 . . .' *Mail on Sunday*, 4 December 1988
'. . . The Intelligence Game' Rusbridger (1989), p. 175–7
'Gibbon eventually . . .' After the Battle #100, p. 62
'. . . ADM 223/794' Morgan (1996), p. 31
'At one time . . .' Montagu (1953), pp. 25–6
'. . . searched and searched' Montagu (1977), p. 145
'I gave a . . .' Montagu (1977), p. 145
'. . . a raft of legislation' Morgan (1986), pp. 15–6
'. . . various reasons' Montagu (1953), p. 53
'. . . in September 1961' Jackson (1963), p. 312
'Purchase insisted . . .' Jackson (1963), p. 150. Jackson based his book on 'many protracted conversations' with Purchase, but observes that the coroner 'soon began to embroider the part he played in the affair' after it became public in 1953.
'Although Barclay was . . .' Morgan (1986), pp. 9–10
'According to Masterman . . .' Masterman (1972), pp. 137–8
'The operation . . .' Montagu (1953), p. 12

'Montagu repeated . . .' Montagu (1977), p. 150
'. . . 1st Panzer Division' Bennett (1989), p. 224
'. . . to Corsica' Bennett (1989), p. 225
'. . . by July' Bennett (1989), p. 226
'Mussolini alone . . .' Colvin (1953), p. 185
'. . . ongoing and methodical' Stripp (1996), pp. 4–5
'. . . insufficient landing craft' Bennett (1989), p. 223
'bogus radio . . .' Bennett (1994), p. 204
'. . . Mediterranean convoys' Montagu (1953), p. 112
'Forceful objections . . .' Bennett (1994), p. 203
'Eisenhower later tried . . .' Bennett (1994), p. 203
'It can hardly . . .' Colvin (1953), p. 190
'While this courier . . .' quoted in Howard (1990), p. 89
'. . . highly competent' Howard (1990), p. 89
'. . . very active German agent' Montagu (1953), p. 28
'. . . Spanish naval headquarters' MI4 analysis dated 22 October 1945 reproduced in Morgan
    (1986), p. 23
'. . . straight to Madrid' Montagu (1977), p. 150; Stripp (1996), p. 7
'. . . absolutely convincing' quoted in Howard (1990), p. 91
'. . . above suspicion' original document and translation in Morgan (1986), p. 22

CHAPTER TEN

'. . . Mata Hari' Cookridge (1948), pp. 41–4; Deacon (1991), p. 258
'. . . Stewart Menzies' Cave Brown (1976), p. 143
'Some accounts . . .' Abshagen (1956), p. 9
'. . . the *Royal Oak*' Deacon (1978), p. 155
'. . . Reinhard Heydrich' Brissaud (1973), p. 3
'. . . Konstantin Kanaris' Klemperer (1992), p. 23
'. . . in Argentina' Cookridge (1948), p. 47
'. . . Nigel West' West (1983), p. 199–201
'. . . Andrew King' *Sunday Times*, 16 October 1983
'. . . Gisevius too' West (1983), p. 364
'. . . Sir Christopher Warner' Colvin (1957)
'British intelligence . . .' Colvin (1951), p. 5
'. . . living in Surrey' Colvin (1951), pp. 89–92
'I am able . . .' Brissaud (1973), p. 15
'He [Colvin] plunged . . .' Churchill (1948), p. 64
'The matter was left . . .' Brissaud (1973), p. 15
'. . . free to fight' Mure (1980), pp. 159–60
'. . . served the Allies' West (1981), pp. 238–9
'In recent years . . .' see Bennett (1994), p. 252; Mure (1980), pp. 159–68, pp. 186–93
'I had not been . . .' Mure (1980), p. 165
'. . . long after others' West (1983), p. 342; Mure (1980), p. 169
'It never appeared . . .' Mure (1980), p. 165
'Another possible example . . .' Jowitt (1954), pp. 18–31; West (1981), pp. 244–50
'. . . champagne cider' *After the Battle*, 11, p. 15
'. . . Oreste Pinto' *After the Battle*, 11, pp. 13–14
'Pinto received a decoded . . .' Pinto (1962), pp. 57–64
'I clenched my . . .' Pinto (1962), p. 64
'In reality, Kieboom . . .' Jowitt (1954), p. 23
'. . . by means of' Masterman (1972), p. 3
'Innumerable precautions . . .' Masterman (1972), p. 3

'. . . Counterfeit Spies' West (1998), pp. 236–54
'. . . West himself' Schellenberg (2000), pp. xxxiii–xxxiv
'. . . George Armstrong' West (1981), pp. 254–5
'It is more . . .' Masterman (1972), pp. 53–4
'Although some accounts . . .' *After the Battle*, 64, pp. 32–3
'. . . MI5 only learned' West (1981), pp. 273–4
'. . . anecdotal evidence' *After the Battle*, 64, p. 34

CHAPTER ELEVEN

'An instance . . .' *Eastern Daily Press*, 19 September 1939
'. . . an elite force' *The Times*, 6 September 1939
'. . . dismounted infantry' Kaufmann (1993), p. 90
'. . . the 18th Lancer' Kaufmann (1993), p. 83
'. . . Italian journalists' Zaloga (1982), p. 8
'. . . 674 German tanks' Kaufmann (1993), p. 91
'. . . the Polish air force' Kaufmann (1993), p. 79
'. . . are legion' for example Longmate (1981), pp. 60–1
'. . . near Newport' Calder & Sheridan (1984), p. 82
'We never found out . . .' Armstrong (1941), p. 213
'. . . Hawkinge airfield' Collier (1979), p. 234
'. . . in East Anglia' Longmate (1971), p. 111
'. . . never been confirmed' Brown (1981), p. 120
'Station Officer . . .' Collier (1979), p. 234
'In The Big Lie . . .' White (1955), p. 22
'It as about midnight . . .' Collyer (1995), pp. 142–3
'George Wright told . . .' Johnson (1992), pp. 126–7
'. . . is a nonsense' Hayward (2001), p. 88
'. . . elderly Home Guards' Hayward (2001), pp. 105–6
'Being a 1914–18 . . .' Hayward (2001), p. 106
'. . . unknown assassins' Hayward (2002), pp. 4–5
'. . . deadly motorcyclist' Hayward (2002), p. 19
'Between 1940 and 1944 . . .' unpublished letter to *Sunday Telegraph*, 3 May 1992.
'. . . Great Circle' Gardner (1954), p. 122
'. . . a serious drain' Howard (1989), pp. 138–9
'I am not saying . . .' Gardner (1954), p. 123
'. . . Hampshire coven' King (1970), pp. 178–9
'Fire and wind . . .' McCormick (1968), p. 151
'A 'Cape-coloured . . .' Bonaparte (1947), p. 98
'. . . by Paul Fussell' Fussell (1989), p. 119
'. . . bite off the nipples' Bonaparte (1947), p. 98
'. . . neatly packed suitcases' Regan (2000), p. 136
'. . . a lot of opera' Fussell (1989), p. 124
'. . . pomaded and scented' Fussell (1989), p. 123
'. . . The Tuscana' Longmate (1971), p. 422
'. . . cardboard boots' Sullivan (1997), p. 181; Regan (2000), p. 134
'. . . by Brian Sullivan' Sullivan (1997), pp. 177–205
'The problem was . . .' Regan (2000), pp. 134–5
'Throughout the war . . .' Sullivan (1997), p. 205
'. . . of the 4,963' Ramsey (1974), p. 23
'. . . lost more prisoners' Thompson (1956), p. 197
'. . . Louis Mountbatten' PRO, CAB 98/22/3830
'. . . the postal censor' Robertson (1963), p. 387

'Lord Beaverbrook . . .' Villa (1994), p. 260
'. . . prove to Stalin' Villa (1994), p. 2
'One fact emerged . . .' Maguire (1963), p. 157
'It is said . . .' Hodgson (1976), p. 263
'. . . Stanley Lovell' West (1984), pp. 120–2
'The message was . . .' Lovell (1963), pp. 153–4
'. . . John Masterman' Masterman (1972), p. 108
'A great question . . .' Peis (1977), pp. 122–3
'. . . a very reliable' Peis (1977), pp. 123–4
'. . . Unreliable Witness' West (1984), pp. 124–8
'. . . Counterfeit Spies' West (1988), p. 245
'It was quite . . .' Mosley (1982), p. 116; p. 104
'. . . Hitler had already' Brown (1976), p. 84
'. . . 302 Division' Maguire (1963), p. 157
'The information . . .' Robertson (1963), p. 206
'. . . fully clothed' West (1984), p. 119
'. . . John Campbell' West (1984), p. 132
'. . . signal traffic' West (1984), p. 132
'. . . a testing and rehearsing' Austin (1943), p. 51
'. . . Sir Leslie Hollis' Villa (1994), p. 3
'. . . John Hughes-Hallett' Villa (1994), p. 4
'. . . Eisenhower credited' Villa (1994), p. 17
'. . . mine of experience' Churchill (1951), p. 459
'. . . Reynolds's book . . .' Villa (1994), p. 24
'. . . King of Holland' Regan (2000), p. 112
'. . . perhaps the most' Pinto (1952), p. 111
'. . . July 1946' West (1984), p. 149
'. . . warned Langley privately' Langley (1974), p. 227
'One man . . .' Pinto (1952), p. 112
'. . . all the secret facts' Pinto (1952), p. 139
'It is true . . .' Pinto (1952), pp. 139–40
'He knew that . . .' Giskes (1953), p. 171
'The traffic heard . . .' Giskes (1953), p. 172
'When I went . . .' Pinto (1952), p. 142
'. . . John Bulloch' Bulloch (1966), p. 101
'The *Abwehr* had . . .' Laurens (1969), p. 119
'Finally, the last . . .' Laurens (1969), p. 119
'They had only . . .' Laurens (1969), p. 134
'. . . countless amours' Pinto (1952), p. 122
'. . . gross appetites' Pinto (1952), p. 149
'. . . superb muscular' Pinto (1952), p. 145
'. . . famed for his' Pinto (1952), p. 144
'A curious moral . . .' Laurens (1969), p. 169
'. . . Kurt Student' Ryan (1974), p. 117
'. . . already in position' Ryan (1974), p. 117
'He asked to be . . .' Langley (1974), pp. 226–7
'Exhaustive enquiries . . .' Langley (1974), p. 228–9
'Months later . . .' Langley (1974), p. 229

CHAPTER TWELVE

'The events leading . . .' Way (1996), pp. 137–45
'. . . save for one report' Butcher (1986), p. 261

'. . . on January 20th 1945' Way (1996), pp. 143

'. . . Paris brothel' Butcher (1986), p. 257; Way (1996), p. 143

'. . . black marketeer' Fussell (1989), p. 41

'. . . psychological wreck' Butcher (1986), p. 257

'. . . had been murdered' *Glenn Miller's Last Flight*, Channel 4 (UK) television programme, 2001

'. . . disfigured in a fire' TV (2001)

'. . . by the SS' TV (2001)

'. . . Down Beat' Down Beat, 27 July 1951

'The following facts . . .' quoted in Butcher (1986), p. 267

'. . . a ferry pilot' Way (1996), p. 140; Butcher (1986), p. 260

'. . . lacked sufficient range' Butcher (1986), p. 258

'. . . Chiltern Hills' Butcher (1986), p. 262

'. . . wreckage recovered' Butcher (1986), p. 262

'. . . Fred Shaw' *Sunday Mirror*, 16 November 1984

'. . . incident was discussed' *Glenn Miller's Last Flight*, Channel 4 (UK) television programme, 2001

'. . . only eight degrees' *Glenn Miller's Last Flight* (2001)

'. . . auctioned by Sotheby's' *Brighton & Hove Argus*, 14 April 1999

'The first prisoner . . .' Johnson (1992), pp. 112–4

'. . . over the English Channel' eg Whalen (1965), pp. 370–1

'. . . the Katyn Forest' West (1981), p. 306

'. . . fled to Manchuria' Piekalkiewicz (1974), p. 320

'On April 26th . . .' Irving (1967), p. 36

'. . . British Secret Service' Irving (1967), p. 83

'. . . last victim of Katyn' Irving (1967), p. 175

'. . . future Honours List' Irving (1967), p. 91

'. . . Erwin Lahousen' Wighton & Peis (1958), p. 35; Hinchley (1963), pp. 203–11

'. . . diaries make no mention' Irving (1967), p. 178ff

'In March 1942 . . .' Irving (1967), pp. 149–52

'. . . De Gaulle' Irving (1967), pp. 163–5

'. . . Stalin was apparently' Djilas (1962), pp. 70–1

'. . . Pinder and Lock' West (1981), p. 305

'. . . Irving 'failed to obtain' Irving (1969), p. 194

'. . . English colonel' West (1981), p. 307

'. . . Swiss bank vault' Thompson (1969), p. 5; Irving (1967), p. 177

'. . . a large amount of money' Thompson (1969), p. 13

'. . . in a bar brawl' Thompson (1969), p. 8

'. . . sued for libel' McCormick (1993), p. 150

'. . . W.S. Herring' Irving (1967), pp. 107–8

'. . . later Prchal denied' Thompson (1969), p. 251–2

'. . . furs and oranges' Thompson (1969), p. 249

'. . . Sikorski himself selected' Irving (1967), p. 55

'There was one . . .' Thompson (1969), Appendix C, p. 4

'. . . ordered by Churchill' Piekalkiewicz (1974), p. 336

'. . . Lionel 'Buster' Crabb' Piekalkiewicz (1974), p. 332

'. . . Christine Granville' McCormick (1993), p. 149

'. . . Teresa Lubienska' McCormick (1993), p. 149; Hinchley (1963), pp. 59–64

'. . . tram or lorry' Thompson (1969), p. 4; Irving (1967), p. 157

'. . . succumbed to pneumonia' Thompson (1969), p. 329

'. . . House of Commons' Hansard (Commons), oral answers 10 June 1943 ('Lost Air Liner')

'. . . his own double' Thompson (1969), p. 82

'The regular commercial . . .' Churchill (1951), p. 742

'The 'thickset man'. . . ' Howard (1981), pp. 234–5

'. . . a British agent' Howard (1981), p.2 29

'. . . inestimable value' Jackson (2000), p. 93

'Wilfrid Israel' Howard (1981), p. 233

'. . . important documents' Howard (1981), p. 226

'. . . reluctant to discuss' Howard (1981), p. 219

'. . . remained unequalled' Kinsey (1992), p. 98

'The Air Officer . . .' Kinsey (1992), p. 99

'. . . daily newspapers' eg *Daily Telegraph*, 31 May 1940

'. . . several diarists' Panter-Downes (1971), p. 65

'Thirty-five Junkers . . .' Kinsey (1992), p. 99

'. . . grounded in January' Brew (1993), pp. 247–8

'. . . very next day' Brew (1993), p. 249

'. . . over four days' Brew (1993), p. 253

'. . . 141, lost six' Brew (1993), p. 250

'. . . 15 Bf 109' Brew (1993), pp. 249–50

'. . . just 14 machines' Brew (1993), p. 250

'. . . two of these Bf 109s' Brew (1993), p. 249

'. . . 1,062 examples' Brew (1993), p. 235

'. . . John Cunningham' Golley (1999), pp. 41–2

'. . . detested the nickname' Rawnsley and Wright (1957), p. 67

'. . . Going to Brighton' Wegmann and Widfelt (1997), foreword

'. . . RAF or USAAF personnel' Wegmann and Widfelt (1997), p. 287

'The story concerned . . .' Johnson (1992), p. 108

'. . . 861st Engineer' Burgess and Rance (1988), p. 49

'A certain stone . . .' Burgess and Rance (1988), p. 49

'. . . local workers' Johnson (1992), p. 108

'. . . a Thunderbolt' Burgess and Rance (1988), p. 51

'. . . a heart attack' Johnston (1992), p.109

'. . . in East Dereham' *Dereham & Fakenham Times*, 11 January 1941; News Chronicle, 6 January
    1941

'. . . phantom Los Angeles' Good (1987), pp. 15–18

'Residents from Santa . . .' *New York Times*, 26 February 1942

'During the blackout . . .' *New York Times*, 26 February 1942

'Most of the [30] arrests . . .' *New York Times*, 26 February 1942

'. . . on Oahu' Fussell (1989), p. 40

'. . . as 27 aircraft' *New York Times*, 26 February 1942

'They seemed to be . . .' Collins (1968), quoted by Good (1987), p. 16

'Taking into account . . .' Collins (1968), quoted by Good (1987), p. 16

'. . . between Santa Monica' Good (1987), p. 15

'As many as 15 . . .' quoted by Good (1987), p. 17

'. . . Long Beach Independent' quoted by Good (1987), p. 16

'Admiral Knox . . .' Good (1987), p. 16

'. . . ignition systems' Good (1987), p. 19

'. . . official reports' Harbinson (1995), p. 46

'A new German . . .' *New York Times*, 14 December 1944

'According to Reuters . . .' *New Orleans Item*, 13 December 1944;
South Wales Argus, 13 December 1944

'Phoo fighters are . . .' *Daily Telegraph*, 1 January 1945

'It was in . . .' Wilkins (1954), p. 21

'. . . through a hatch' Creighton (1962), p. 12

'. . . Rudolph Schriever' Harbinson (1995), p. 71; p. 259

'During the war . . .' Lusar (1959), p. 165

'. . . General Massey' Good (1987), pp. 18–19; pp. 25–6

'. . . myth of Scrarecrows' Hastings (1979), p. 167

Bibliography

Abshagen, Karl Heinz, *Canaris*, Hutchinson, 1956

Addison, Paul and Calder, Angus, *A Time to Kill*, Random House, 1997

Aitken, Leslie, *Massacre on the Road to Dunkirk*, William Kimber, 1977

Allingham, Margery, *The Oaken Heart*, Hutchinson, 1941

Anderson, Ken, *Hitler and the Occult*, Prometheus (New York), 1995

Ansel, Walter, *Hitler Confronts England*, Duke University Press, 1960

Armstrong, Anthony, *Village at War*, Collins, 1941

Aston, George, *Secret Service*, Faber & Faber, 1930

Atkin, Ronald, *Pillar of Fire – Dunkirk 1940*, Sidgwick and Jackson, 1990

Bacque, James, *Other Losses*, Macdonald & Co, 1989

——, *Crimes and Mercies*, Little Brown, 1997

Barber, Noel, *The Week France Fell*, Stein & Day, 1976

Barlone, D., *A French Officer's Diary*, Cambridge University Press, 1942

Bennett, Ralph, *Ultra and Mediterranean Strategy*, Hamish Hamilton, 1989

——, *Behind the Battle*, Sinclair-Stevenson, 1994

Bezymenski, Lev, *The Death of Adolf Hitler*, Michael Joseph, 1968

Biddle, A.J. Drexel, *Poland and the Coming of the Second World War*, Ohio State University Press, 1976

Blaxland, Gregory, *Destination Dunkirk*, William Kimber, 1973

Bloom, Ursula, *The Log of No Lady*, Chapman and Hall, 1940

Blundell, Nigel, *A Pictorial History of Adolf Hitler*, Sunburst Books, 1995

Bonaparte, Marie, *Myths of War*, Imago, 1947

Brew, Alec, and Boulton Paul, *Aircraft Since 1915*, Putnam, 1993

Brissaud, André, *Canaris*, Weidenfeld & Nicolson, 1973

Brittain, Vera, *England's Hour*, Macmillan, 1941

Brown, R. Douglas, *East Anglia 1940*, Terence Dalton, 1981

Brown, Richard, *Mr Brown's Diary*, Sutton, 1998

Bulloch, John, *MI5*, Arthur Barker, 1963

Burgess, Eleanor, *Rance, Mary, Boreham*, BHPG, 1988

Butcher, Geoffrey, *Next to a Letter From Home*, Mainstream, 1986

Butler, Ewan and Bradford, Selby, *The Story of Dunkirk*, Hutchinson, 1950

Byford-Jones, Wilfred, *Berlin Twilight*, Hutchinson, 1947

Calder, Angus, *The People's War*, Jonathan Cape, 1969

—— and Sheridan, Dorothy (eds.), *Speak for Yourself*, Jonathan Cape, 1984

Calder, Angus, *The Myth of the Blitz*, Jonathan Cape, 1991

Cave Brown, Anthony, *Bodyguard of Lies*, W.H. Allen, 1976

——, *The Secret Servant*, Michael Joseph, 1988

Chatterton, E. Keble, *The Epic of Dunkirk*, Hurst & Blackett, 1940

Churchill, Winston, *The Second World War Vol 2 – Their Finest Hour*, Cassell, 1949

——, *The Second World War Vol 4 – The Hinge of Fate*, Cassell, 1951

Cole, J.A., *Lord Haw Haw*, Faber, 1964

Collier, Richard, *The Sands of Dunkirk*, Collins, 1961

——, *1940 – the World in Flames*, Hamish Hamilton, 1979

Collyer, David, *Deal and District at War*, Sutton, 1995

Colville, John, *The Fringes of Power*, Hodder & Stoughton, 1985

Colvin, Ian, *Chief of Intelligence*, Victor Gollancz, 1951

——, *The Unknown Courier*, William Kimber, 1953

——, *Hitler's Secret Enemy*, Pan, 1957

Cookridge, E.H., *Secrets of the British Secret Service*, Sampson Low, Marston & Co, 1948

——, *The Third Man*, Arthur Barker, 1968

Cooksey, Jon, *Calais*, Leo Cooper, 2000

Cooper, Duff, *Operation Heartbreak*, Hart-Davis, 1950

Cousins, Geoffrey, *The Story of Scapa Flow*, Frederick Muller, 1965

David, Saul, *Churchill's Sacrifice of the Highland Division*, Brassey's, 1994

De Wilde, John, *Handbook of the War*, Constable, 1940

Deacon, Richard, *The Silent War*, David and Charles, 1978

——, *British Secret Service* (rev. edn.), Grafton, 1991

Deighton, Len, *Fighter*, Jonathan Cape, 1977

——, *Blitzkrieg*, Jonathan Cape, 1979

——, *Battle of Britain*, Jonathan Cape, 1980

Delmer, Sefton, *Black Boomerang*, Secker & Warburg, 1962

Djilas, Milovan, *Conversations With Stalin*, Hart Davis, 1962

Driberg, Tom, *Colonnade 1937–47*, Pilot Press, 1949

Ellis, L.F., *The War in France and Flanders 1939–14* (Official History), HMSO, 1953

Farago, Ladislas, *Aftermath*, Hodder & Stoughton, 1974

Felix, Christopher, *The Spy and his Masters*, Secker & Warburg, 1963

FitzGibbon, Constantine, *The Blitz*, Allan Wingate, 1957

Fleming, Peter, *Invasion 1940*, Rupert Hart-Davis, 1957

Foot, M.R.D., *Resistance*, Eyre Methuen, 1976

Foynes, Julian, *The Battle of the East Coast 1939–45*, private printing, 1994

Frank, Wolfgang, *Enemy Submarine*, William Kimber, 1954

Fraser, David, *And We Shall Shock Them*, Hodder & Stoughton, 1983

Fussell, Paul, *Wartime*, Oxford University Press, 1989

Gardiner, Geoff, *Airfield Focus 30 – Watton*, GMS Enterprises, n.d.

Gardner, Gerald, *Witchcraft Today*, Rider, 1954

Garlinski, Josef, *Poland in the Second World War*, Macmillan, 1985

Gelb, Norman, *Dunkirk*, Michael Joseph, 1990

Gibson, Guy, *Enemy Coast Ahead*, Michael Joseph, 1946

Gillman, Peter, *Collar the Lot!*, Quartet, 1980

Glover, Michael, *The Fight for the Channel Ports*, Leo Cooper, 1985

——, *Invasion Scare 1940*, Leo Cooper, 1990

Goebbels, Josef, *The Goebbels Diaries*, Hamish Hamilton, 1982

Golley, John, *John 'Cat's Eyes' Cunningham*, Airlife, 1999

Good, Timothy, *Above Top Secret*, Sidgwick & Jackson, 1987

Goodrick-Clarke, Nicholas, *The Occult Roots of Nazism*, Aquarian Press, 1985

Goris, Jan-Albert, *Belgium in Bondage*, LB Fischer, 1943

Gray, Bernard, *War Reporter*, Robert Hale, 1942

Guderian, Heinz, *Panzer Leader*, Michael Joseph, 1952

Gun Buster, *Return Via Dunkirk*, Hodder & Stoughton, 1940

Hadley, Peter, *Third Class to Dunkirk*, Hollis & Carter, 1944

Harbinson, W.A., *Projekt UFO*, Boxtree, 1995

Harman, Nicholas, *Dunkirk – the Necessary Myth*, Hodder & Stoughton, 1980

Harris, John, *Dunkirk – The Storms of War*, David & Charles, 1980

Harris, Robert, *Selling Hitler*, Faber & Faber, 1986

Harrisson, Tom, *Living Through the Blitz*, Collins, 1976
—— and Madge, Charles, *War Begins at Home*, Chatto & Windus, 1940
Hart, Basil Liddell (ed.), *The Rommel Papers*, Collins, 1953
Hastings, Max, *Bomber Command*, Michael Joseph, 1979
Hatherill, George, *The Detective's Story*, André Deutsch, 1971
Hayward, James, *The Bodies on the Beach*, CD41 Publishing, 2001
——, *Myths & Legends of the First World War*, Sutton, 2002
Heide, Dirk van der, *My Sister and I*, Faber, 1941
Hickman, Tom, *What Did You Do in the War, Auntie?*, BBC, 1995
Hinchley, Vernon, *Spy Mysteries Unveiled*, George Harrap, 1963
Hinsley, F.H., *British Intelligence in the Second World War* (abridged edn.), HMSO, 1993
Hoare, Samuel, *Ambassador on Special Mission*, Collins, 1946
Hodgson, Vere, *Few Eggs and No Oranges*, Dennis Dobson, 1976
Hodson, James, *Through the Dark Night*, Gollancz, 1941
Hohne, Heinz, *Canaris*, Secker & Warburg, 1979
Hooper, David, *Official Secrets*, Secker & Warburg, 1987
Horne, Alistair, *To Lose a Battle – France 1940*, Macmillan, 1969
Howard, Michael, *The Occult Conspiracy*, Rider, 1989
——, *Strategic Deception in WW2*, HMSO, 1990
—— and Sparrow, John, *The Coldstream Guards 1920–46*, Oxford University Press, 1951
Howard, Ronald, *In Search of My Father*, William Kimber, 1981
Howe, Ellic, *Urania's Children*, William Kimber, 1967
——, *The Black Game*, Michael Joseph, 1982
Infield, Glenn, *Hitler's Secret Life*, Hamlyn, 1980
Ironside, Edmund, *The Ironside Diaries 1937–40*, Constable, 1962
Irving, David, *Accident: The Death of General Sikorski*, William Kimber, 1967
Jackson, Robert, *Coroner*, George Harrap, 1963
——, *Unexplained Mysteries of World War II*, Quantum, 2000
James, Robert Rhodes, *Chips: The Diaries of Sir Henry Channon*, Harmondsworth, 1970
Johnson, Derek, *East Anglia at War* 2nd edn., Jarrold, 1992
Jolly, Cyril, *The Vengeance of Private Pooley*, William Heinemann, 1956
Jones, R.V., *Most Secret War*, Hamish Hamilton, 1978
——, *Reflections on Intelligence*, Heinemann, 1989
Jones, Stephen, *James Herbert: By Horror Haunted*, Hodder & Stoughton, 1992
Karslake, Basil, *1940 – The Last Act*, Leo Cooper, 1979
Kaufmann, J.E., *Hitler's Blitzkrieg Campaigns*, Combined Books, 1993
Keegan, John, *The Battle for History*, Hutchinson, 1995
Kersaudy, François, *Churchill and De Gaulle*, Collins, 1981
King, Cecil, *With Malice Towards None*, Sidgwick & Jackson, 1970
King, Francis, *Satan and Swastika*, Mayflower, 1970
Kinsey, Gordon, *Bawdsey – Birth of the Beam*, Terence Dalton, 1983
——, *Boulton & Paul Aircraft*, Terence Dalton, 1992
Kleffens, E.N. Van, *The Rape of the Netherlands*, Hodder & Stoughton, 1940
Klemmer, Harvey, *They'll Never Quit*, Peter Davies, 1941
Klemperer, Klemens von, *German Resistance to Hitler*, Oxford University Press, 1992
Knightley, Phillip, *The First Casualty*, Quartet, 1982
Knowles, David, *Escape from Catastrophe*, Knowles, 2000
Koestler, Arthur, *The Scum of the Earth*, Gollancz, 1941
Korganoff, Alexandre, *The Phantom of Scapa Flow*, Ian Allen, 1974
Kuby, Erich, *The Russians and Berlin*, Hill & Wang, 1968
Lafitte, L., *The Internment of Aliens*, Penguin, 1940
Lampe, David, *The Last Ditch*, Cassell, 1968
Le Tissier, Tony, *Berlin Then and Now*, After The Battle, 1992
——, *Farewell to Spandau*, Ashford, Buchan & Knight, 1994

Leasor, James, *Rudolf Hess: The Uninvited Envoy*, Allen & Unwin, 1962

Lehmann, John, *Thrown to the Woolfs*, Weidenfeld & Nicolson, 1978

Lewis, Peter and English, Ian, *8th Battalion Durham Light Infantry 1939–45*, J & P Bealls Ltd, 1949

Longmate, Norman, *How We Lived Then*, Hutchinson, 1971

——, *The Home Front*, Chatto & Windus, 1981

Lord, Walter, *The Miracle of Dunkirk*, Allen Lane, 1983

Lovell, Stanley, *Of Spies and Stratagems*, Prentice-Hall, 1963

Lusar, Rudolf, *German Secret Weapons of the Second World War*, Neville Spearman, 1959

McCormick, Donald, *Murder by Witchcraft*, John Long, 1968

——, *17F: The Life of Ian Fleming*, Peter Owen, 1993

Machtan, Lothar, *The Hidden Hitler*, Perseus Press, 2001

McInnis, Edgar, *The War – First Year*, Oxford University Press, 1940

McKale, Donald, *Hitler: The Survival Myth*, Stein & Day, 1981

Mackenzie, S.P., *The Home Guard*, Oxford University Press, 1995

Macksey, Kenneth, *The Shadow of Vimy Ridge*, William Kimber, 1965

MacLean, Hector, *Fighters in Defence*, private printing, 1999

Maguire, Eric, *Dieppe August 19*, Jonathan Cape, 1963

Mannheim, Hermann, *War and Crime*, Watts & Co, 1941

Martel, Giffard, *An Outspoken Soldier*, Sifton Praed, 1949

Marwick, Arthur, *The Home Front*, Thames & Hudson, 1976

Maser, Werner, *Adolf Hitler: Legend, Myth and Reality*, Allen Lane, 1973

Masterman, J.C., *The Double Cross System*, Yale University Press, 1972

Masters, Anthony, *The Man Who Was M*, Blackwell, 1984

Mitchison, Naomi, *Among You Taking Notes*, Victor Gollancz, 1985

Moen, Lars, *Under the Iron Heel*, Robert Hale, 1941

Monsarrat, Nicholas, *Life is a Four-Letter Word*, Cassell, 1966

Montagu, Ewen, *The Man Who Never Was*, Evans Brothers, 1953

——, *Beyond Top Secret U*, Peter Davies, 1977

Montgomery, Bernard, *Memoirs*, Collins, 1958

Moore, Bob and Fedorowich, Kent, *Prisoners of War and Their Captors in WW2*, Berg, 1996

Moore, Bob (ed.), *Resistance in Western Europe*, Berg, 2000

Mosley, Leonard, *Backs to the Wall*, Weidenfeld & Nicolson, 1971

Moynihan, Michael, *People at War*, David & Charles, 1974

Muggeridge, Malcolm, *The Infernal Grove*, Collins, 1973

Mure, David, *Master of Deception*, William Kimber, 1980

Neillands, Robin, *The Bomber War*, John Murray, 2001

Nesbit, Roy Conyers, *The Flight of Rudolf Hess*, Sutton, 1999

Newton, Scott, *Profits of Peace*, Clarendon Press, 1996

Nicholas, Sian, *Echoes of War*, Manchester University Press, 1996

Nicolson, Harold, *Diaries and Letters 1930–64*, Collins, 1980

Nixon, Barbara, *Raiders Overhead*, Lindsay Drummond, 1943

O'Donnell, James, *The Berlin Bunker*, J.M. Dent, 1979

Paassen, Pierre van, *That Day Alone*, Dial Press, 1941

Padfield, Peter, *Hess: Flight for the Führer*, Weidenfeld & Nicolson, 1991

Paine, Lauran, *The Abwehr*, Robert Hale, 1984

Pallud, Jean-Paul, *Blitzkrieg in the West – Then and Now*, Plaistow Press, 1991

Panter-Downes, Mollie, *London War Notes 1939–45*, Longman, 1971

Patton, George S., *The War As I Knew It*, Houghton Mifflin, 1947

Perry, Colin, *Boy in the Blitz*, Colin Perry, 1972

Picknett, Lynn, Prince, Clive and Prior, Stephen, *Double Standards*, Little Brown, 2001

Piekalkiewicz, Janusz, *Secret Agents, Spies and Saboteurs*, David & Charles, 1974

Pinto, Oreste, *Spycatcher*, Werner Laurie, 1952

——, *The Spycatcher Omnibus*, Hodder & Stoughton, 1962

Ponting, Clive, *1940: Myth and Reality*, Hamish Hamilton, 1990

Prien, Gunter, *I Sank the Royal Oak*, Grays Inn Press, 1954
Ramsey, Winston (ed.), *Battle of Britain – Then & Now*, Plaistow Press, 1980
—— (ed.), *The Blitz – Then & Now* (vol. 1), Plaistow Press, 1987
—— (ed.), *The Blitz – Then & Now* (vol. 2), Plaistow Press, 1988
—— (ed.), *The Blitz – Then & Now* (vol. 3), Plaistow Press, 1990
Ravenscroft, Trevor, *The Spear of Destiny*, Neville Spearman, 1973
Rawnsley, C.F and Wright, Robert, *Night Fighter*, Collins, 1957
Read, Anthony and Fisher, David, *Colonel Z*, Hodder & Stoughton, 1984
Redlich, Fritz, *Hitler: Diagnosis of a Destructive Prophet*, Oxford University Press, 1999
Regan, Geoffrey, *Great Military Blunders*, Channel 4 Books, 2000
Rhodes, Anthony, *Sword of Bone*, Faber & Faber, 1942
Rissik, David, *The DLI at War 1939–45*, private printing, 1953
Robertson, Terence, *Dieppe*, Hutchinson, 1963
Roos, Hans, *A History of Modern Poland*, Eyre & Spottiswoode, 1966
Royde Smith, Naomi, *Outside Information*, Macmillan, 1941
Rubinstein, William, *The Myth of Rescue*, Routledge, 1997
Ruby, Marcel, *F Section SOE*, Leo Cooper, 1988
Rusbridger, James, *The Intelligence Game*, The Bodley Head, 1989
Ryan, Cornelius, *A Bridge Too Far*, Hamish Hamilton, 1974
Savignon, André, *With Plymouth Through Fire*, SE Ouston, 1968
Sayer, Ian and Botting, Douglas, *Hitler's Last General*, Bantam Press, 1989
Scannell, Vernon, *Argument of Kings*, Robson Books, 1987
Schellenberg, Walter, *The Schellenberg Memoirs*, André Deutsch, 1956
——, *Invasion 1940*, St Ermin's Press, 2000
Schenk, Peter, *The Invasion of England 1940*, Conway Maritime Press, 1990
Scotland, A.P., *The London Cage*, Evans Brothers, 1957
Seth, Ronald, *The Truth Benders*, Leslie Frewin, 1969
Shirer, William, *Berlin Diary*, Alfred Knopf, 1941
——, *The Rise and Fall of the Third Reich*, Secker & Warburg, 1960
Singer, Kurt, *Spies and Traitors*, W.H. Allen, 1953
——, *Spy Omnibus*, W.H. Allen, 1959
Smithies, Edward, *Crime in Wartime*, Allen & Unwin, 1982
Snagge, John & Barsley, Michael, *Those Vintage Years of Radio*, Pitman, 1972
Snyder, Gerald, *The Royal Oak Disaster*, William Kimber, 1976
Spaight, J.M., *The Battle of Britain 1940*, Geoffrey Bles, 1941
Spence, Lewis, *The Occult Causes of the Present War*, Rider & Co, 1943
Stein, George, *The Waffen-SS*, Oxford University Press, 1966
Stockman, Rocky, *The History of RAF Manston* (3rd edn.), RAF Association, 1986
Sydnor, Charles, *Soldiers of Destruction*, Princetown University Press, 1977
Tabori, Paul, *The Private Life of Adolf Hitler*, Aldor, 1949
Thomas, Hugh, *The Murder of Rudolf Hess*, Hodder & Stoughton, 1979
——, *Doppelgänger*, Fourth Estate, 1995
——, *SS1 – The Untimely Death of Heinrich Hitler*, Fourth Estate, 2001
Thompson, Carlos, *The Assassination of Winston Churchill*, Colin Smyth, 1969
Thompson, Laurence, *1940 – Year of Legend, Year of History*, Collins, 1966
Thomson, George, *Blue Pencil Admiral*, Sampson Low, 1947
Trevor-Roper, Hugh, *The Last Days of Hitler*, Macmillan, 1947
Troy, Thomas, *Wild Bill and Intrepid*, Yale University Press, 1996
Turner, E.S., *The Phoney War on the Home Front*, Michael Joseph, 1961
Villa, Brian, *Unauthorized Action*, Oxford University Press, 1994
Vince, Charles, *Storm on the Waters*, Hodder & Stoughton, 1946
Wahlen, Richard, *The Founding Father*, Hutchinson, 1965
Waite, Robert, *The Psychopathic God: Adolf Hitler*, Basic Books (New York), 1977
Watson, Peter and Petrova, Ada, *The Death of Hitler*, Richard Cohen, 1995

Wavell, Archibald, *Allenby – A Study in Greatness*, George Harrap, 1940
Way, Chris, *Glenn Miller in Britain Then and Now*, After the Battle, 1996
Weaver, H.J., *Nightmare at Scapa Flow*, Cressrelles, 1980
Wegmann, Rolph and Widfeldt, Bo, *Making for Sweden*, Air Research Publications, 1997
West, Nigel, *MI5 (1909–1945)*, The Bodley Head, 1981
——, *MI6 (1909–1945)*, Weidenfeld & Nicolson, 1983
——, *Unreliable Witness*, Grafton, 1986
——, *Counterfeit Spies*, St Ermin's Press, 1998
——, *British Security Co-ordination*, St Ermin's Press, 1998
Westphal, Siegfried, *The German Army in the West*, Cassell, 1951
Wheatley, Dennis, *Black August*, Hutchinson, 1934
——, *Stranger Than Fiction*, Hutchinson, 1959
White, John Baker, *The Big Lie*, Evans Brothers, 1955
Wighton, Charles and Peis, Gunter, *They Spied on England*, Odhams, 1958
Wilkins, Harold, *Flying Saucers on the Moon*, Peter Owen, 1954
Williams, Douglas, *The New Contemptibles*, John Murray, 1940
Wilson, Patrick, *Dunkirk*, Leo Cooper, 2000
Winterbotham, F.W., *The Ultra Secret*, Weidenfeld & Nicolson, 1974
Wolff, Helmut, *Die Deutschen Kriegsgefangen in Britischer Hand*, Verlag Gieseking, Munich, 1974
Woon, Basil, *Hell Came to London*, Peter Davies, 1941
Young, Martin and Stamp, Robbie, *Trojan Horses*, Bodley Head, 1989
Zaloga, Steven J., *The Polish Army 1939–45*, Osprey, 1982
Ziegler, Philip, *London at War 1939–45*, Sinclair-Stevenson, 1995

Essays
Alexander, Martin, 'No Taste for the Fight?', in Addison & Calder (1997)
Anonymous, 'The Rumor Racket' (in *20 Army Talks*), US Army publication, July 1945
Bond, Brian, 'The British Field Force in France and Belgium 1939–40', in Addison & Calder (1997)
Sullivan, Brian, 'The Italian Soldier in Combat', in Addison & Calder (1997)

Forewords and Introductions
Colvin, Ian, *Canaris* (Brissaud), Weidenfeld & Nicolson, 1973
Stripp, Alan, *The Man Who Never Was* (Montagu), Oxford University Press, 1996
Trevor-Roper, Hugh, Preface to 7th edn. of *The Last Days of Hitler*, Papermac/Macmillan, 1995
West, Nigel, *Invasion 1940* (Schellenberg), St Ermin's Press, 2000

Magazine Articles
Bateman, Denis C., 'Rudolf Hess', *After the Battle* 58, 1987
Collins, Paul, 'The UFOs of 1942, Exploring the Unknown' 48, 1968
Creighton, Gordon, 'Foo Fighters', *Flying Saucer Review*, March–April 1962
——, 'The Man Who Almost Is', *After the Battle* 54, 1986
Morgan, Roger, 'The Second World War's Best Kept Secret Revealed', *After the Battle* 94, 1996
Ramsey, Winston, 'Dieppe 1942', *After the Battle* 5, 1974
——, 'Himmler's Suicide', *After the Battle* 14, 1976
——, 'Major Martin – the Story Continues', *After the Battle* 64, 1989
——, 'From the Editor', *After the Battle* 100, 1998
Smith, David J., 'The Death of the Duke of Kent', *After the Battle* 37, 1982

Index